ALSO BY BURT WOLF

EATING WELL

WHAT'S COOKING

BURT WOLF'S
TABLE

BURT WOLF'S TABLE

BURT WOLF

WITH PHOTOS AND DRAWINGS BY THE AUTHOR

A JENIFER LANG BOOK

DOUBLEDAY

New York   London   Toronto   Sydney   Auckland

PUBLISHED BY DOUBLEDAY
a division of Bantam Doubleday Dell Publishing Group, Inc.
1540 Broadway, New York, New York 10036

DOUBLEDAY and the portrayal of an anchor
with a dolphin are trademarks of Doubleday,
a division of Bantam Doubleday Dell
Publishing Group, Inc.

Library of Congress Cataloging-in-Publication Data

Wolf, Burton.
    [Table]
    Burt Wolf's table / Burt Wolf. — 1st ed.
        p.   cm.
    1. Cookery, International.   I. Title.   II. Title: Table.
TX725.A1W5833   1994   93–43380
641.59—dc20   CIP

ISBN 0-385-47274-9

BOOK DESIGN BY CAROL MALCOLM RUSSO/SIGNET M DESIGN, INC.

◆

This book is dedicated to my uncle,

MAXWELL M. POWELL

1916–1993

THE PICTURE ABOVE WAS TAKEN IN 1941. MY UNCLE IS ON THE LEFT; THAT'S ME ON THE RIGHT. IT WAS MY UNCLE MAXWELL WHO INTRODUCED ME TO THE PLEASURES OF THE TABLE.

TWO ANNIVERSARIES

January 1994 marks the beginning of my twentieth year of working with Emily Aronson. She has been the executive producer and director for all of my shows. As I wrote the words, she produced the pictures. During these two decades she has also become my dearest friend and partner. If you enjoy my television shows or this book, you are enjoying the creativity and talents of Emily.

January 1994 also marks the beginning of my seventh year with Caroline McCool as my senior producer. Once I decide on the subject for the stories, Caroline finds the proper spot on the globe for filming. She then sets all the arrangements that make the trip possible. She is the rudder on our ship.

ACKNOWLEDGMENTS

All the television reports used as the basis for this book were videotaped on location in the United States, Canada, the Caribbean, Europe, Australia, and Asia. Over two thousand people were involved in the development, production, and distribution of the series. As I look through the pages of this book, I recall the people who made it possible for us to follow the stories, and in spite of my advancing age, I honestly believe that I remember all of them. Researchers, press officers, government representatives, airline staff, hotel and restaurant personnel, chefs, manufacturers, television producers, cameramen, sound engineers, lighting directors, television editors, book editors, designers, and talented specialists in dozens of other crafts, who helped me get the job done. I thank each of them and I hope they realize how much I appreciate their efforts on my behalf.

There are, however, a few individuals whom I would like to mention by name, because their contributions run throughout the entire undertaking.

THE TELEVISION PRODUCTION TEAM
Emily Aronson, Executive Producer
Caroline McCool, Senior Producer
David Dean, Senior Editor
Hillary Davis, Mardee Haidin Regan, Gary Regan,
    Recipe Testing and Development
Bernard Couture, Director of Photography
Vanessa Stark, Production Assistant

CABLE NEWS NETWORK
Tom Johnson
Burt Reinhart
Jay Suber
Ted Turner

PUBLIC TELEVISION
Mike LaBonia
Gene Nichols

GREY ADVERTISING
John Fox
Ken Levy
Tony Pugliese
Hy Rosen

IN ADDITION
William G. Barry
Bill Dreher
Kenneth Jackier
Judith Kern
Joel Kleiman
Jonathan Korn
Jenifer Harvey Lang
May Mendez
Larry Ossias
Janet Pappas
Lynn Prime
Steven J. Ross
Susan Van Velson

Stephen.

Andrew.

James.

My sons, Stephen, Andrew, and James. Stephen is a director of special effects for feature films but he took time out here and there to give his dad a hand. Andrew is a cameraman for an international television network but was kind enough to take some of his vacation days to do the camera work on a few of our shows. James is an industrial designer studying in Japan, but he took a few breaks so he could help out in Canada, the U.S. Virgin Islands, and Australia. They all took a paycheck.

And at the core of every project for almost thirty years, my legal counsel, confidante, and loyal friend, Raymond Merritt of Willkie, Farr & Gallagher.

David Dean is responsible for the editing of all of our television shows.

Raymond Merritt.

CONTENTS

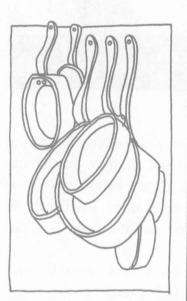

INTRODUCTION

The story of a person, a family, a religion, or a nation is inseparable from the subject of food. What and how we eat and drink are the very basis of our physical existence. Our eating and drinking are also the way we define our relationships. The very word "companion" is derived from a Latin phrase that means "the one we eat bread with."

Brillat-Savarin, a French writer of the eighteenth century, said, "Tell me what you eat, and I will tell you who you are." For me, the opposite is also true. Tell me who you are and I'll tell you what you eat. And I hope I will also be able to tell you why you eat it.

The United States is an English-speaking nation with many of its political and cultural institutions based on the English models of the colonial period. The English were tea drinkers and yet the people of the United States drink over half a billion cups of coffee each day. I wanted to know why.

The hot foods of the Chinese provinces of Szechwan and Hunan get their heat from chili peppers, which are not among the traditional plants of the area. How did they get there and why did they become part of the cuisine? I wanted to know.

In 1989 I decided that the only way I was going to make even the slightest dent in my list of questions was to get on the road—to visit those parts of the world where the local history, culture, and religion would answer my questions.

So I took my television crew and headed off. Each month I settled down in a different part of the world and spent the weeks trying to understand what the people of the town were eating and drinking and why. The information I gained is presented in two forms. The first is a series of television reports; the second is a group of books containing the same material. The first twenty-six trips became a series and book called *Eating Well*. The second twenty-six trips are part of a new series and this companion book, both entitled *Burt Wolf's Table*.

The recipes have been chosen to reflect the history of the communities in which we videotaped, but an effort was made to avoid ingredients that are hard to find in the United States and Canada. I like recipes that are simple, easy, and worth the time, effort, and money.

As I write this, I am also waiting for my laundry to be finished, because I am, once again, about to go on the road, starting my third series of adventures in search of good things to eat and the reasons why people eat them.

BURT WOLF
NEW YORK CITY
JANUARY 1994

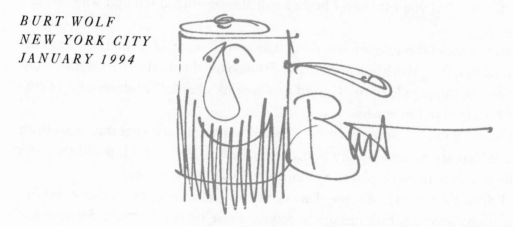

BURT WOLF'S TABLE

SOUPS

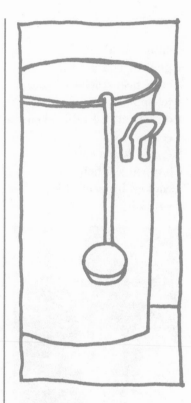

CHINESE BEEF SOUP
THE GRAND FORMOSA REGENT HOTEL ◆ TAIPEI, TAIWAN

MAKES 4 SERVINGS

4 cups water
1 pound ground beef
4 cups beef stock or broth
1 teaspoon cornstarch
   dissolved in 1 tablespoon
   cold water
2 egg whites, beaten
Chopped scallions or
   cooked broccoli, for
   garnish

The Dream of the Red Chamber *is clearly the most important novel in Chinese literature. It is also the basis of an entire school of cooking. It is the only work of fiction that has a companion cookbook and a team of culinary experts that travel around the world teaching the recipes for the dishes described in the original work. Many of those recipes are for soups which were and still are an essential part of every Chinese meal. The following beef soup was prepared by Chef Kow of the Grand Formosa Regent Hotel in Taipei, Taiwan, and is an excellent example of the Red Chamber style.*

1. In a large saucepan over high heat, bring the water to a boil. Add the ground beef and break it up with a spoon or spatula. Cook the beef for 2 minutes. Drain the beef and rinse well with fresh water.

2. Pour the beef stock or broth into the pan and bring to a boil over high heat. Stir in the beef. Add the cornstarch mixture and bring to a boil. Pour in the egg whites in a thin, steady stream and cook until the egg solidifies, about 1 minute. Serve hot, garnished with the scallions or broccoli.

Of all the cultures on our planet, the Chinese culture is probably the most preoccupied with eating and drinking. The great Chinese scholar Lin Yutang wrote, "No food is really enjoyed unless it is keenly anticipated, discussed, eaten, and then commented upon." Long before we have any special food we think about it, rotate it in our minds, and anticipate it as a secret pleasure to be shared with some of our closest friends. Taiwan's food is part of almost every conversation. When you meet a friend and ask how they are, you ask, "Have you eaten lately?" The phrase used to ask someone what their profession is translates as "What do you do to eat?" Food is constantly used as a metaphor to tell a story or make a point. A great Taoist teacher explained the role of government by saying that the country should be ruled the same way you fry a small fish: "Don't turn things over too much. Keep the heat low and be careful and delicate." If that scholar were with us today, he might add, looking at the United States and its national debt, that it's a good idea to be able to pay for the fish before you buy it.

Food is also a basic part of Chinese art. Some of the most important paintings deal with people eating, drinking, or preparing food. It is also central to Chinese literature. There are poems about favorite recipes and short stories that revolve around long meals. The Dream of the Red Chamber is the greatest of the classical Chinese novels. It was written in the middle of the 1700s and tells a love story with a sad ending. It is a huge novel with 975 characters winding their way through the narrative. It is also an authentic picture of Chinese life during the time it was written, particularly when it comes to food. There are over 190 scenes in the novel that involve eating and drinking.

The Dream of the Red Chamber became the theme of the Taipei Food Festival in 1992 with chefs creating many of the dishes described in the book. There are a number of general themes that run through the Red Chamber recipes. One common theme is the desire to have attractive presentations for a single serving. There is also a great interest in food that illustrates the delicate skills of carving and shaping. The Chinese respect for age is also presented in the novel and in its recipes. For example, a pork dish is boiled to tenderness with the specific intent of making it easier for older people to chew.

◆

ABOUT LUKANG

The town of Lukang was one of the earliest ports in Taiwan. The first Chinese to arrive in the area came over from the mainland in the early 600s. By the middle of the 1700s it was a major trading center. When the winds were right, a captain could get his craft from the mainland to Lukang in less than a day; almost a thousand ships made that passage each week. It was a busy neighborhood. The traders would bring manufactured goods and immigrants from the mainland to Lukang. Then they would return with locally grown agricultural products.

These days there are parts of Lukang that look very much the way they did almost two hundred years ago during the peak of its commercial history. Yaolin Street is a good example of the old architecture of the town—a narrow roadway lined with homes that open out into the street. Some front rooms are used as family rooms, others are shops or offices. All of them, however, have similar altar tables that are given over to the artifacts of ancestor worship.

Lukang's main street is Chungshan Road. It used to be called "See No Sky Street," because the roofs of the houses had been extended into the road until they met in the center. The covered street that resulted allowed people to conduct their business from shop to shop without being inconvenienced by bad weather. Amazing . . . two hundred years ago the Chinese were building covered malls. About fifty years ago they took down the road cover, but it's still a great place to shop.

Lukang is also home to the Matsu Temple, which was built in 1647. It is a Taoist temple and named after the Goddess of the Sea. She is protected by two of the most powerful guardians. On one side is Thousand-Mile Ears, who has mastered the art of listening through the wind. On the other side is Thousand-Mile Eyes, who can see for a thousand miles. Having just increased the strength of the prescription in my reading glasses, I must say I am particularly impressed. In front of the temple is an area devoted to street food vendors. After all, once you've fed the soul, it's time to feed the body. The stalls are famous for their oyster soups and oyster omelets, meat balls, and moon cookies.

They also have a specialty that I had heard a lot about before I got there. Though I knew I had to taste it for professional reasons, I was not looking forward to the experience. The food in question was described to me as ox-tongue cakes. Fortunately, they are named ox-tongue cakes because of their shape and not their ingredients.

◆

Chicken Egg Drop Soup
THE GRAND FORMOSA REGENT HOTEL ◆ TAIPEI, TAIWAN

It is traditional in Chinese cooking to serve at least one soup at every meal. At breakfast it is always a simple rice recipe called congee. At lunch and dinner you can select from some 10,000 classic soup recipes. An old favorite in the Chinese restaurants of North America is Chicken Egg Drop Soup. Here's how it is prepared by Chef Kow at Taipei's Tsai Fung Shuen Restaurant in the Grand Formosa Regent Hotel.

1. In a saucepan over high heat, bring the chicken stock or broth to a boil. Season with salt and pepper.

2. With the soup boiling, pour in the beaten eggs in a thin, steady stream. Cook for about 2 minutes, until the egg is set. Ladle into 4 bowls and garnish with the scallions and cilantro.

MAKES 4 SERVINGS

4 cups chicken stock or broth
Salt and freshly ground white pepper, to taste
4 eggs, well beaten
¼ cup chopped scallions, for garnish
2 tablespoons chopped cilantro leaves, for garnish

Yaolin Street, Lukang.

THE SAGE ADVICE OF KWAN TZE

The ancient Chinese sage Kwan Tze lived some 2,700 years ago, but he had some very interesting observations about life. He wrote: "To the ruler, the people are Heaven; but to the people, food is Heaven." A nice reminder of the real priorities in life.

◆

TAIWANESE NOODLE SOUP
THE GRAND FORMOSA REGENT HOTEL ◆ TAIPEI, TAIWAN

MAKES 6 SERVINGS

SAUCE
2 cups ground pork
½ cup white wine
½ cup soy sauce
1 teaspoon ground white
  pepper
¼ teaspoon ground
  cinnamon
¼ teaspoon anise powder
  (optional)
2 tablespoons sugar

SOUP
10 cups chicken stock
½ pound thin flat noodles

GARNISHES
6 teaspoons soy sauce
½ teaspoon ground white
  pepper
½ cup minced scallions

T'ai-nan is the cultural center of Taiwan, and for over 200 years it was the island's capital. T'ai-nan also has a long history as a gastronomic center. One of T'ai-nan's most famous dishes is referred to locally as "tan tan noodles." It was once accurately described to me as combining the best qualities of pasta Bolognesa and noodle soup in one dish.

1. To make the sauce: Heat a wok or large sauté pan over high heat. Add the pork and stir-fry for 5 minutes. Add the remaining ingredients. Bring the mixture to a boil, reduce to a simmer, and cook for 30 minutes.

2. To make the soup: In a large saucepan or stockpot over high heat, bring the chicken stock to a boil. Add the noodles and cook until just tender.

3. To serve, put 1 teaspoon of the soy sauce into each of 6 soup bowls. Divide the cooked noodles into the bowls. Pour equal amounts of the chicken stock onto the noodles. Sprinkle some of the white pepper onto each mound of noodles. Divide the meat sauce onto the noodles. Garnish with the scallions.

Street Market, Lukang.

The time period between the fall of Rome and the beginning of the Renaissance is often referred to as the Dark Ages. From the point of view of food it could easily be described as the "dull ages." The ancient Romans had developed a spice trade with Asia and used an almost endless variety of spices in their cooking. But when the structure of Rome fell apart so did the commercial arrangements that brought rare spices into Europe. The birth of the Renaissance reawakened the craving for those flavors to a point where individual spices became worth their weight in gold. Every trader in Europe wanted to make a direct deal with a source. But that wasn't so easy. Between Europe and the spices of India and China lay the vast Muslim world. The Islamic nations controlled the spice trade and the European nations felt a constant frustration over the issue. Every European monarch was interested in eliminating the Arab middlemen. That is precisely why the Portuguese government sent out Vasco da Gama, and the Spanish sent out Ferdinand Magellan and, of course, Christopher Columbus.

The first great European explorers were the Portuguese, and they were the first Europeans to start doing business in Asia. They sailed along the coast of China and made a series of early charts showing the mainland and the island of Taiwan. They gave the land the name Formosa, which is Portuguese for "beautiful island," but they never actually set foot on the territory or considered setting up a colony. The Portuguese set up their trading base in Macao, just as the Spanish set up theirs in Manila; the big deals were being made in the Chinese coastal cities.

In 1602 the Dutch decided that they should have a piece of the action. Accordingly, they formed the Dutch East India Company with the express purpose of taking over a part of the pepper and spice trade from the Portuguese and the Spanish. One of the locations that the Dutch used to develop this trade was Fort Zeelandia. It was constructed in the 1620s on a protected sandbank along the southwest coast. The area was called T'ai-wan which means terraced bay. The Dutch began to use that word to describe the entire island.

The site of the fort is at the edge of the present Taiwanese city of T'ai-nan. One of the original walls is still standing. The bricks were held together with a mixture of sugar syrup, rice, and oysters. Makes a nice recipe and a great wall. It's thirty feet thick and high in complex carbohydrates. There is a small museum on top of the hill that will show you what the fort looked like in its good old days.

Fort Zeelandia became the key trading point for the Dutch interests in Asia and produced extraordinary fortunes for the merchants back home in Holland. The amazing canal houses that stand in Amsterdam today, the great furniture inside them, and the fabulous art of the 1600s from people like Rembrandt or the Van Loons are all things that came from the wealth created in Asia, with the aid of Fort Zeelandia.

◆

DUTCH CHEESE SOUP ✓
MUSEUM VAN LOON ◆ AMSTERDAM, HOLLAND

MAKES 6 TO 8 SERVINGS

2 tablespoons butter
1 cup sliced leeks
2 cups peeled, cubed new
  potatoes
1 bunch broccoli, stalks
  sliced and florets kept
  separate from the stalks
6 cups chicken stock or
  broth
1 cup milk
1 cup grated Gouda or
  Edam cheese, plus extra
  grated cheese, for garnish

The Van Loon Museum is a fascinating restoration of a private home as it was in Amsterdam during the 1700s. The dining room has a 240-piece Amstel China service, particularly impressive because it was purchased before dishwashing machines. There are also portraits of the Van Loon brothers as newlyweds with their wives. It is the perfect setting for a romantic supper and is available as a location for such dinners, as well as for parties. If you go to dinner there, one of KLM's master chefs like Paolo-Arpa Sanna will cook any menu that you like. The following is his recipe for Dutch Cheese Soup.

1. In a large saucepan over medium heat, melt the butter. Add the leeks, potatoes, broccoli stalks, and chicken stock and bring to a boil. Reduce the heat to medium-low, cover, and simmer for 20 minutes.

2. Stir in the broccoli florets and cook for 3 minutes. Working in batches, puree the soup in a blender or food processor. Return the soup to the saucepan.

3. Add the milk and reheat the soup until hot. Add the cheese and stir until the cheese melts, about 1 minute. Serve hot, garnished with extra cheese.

Holland's mild climate, high-quality marshy soil, and regular rainfall promote the year-round growth of excellent grass. The grass, in turn, produces excellent cattle. The cattle have been used to produce milk for at least four thousand years and cheese for at least one thousand years. Archaeologists have found various pots that indicate that milk was being turned into cheese as early as 200 B.C., and trading records from the Middle Ages show that by the 1100s, Holland had already become a major exporter of cheese.

The country's natural waterways played a big part in the development of the cheese business. Almost every farmer had a waterway touching some point of his land. When his cheese was made he would load it onto a barge and sail off to a market. It could be a nearby town just down the canal from his farm or he could join up with a major river like the Rhine and go off to Germany or France. Because the Dutch sailors were so skilled at coastal navigation, they were able to develop a cheese trade with Portugal and Spain. Cheese became such an important commodity that at one point it was used as a form of money, though it was somewhat difficult to keep small change in your pocket. Today the technology has changed some but the story is pretty much the same. Holland is the world's largest exporter of cheese, shipping out millions of pounds of cheese each year.

North America imports about forty thousand metric tons of cheese from Holland each year, and most of the exported cheese from Holland is named after the towns from which they come: Edam is made from skim milk, has a mild flavor, smooth texture, and is easy to spot because it usually comes in a red ball; Leerdammer is Holland's answer to Swiss cheese with a mild, musty flavor; and of course, Gouda is the most famous cheese produced in Holland and accounts for about 60 percent of all the cheese produced in Holland. Gouda cheese starts with a mild and creamy flavor that becomes more robust the longer it is aged.

ABOUT KLM'S HISTORY AND INTERNATIONAL KITCHEN

KLM, the Royal Dutch Airline of Holland, is the oldest airline still operating. Most airlines started by flying people around in their home country from one local town to another. But that was not true for KLM. Holland is a country with such a small area that you are much better off getting around in a car, on a bike, or even in a canal boat. KLM made its first flight in 1920 from London to Amsterdam. The airport in Amsterdam has an aircraft museum and an actual KLM plane from the 1920s. The plane was designed like a horse carriage of the period. The two drivers would sit up front in the open air, which gave them better visibility and greater knowledge of the weather conditions. The passengers sat inside the coach area. Before you got on board you were issued a leather jacket, flying goggles, a hot-water bottle, and a set of ear plugs. The final destination might have been half a world away, but the actual trip was made up of many short flights. Stops were often scheduled to match up with mealtimes, and passengers were taken to local hotels and restaurants so they could dine properly. Even on transcontinental flights there was very little food on board. The concept of eating or drinking on an aircraft was unheard of.

These days, however, in-flight food is a major consideration and an essential part of airline activities. The average KLM 747 takes on five and a half tons of food for each flight, offering fourteen different types of special meals. KLM has two menus on its flights. One has traditional European dishes while the other menu is Indonesian food. The airline also features many other ethnic kitchens, including Japanese, Italian, Indian, and Chinese. The latest and fastest-growing trend in the kitchens of KLM is for meals that reflect the public's interest in food for good health. Accordingly, you can call in for a low-salt meal, a low-cholesterol meal, or a low-calorie meal. Or, you can just live it up, in moderation of course.

◆

ESCAROLE AND WHITE BEAN SOUP ✓
TRIBECA GRILL ◆ NEW YORK, NEW YORK

On the first floor of Robert De Niro's Film Center in New York City is a restaurant called the TriBeCa Grill. It is owned by De Niro, Bill Murray, Mikhail Baryshnikov, and other famous eaters. It has high ceilings, bare brick walls, and a relaxed, informal atmosphere. The place has become popular for its seafood, homemade pastas, and a series of dishes with an interesting blend of French, Italian, and Asian influences. The executive chef is Don Pintabona, and the following is his recipe for Escarole and White Bean Soup.

1. To make the basil puree: Place the basil in a food processor or blender and blend with the olive oil, 1 tablespoon at a time. Process to a thick puree. Add salt.

2. To make the soup: In a large pot over medium-low heat, heat the olive oil and add the pancetta, prosciutto, or bacon and cook slowly for 3 to 5 minutes. Add the onion and cook gently for 3 minutes more.

3. Add the garlic, celery, and carrots to the pot and continue cooking for an additional 5 minutes. Do not let the onion or celery turn brown.

4. Add the greens to the pot and turn up the heat, stirring until wilted. Add the chicken stock and thyme, lower the heat, and cook slowly for 30 minutes. Add the beans, salt (if needed) and pepper. Cook for another 30 minutes. Check the seasoning.

5. Drizzle the basil puree onto each serving of soup along with a sprinkle of Pecorino Romano cheese.

MAKES 4 SERVINGS

FRESH BASIL PUREE
1 cup fresh basil
1 to 3 tablespoons olive oil
Salt, to taste

ESCAROLE AND WHITE BEAN SOUP
¼ cup olive oil
3 ounces pancetta, prosciutto, or bacon, finely diced
1 large onion, thinly sliced (about 1½ cups)
2 cloves garlic, chopped
2 stalks celery, chopped
2 carrots, chopped
2 heads escarole (kale, collard greens, or Swiss chard may be substituted), (about 12 cups) loosely packed
6 cups chicken stock, warmed
2 teaspoons fresh thyme leaves, or 1 teaspoon dried
2 cups cooked white beans, drained
Salt and freshly ground black pepper, to taste
½ to ¾ cup grated Pecorino Romano cheese

JAMAICAN PUMPKIN SOUP
THE ENCHANTED GARDEN RESORT ◆ OCHO RIOS, JAMAICA

MAKES 8 SERVINGS

6 cups chicken stock
2 cups fresh or canned
  pumpkin meat or your
  favorite winter squash
  (such as butternut, acorn,
  etc.), cut into 1-inch
  cubes
2 cups all-purpose potatoes,
  peeled and cut into 1-inch
  cubes
1 onion, minced
2 cloves garlic, minced
½ teaspoon dried thyme
1 bay leaf
2 teaspoons minced
  jalapeño pepper, or more
  to taste
Salt and freshly ground
  black pepper, to taste
Freshly ground nutmeg, to
  taste
¼ cup low-fat buttermilk or
  evaporated milk
¼ cup minced fresh
  coriander, for garnish

The Enchanted Garden is a resort in the Ocho Rios area of the island of Jamaica. It is set on twenty acres of tropical garden. The structures are so cleverly placed that you can barely see them. Twelve magnificent waterfalls run through the Enchanted Garden property and their gentle sound lulls you into a state of relaxation. Indian tents are set out on the lawn, where traditional afternoon tea is served. You can have a table set up in a deserted pad by a waterfall, and a trained masseuse will gently rub you and calm your shattered nerves. The objective of the management is to produce an environment that will refresh the soul—a place to recharge and rejuvenate. They are also interested in refreshing your palate and they present the following pumpkin soup recipe to perform that task.

1. In a saucepan, or stockpot (large enough to hold all the ingredients) over medium heat, bring the chicken stock to a simmer. Add all the ingredients except the buttermilk and coriander and simmer for 20 minutes, or until the potatoes and pumpkin are tender. The stock should completely cover all ingredients by at least 2 inches.

2. Remove the bay leaf and pour the soup into a blender or food processor and process until smooth.

3. Return the soup to the pot and heat through. Stir in the buttermilk or evaporated milk. Divide the soup into serving bowls and garnish with the coriander.

PINEAPPLE GAZPACHO
THE BUCCANEER RESORT ◆ ST. CROIX, U.S. VIRGIN ISLANDS

The first Europeans to set foot on what is now the U.S. Virgin Island of St. Croix were a group of sailors who came ashore from Christopher Columbus's ship, during his second voyage in 1493. Since then there has been considerable Spanish influence on the island's history, not the least of which can be found in the kitchens. Mike Smith, the executive chef at The Buccaneer resort, prepares a gazpacho, which is a classic soup in Latin countries. But Mike makes his with pineapple, which produces a refreshing and interesting soup.

1. Cut off the top, bottom, and peel from the pineapple; core it if necessary. Coarsely chop the pineapple into large pieces, and place it in a blender. Add the oil, Tabasco, and salt. Blend on high speed until thoroughly liquid.

2. Add the mint, bell pepper, scallions, and red onion to the blender. Blend briefly at high speed until the mixture is thoroughly pureed.

3. Refrigerate the gazpacho for at least 3 hours before serving.

MAKES 6 TO 8 SERVINGS

1 large ripe pineapple
1 tablespoon vegetable oil
1 teaspoon Tabasco sauce
½ teaspoon salt
¼ cup finely chopped fresh mint leaves
1 small red bell pepper, seeded and finely chopped
8 scallions, finely chopped
1 small red onion, finely chopped

Thelma Clark, Estate Whim.

◆

THE NEW ENGLANDERS IN CANADA

The original French settlers to arrive in Nova Scotia, on the northeast coast of Canada, called themselves "Acadians" after an ancient Greek word that meant "dwellers in the land of innocence." They had been the first European colonists in the area. But by 1755, they were living in territory controlled by the British and there were ten thousand Acadians, which made the British nervous. The British were afraid that the Acadians would side with the French during the constant Anglo-French wars of the period. As a result, the British troops forced the Acadians to leave Nova Scotia and physically scattered them throughout North America, sending them as far south as New Orleans. The British then took the Acadian farms, which were on the best soil, and sold them to loyal British colonists from New England. This influx of New Englanders was shortly followed by an even greater immigration from the original U.S. colonies. Over thirty thousand people loyal to the King of England went to Nova Scotia as a result of the American Revolution. They went there not only from New England but from places as far south as Florida. These new arrivals eventually came to represent some two thirds of the residents of Nova Scotia.

The new residents also gave the cooking of the area a distinctly American colonial flavor. There are recipes all over Nova Scotia that clearly come from the kitchens of eighteenth-century Virginia and the Carolinas. The local hearts may be up north, but part of the local stomachs are down south.

◆

SEAFOOD CHOWDER
THE UPPER DECK ◆ HALIFAX, NOVA SCOTIA

The waters of Nova Scotia produce an enormous amount of seafood. The vast majority comes from the clear, clean seas just the way Mother Nature set things up. There is also a farm-raised source. Fish farms have been around for thousands of years and the people of Nova Scotia put them to good use, as do the local chefs. Alan Johnston is the executive chef at the Upper Deck restaurant in Halifax, Nova Scotia, and uses the local seafood to make a chowder.

1. In a large saucepan over medium-high heat, melt the butter until foamy. Add the celery, onion, and bacon and sauté until the onion is translucent, about 5 minutes.

2. Stir in the flour and cook, stirring, for 3 minutes. Add the fish stock in 3 parts, stirring well after each addition. Bring the soup to a boil.

3. Reduce the heat to a simmer, add the remaining ingredients, and stir well. Cook uncovered for 10 minutes. Serve hot, with crusty bread.

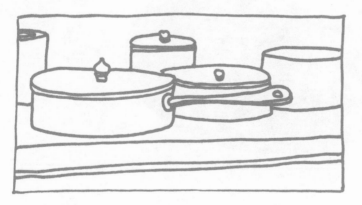

MAKES 8 TO 12 SERVINGS

3 tablespoons unsalted butter
½ cup roughly chopped celery
1 medium onion, roughly chopped
6 ounces bacon, cooked until almost crisp, drained, and cut into ½-inch pieces
3 tablespoons all-purpose flour
2 quarts fish stock, or 1 quart bottled clam juice diluted with 1 quart water
1 pound haddock fillets, cut into bite-size pieces
8 ounces uncooked small shrimp, cleaned and shelled
8 ounces uncooked sea scallops
6 ounces cooked, shelled clams
2 medium potatoes, diced, boiled until tender
2 tablespoons chopped fresh parsley
½ teaspoon paprika
½ teaspoon white pepper
½ teaspoon cayenne pepper

◆

ABOUT TUGBOAT ANNIE

During the 1930s the Saturday Evening Post magazine carried a series called "Tugboat Annie." The story line was so popular that it became the basis for two movies. There actually was a "Tugboat Annie" but her real name was Thea Foss. She and her husband Andrew were immigrants from Norway who arrived in Seattle in 1889. Her husband was a boat builder, and one day while he was away working at a yard, Thea bought an old beat-up rowboat from a neighbor who was moving away. She paid $5 for it, fixed it up, and sold it for $10. She liked the experience and for a while she continued to buy and sell rowboats. Then one day she realized that she could make more money renting the boats to people who just wanted to relax on the water, and she began to amass a sizable fleet. Eventually, some of the boats began to be used to take people and supplies to the larger ships anchored in the harbor. Gradually, Thea went out of the rowboat-rental business and into commercial maritime services. Her husband stopped making boats for other people and concentrated on the design and construction of boats for Thea. He developed the teardrop design that eventually became the world standard for tugs. These days the Foss Tug Company is one of the most important organizations in the business, operating on a worldwide basis. To honor their contribution to maritime history, Thea and Andrew have been inducted into the Maritime Hall of Fame.

Now, quite frankly, I went onboard to track down a story. For years I have been hearing that tugboat crews are very serious about food and that there is some great cooking on these boats. The first indication that the stories I heard were true was the fact that Foss had its own cookbook. Another obvious indication was that the largest space on the boat after the engine room was the cooking area. A good sign. Finally, I tasted Joe Goodman's seafood stew and officially confirmed the legend of tugboat cooking.

TUGBOAT CHOWDER
FOSS TUG COMPANY ◆ SEATTLE, WASHINGTON

1. In a large saucepan or stockpot over medium-high heat, warm the butter until bubbling. Add the onion and celery and sauté until the onion is translucent, about 5 minutes.

2. Add the clam juice, chicken broth, and potatoes and bring the mixture to a boil. Reduce the heat to medium and cook uncovered for 8 to 10 minutes, or until the potatoes are tender.

3. Stir in the halibut, shrimp, evaporated milk, clams, oysters, and thyme. Cook for 5 minutes, or until the fish is opaque. Season with salt and pepper. Serve hot, in soup bowls, with a pinch of the fresh parsley sprinkled on top.

MAKES 6 TO 8 SERVINGS

2 tablespoons unsalted
   butter
1 medium onion, finely
   chopped
2 stalks celery, finely
   chopped
1 cup bottled clam juice
One 14½-ounce can chicken
   broth
2 medium potatoes, peeled
   and cut into ¼-inch cubes
One 1-pound halibut fillet,
   cut into bite-size pieces
1 pound uncooked medium
   shrimp, peeled, deveined,
   and halved lengthwise
Two 12-ounce cans
   evaporated milk
2 cups chopped fresh clams
24 fresh oysters, shucked,
   with liquid reserved
1 tablespoon chopped fresh
   thyme leaves
Salt and freshly ground
   black pepper, to taste
1 tablespoon chopped fresh
   parsley, for garnish

CRABMEAT AND CORN SOUP
GRAND FORMOSA REGENT HOTEL ◆ TAIPEI, TAIWAN

MAKES 4 SERVINGS

2 cups chicken stock
1 cup precooked crabmeat
1½ cups cream style corn
1 tablespoon cornstarch
   dissolved in 1 ounce water
2 egg whites
Salt and pepper, to taste
½ cup sliced scallion

1. In a saucepan or wok, over medium heat, warm the chicken stock to a simmer. Add the crab and cook for 1 minute. Add the corn and cook for 1 minute.

2. Add the cornstarch mixture and cook for 1 minute. Stir in the egg whites, salt and pepper, and simmer for 2 minutes. Pour the soup into serving bowls and sprinkle some of the sliced scallion on top.

> ### ABOUT STORING CHICKEN BROTH
>
> *Instead of storing cans of chicken broth in a cabinet at room temperature, keep them in the refrigerator. Take them out and open them up just before you're going to use the stock. The cold air has turned the fat in the stock to a solid and you'll find it floating on top. Spoon it off and you have saved yourself at least 100 fat calories.*

Gordon Tang, our guide in Taiwan.

NYDIA'S GAZPACHO
NYDIA CARO ◆ SAN JUAN, PUERTO RICO

Born and raised in the Bronx, Nydia Caro moved to Puerto Rico as a teenager and became a television sensation singing rock and roll in English. Soon after, she had her own weekly variety show and remains one of Puerto Rico's most popular entertainers. Because I was also born in the Bronx, she gave me her favorite recipe for gazpacho.

1. Combine all the ingredients except the bell pepper rings in a blender or the bowl of a food processor. Blend until smooth.

2. Transfer to a serving bowl, and chill for at least 2 hours before serving. Garnish with the green pepper rings.

MAKES 4 TO 6 SERVINGS

¼ cup olive oil
4 large tomatoes, cored and cut into chunks
1 green bell pepper, cored, seeded, and cut into chunks
1 red bell pepper, cored, seeded, and cut into chunks
½ onion, chopped
3 cloves garlic
1 tablespoon fresh oregano, or 1 teaspoon dried oregano
1 cup tomato juice
1 teaspoon salt
¼ teaspoon freshly ground black pepper
6 green bell pepper rings, for garnish (optional)

RIPENING YOUR TOMATOES AT HOME

There are a number of fruits that are picked at a point where they still need a little ripening. Bananas, pears, avocados, and tomatoes are the most common of such fruits. This means that when you get your tomatoes home from the market, let them sit for a few days at room temperature. Keep them out of the refrigerator and with the stem up. The shoulders of the tomato are the most delicate part and they bruise easily. Also, store tomatoes out of direct sunlight, which can dry them out. Three to five days of ripening at home and they are ready to eat.

BERMUDA FISH CHOWDER
ONCE UPON A TABLE ◆ HAMILTON, BERMUDA

MAKES 10 SERVINGS

1 tablespoon vegetable oil
3 strips bacon, cut into
   ¼-inch pieces
1 cup onion, thinly sliced
3 cloves garlic, minced
1 teaspoon dried thyme
1 cup chopped celery
1 cup chopped carrots
1 cup tomatoes and their
   juices, canned or fresh
Two 13¾-ounce cans
   chicken stock
2 cups water
2 bay leaves
2 pounds boneless skinless
   scrod, grouper, or other
   firm-fleshed fish
1 tablespoon
   Worcestershire Sauce
¼ cup chopped fresh
   parsley

Track down the history of the word "chowder" and you will end up along the northeast coast of North America. The first printed use of the phrase "fish chowder" shows up in New England during the middle of the 1700s. Herman Melville, the New Englander who wrote **Moby Dick,** *said that parts of the area where he grew up served seafood chowder for breakfast, seafood chowder for lunch, and seafood chowder for dinner, until you started looking at your clothing to see if there were fish bones coming through.*

The following recipe is for a traditional Bermudan fish chowder, and it is excellent. No bones about it.

1. In a large saucepan or stockpot, over medium heat, heat the oil until just shimmering. Add the bacon and cook for 5 minutes. Add the onion and cook for 5 minutes. Add the garlic and thyme and cook for 1 minute. Add the celery and carrots and cook for 5 minutes. Add the tomatoes and their juices, the chicken stock, the water, and the bay leaves. Bring to a boil, reduce the heat to a simmer, and simmer for 1 hour. Add the fish and simmer for 30 minutes longer. Stir in the Worcestershire and parsley.

2. Ladle the soup into serving bowls and garnish.

◆

THE GARNISH

The traditional garnish for this soup is a tablespoon of Goslings Black Seal Rum and a ½ teaspoon of Outerbridge's Sherry Pepper Sauce, both added to the individual soup bowl at the table. If Goslings is not available, a dark, full-flavored rum like Myers's may be substituted. A touch of vinegar and a drop of Tabasco is as close as I can get to Outerbridge's Sherry Pepper Sauce.

Gerhard Lipp.

ABOUT BERMUDA TOURISM

Princess Louise was the daughter of England's Queen Victoria, but because she was married to the Governor General of Canada, she lived in North America. North was the operative word there. Canadian winters can be quite cold and can quickly turn one's mind to thoughts of vacations in the south. But these were the days before air travel, and most winter vacations were limited by the amount of time you were willing to spend on a boat. Florida and the Caribbean had warm weather but they were far away. Bermuda, because it sits in the middle of the warm Gulf Stream, also has warm weather but it is right off the east coast. Take a look at a map and you can see. Bermuda is a three-hour flight from Toronto, less than two hours from New York, and only 2½ from Atlanta. Princess Louise must have had a similar view of the geography because she was the original "discoverer" of Bermuda as a vacation destination. Her first vacation in Bermuda attracted a great deal of press and public attention, and transformed the island into a major holiday spot.

VEGETABLE SOUP WITH PRAWNS OR SHRIMP
QANTAS JET BASE ◆ SYDNEY, AUSTRALIA

MAKES 4 SERVINGS

SOUP
1 tablespoon vegetable oil
1 cup carrots, cut into
  small pieces
1 cup fresh or frozen peas
1 cup tomato, cut into small
  pieces
1 cup zucchini, cut into
  small pieces
4 cups chicken broth

SHRIMP
1 tablespoon vegetable oil
1 clove garlic, thinly sliced
12 medium uncooked
  prawns or shrimp, shelled
  and cleaned
2 tablespoons minced fresh
  basil, or 1 tablespoon
  dried
1 red bell pepper, thinly
  sliced
Juice of 1 lemon
Freshly ground black
  pepper, to taste
12 coriander leaves, for
  garnish

Cheong Tse is the executive chef at Qantas. He was born in Hong Kong and has cooked all over the world, from the classic kitchens of The Dorchester in London, to the Camino Real in Mexico, and back home to The Mandarin in Hong Kong. His extensive knowledge of herbs and spices has given him the ability to produce intensive flavors without the use of salt. He used this skill to develop a series of very interesting salt-free menus for Qantas. A perfect example is this dish of vegetable soup accompanied by sautéed Australian prawns.

1. To make the soup: In a saucepan over medium heat, warm the oil. Then add the vegetables, stir, and cook for 5 minutes. Add the chicken broth, and simmer for 5 minutes.

2. To make the shrimp: In a frying pan over medium-high heat, warm the oil. Then add the garlic, prawns or shrimp, basil, red pepper, lemon juice, and pepper. Stir-fry for 2 minutes, or until the shrimp are cooked.

3. Place 3 shrimp and some of the basil and peppers on one side of a larger serving plate. Garnish with coriander leaves. Pour the soup into a small cup or mug and place the soup on the serving plate next to the shrimp.

HERBS AND SPICES THAT SIMULATE THE TASTE OF SALT

The interaction of basil, garlic, coriander, lemon juice, and pepper stimulates many of the same taste buds that are stimulated by salt. The result is that very often you don't feel the absence of salt in the final flavor.

◆

ABOUT AUSTRALIAN FOOD

Australia is often described as "down under." Well, it may be down under when it comes to geography, but it is clearly on top when it comes to good food. Because Australia is so far away from every other place on the planet, it had to become self-sufficient in terms of food production. Additionally, the food that it produces comes from an environment that is quite unpolluted.

They have fish farms in Tasmania, which is a devil of a place to get to. It's actually an island between the continent of Australia and the Antarctic. The deep cold waters around it produce some of the finest fish in the world. The Australians also come up with great prawns which North Americans call "shrimp." There's wonderful salmon, lobster, orange roughy, and just about every other type of seafood you could possibly want; they have over three thousand different varieties. They produce excellent lamb, which is delivered fresh to North America within four days of processing. The Australians developed the Granny Smith apple and the William pear. They even have an olive oil industry. During the 1980s their wine producers won many of the world's most important competitions and began to develop a major overseas market for their vintages.

Because Australia has a landmass about as large as the United States, with as varied a climate, you can find production areas that range from subtropical banana plantations, to wheat- and rye-producing regions similar to those found in Canada. But food in Australia wasn't always what it is today. For the first 150 years it was tough going for the settlers. They often gave the recipe for galah soup as the most typical recipe of the Australian kitchen. A galah is a local bird, and the recipe is as follows: Place a galah and a large stone in a pot of water. Bring the water to a boil. When the stone is tender, discard the galah and eat the stone.

◆

BERMUDA ONION SOUP
WYNDHAM'S ELBOW BEACH RESORT ◆ BERMUDA

MAKES 8 SERVINGS

2 tablespoons butter
2 tablespoons vegetable oil
3 Bermuda onions, thinly
  sliced, about 5 cups
2 cloves garlic, 1 minced, 1
  sliced in half
½ teaspoon dried thyme
1 bay leaf
8 cups chicken stock
2 tablespoons Outerbridge's
  Sherry Pepper Sauce
  (optional)
16 thin slices French or
  Italian bread
½ cup grated mozzarella
  cheese

Norbert Stange.

There is an ancient legend about the first two steps Satan took when he was cast out of heaven. The spot where he first placed his left foot began to grow garlic, and the area marked by his right foot produced onions.

I wouldn't want to give credit to Satan for two foods that do so much to improve the taste of a recipe, and both garlic and onions have had a long association with good health, especially for the heart. I feel that things that are good for my heart are heavenly. Which is more in line with what the ancient Egyptians felt about onions. They considered them one of the more important foods at temple offerings, and onions are often painted on the walls of the great Egyptian tombs, which is an excellent reminder to store your onions in a cool, dark, and dry place.

1. In a stock pot or sauce pan large enough to hold all the ingredients, over medium heat, heat the butter and the oil together until the butter melts. Add the onions and sauté until the onions begin to turn a milky transparent white.

2. Add the minced garlic, and sauté for 3 minutes more. Add the thyme and the bay leaf, and sauté for 1 minute. Add the chicken stock and the Sherry Pepper Sauce, bring the mixture to a boil, reduce to a simmer, and simmer for 30 minutes.

3. While the soup is cooking, toast the slices of bread until they have a crisp surface. Rub one side of each slice with the cut surface of the sliced garlic clove.

4. Preheat broiler. Remove the bay leaf from the soup. Ladle the soup into individual heat-proof serving bowls. Place two slices of bread on top of the soup. Sprinkle some of the mozzarella cheese on top of the bread. Melt the cheese under a broiler or in the oven. Serve the soup as soon as the cheese is melted.

ABOUT BERMUDA ONIONS

The first onion seeds to arrive in Bermuda came from England in 1616. They may have been the forefathers and mothers of the famous Bermuda onion, or that honor may belong to an onion variety that came to Bermuda with the Portuguese, who started to arrive during the 1840s. No one knows for sure, but what we do know is that, somewhere along the way, a particular variety of onion seed began to grow extremely well in Bermuda's soil. The seeds, the soil, and the climate combined to produce a very special onion with a wonderfully sweet taste.

As time passed, Bermuda began to devote more and more of its farmland to the cultivation of onions. They grew to a rather large size for an onion and their mildness made them very popular throughout Europe, South America, and the United States. The exporting of onions became such a big business that Bermuda sailors became known as "Onions" and Bermuda itself as "The Onion Patch."

Now, this story may be totally untrue, but I have heard it so often that I'll tell it anyway. Folks say that the Bermuda onion became so popular that a group of farmers from Texas came to Bermuda to make a deal to grow the Bermuda onion in Texas. These were the days before Ralph Lauren and Calvin Klein and Mickey Mouse; the people of Bermuda did not understand the concept of licensing. They actually thought that, if an onion was called a Bermuda onion, it should really be grown by Bermudans in Bermuda. Can you imagine that? So they decided not to make the deal. But the guys from Texas were not going to get caught up in a little detail like having Bermuda onions come from Bermuda. They went home, changed the name of their town to Bermuda, Texas, got a trademark from Washington, D.C., and set up an import duty against Bermuda onions coming to the United States from Bermuda.

CARROT SOUP WITH CORIANDER
THE HERBFARM ◆ FALL CITY, WASHINGTON

MAKES 10 TO 12 SERVINGS

4 to 5 tablespoons
   coriander seeds
¼ cup vegetable oil
2 large onions, sliced
2 cloves garlic, minced
2 teaspoons minced fresh
   ginger
2 pounds sliced carrots
3 quarts or six 13¾-ounce
   cans chicken stock
1 teaspoon salt
½ teaspoon freshly ground
   black pepper
2 tablespoons granulated
   sugar (optional)
2 tablespoons freshly
   squeezed lemon juice
½ cup chopped fresh mint
1 cup plain yogurt or crème
   fraîche, for garnish

1. In a dry skillet over medium-high heat, toast the corian-der seeds until golden, about 3 minutes. Shake the seeds con-stantly until they begin to give off a strong fragrance. Cool and process in a blender or mortar and pestle, into a fine powder. Reserve.

2. In a large saucepan over high heat, warm the oil. Add the onions and cook for 3 minutes, stirring occasionally or until the onions are translucent. Add the garlic, ginger, carrots, chicken stock, salt, pepper, and ground coriander. Bring to a boil.

3. Reduce heat; cover and simmer for 45 minutes, or until the carrots are tender. If the carrots are not sweet, add sugar at this time. Stir in the lemon juice. Remove from heat. Process the soup in a food processor until smooth.

4. Just before serving, stir in the fresh mint and garnish each bowl with a dollop of yogurt or crème fraîche.

Jerry Traunfeld.

THE HERBFARM

Just east of the city of Seattle is a place called The Herbfarm. It was started in 1972 when Bill and Lola Zimmerman purchased a small piece of land and started to prepare for Bill's retirement from Boeing aircraft company. One day Lola had a few extra potted herbs from her garden, so she put them in a wheelbarrow, set them under a walnut tree on the side of the road, and placed instructions for payment next to a jar in the barrow. By the end of the day, the barrow was empty and the jar was full. Lola repeated the process until The Herbfarm grew into a business that produces over a quarter of a million plants. It has a wonderful restaurant that is regularly chosen by the people of Seattle as one of their favorites. There's also a gift shop, a national mail-order catalog, and a herbal educational program that holds classes. These days over eighty thousand people stop by each season.

The Herbfarm did not grow very much until 1986. That was the year that Lola's son Ron, and his wife, Carrie Van Dyck, took over the operation of the business and put Ron's marketing talents to work. The restaurant was originally opened by Ron, who had no formal training as a chef, but clearly knew how to cook. As the business grew, it became necessary for Ron to bring in a professional chef. His choice was Jerry Traunfeld, who prepares a delicious soup based on carrots.

◆

BURT WOLF

ABOUT CARROTS

Carrots were one of the very first foods in the human diet. They got their start in Afghanistan and were spread to both Europe and Asia. When they were brought to North America by the early colonists some of the seeds escaped from the gardens and became wild carrots. You see them all along our roadsides in the form of Queen Anne's lace. The state of California cultivates sixty thousand acres with carrots so the country has a fresh supply all year long.

These days the cultivated carrot is getting the royal treatment because of its nutritional value. Carrots appear to help protect us against heart disease and cancer. There have been over three hundred research studies involving beta-carotene, vitamin A, and carrots. The results of the studies all seem to point in the same direction. Beta-carotene in its natural form appears to help protect both smokers and nonsmokers from lung cancer. It also plays a role in defending our arteries from the fatty buildup that causes heart attacks and strokes. A study by the United States Department of Agriculture showed that seven ounces of carrots each day could reduce cholesterol levels by as much as 11 percent. These days, it looks like it's a carrot a day that will keep the doctor away.

There are, however, a few things to remember about carrots. To get the most vitamin A out of a carrot, it should be cooked. Five minutes of steaming or microwaving will do the trick. The darker the orange color the more beta-carotene in the carrot. If you purchase carrots with the green leaves on top, take them off as soon as you get home. The leaves draw moisture from the roots. Finally, don't store carrots near apples, pears, or other fruits that give off ethylene gas as they ripen. The gas can cause the carrots to develop a bitter taste. The best way to store a carrot is in the refrigerator in the same type of plastic bag in which they are usually packed in your supermarket.

◆

STEWS

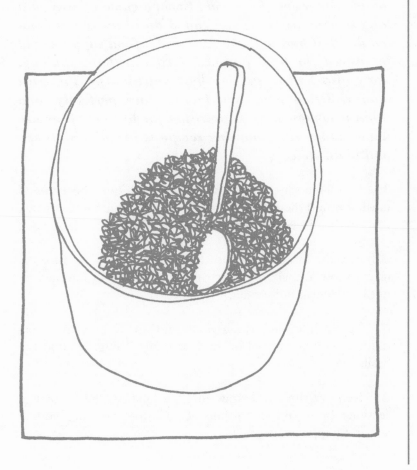

LENTIL STEW
THE BUCCANEER RESORT ◆ ST. CROIX, U.S. VIRGIN ISLANDS

MAKES 6 TO 8 SERVINGS

2 tablespoons vegetable oil
1 cup coarsely chopped
   celery
1 cup coarsely chopped
   carrots
1 medium onion, coarsely
   chopped
1 pound lentils
1¼ cups chicken broth or
   stock
2 oranges
10 fresh basil leaves
2 tablespoons fresh lemon
   juice
Salt and pepper, to taste

When Mike Smith first started cooking at The Buccaneer resort on the U.S. Virgin Island of St. Croix, he noticed that dried peas and lentils were a regular part of the diet, and had been in the St. Croix kitchens for hundreds of years. The reason was quite simple. The people who came here from Europe came by way of a long ocean voyage. They ended up in an island community that had to make sure that a food supply could be stored for long periods of time without spoiling. They also had to get the best nutrition for the least money. Dried peas and lentils store perfectly, and when it comes to good nutrition for low cost they are unbeatable. The following recipe is for Mike's orange and lentil stew.

1. In a large saucepan over medium-high heat, heat the oil until hot. Add the celery, carrots, and onion, and sauté, stirring frequently, until the onion is translucent, about 5 minutes.

2. Add the lentils and broth and bring to a boil. Reduce the heat to low and simmer uncovered for about 45 minutes, or until the lentils are tender.

3. Meanwhile, peel the oranges and divide them into sections, removing any white pith or seeds. Roughly chop the basil.

4. Remove the lentil stew from the heat, stir in the orange sections, basil, and lemon juice. Check for seasoning, adding salt and pepper as needed.

◆

ABOUT LENTILS

The lentil was one of the first foods brought under cultivation. The ancient Greeks had them as part of their diet, and so did the Romans. Lentils are very valuable from the point of view of good nutrition, but they are also very inexpensive. In ancient times, if you became rich but still ate lentils it was a sign that you had not lost touch with reality and become a snob.

Today almost all of the lentils available in the United States are grown in the Northwest, in an area that spans the border between Idaho and Washington State. It's called the Palouse, a French word that means "green lawn," which is rather descriptive for an area that specializes in lentils and peas. Lentils are high in fiber, potassium, and a substance called folate or folic acid. Folic acid is very important in the diet of pregnant women. A series of studies has shown the need for folic acid during pregnancy and a number of health-promoting organizations like the March of Dimes have started programs to make people aware of the importance of folic acid.

Lentils also contain a lot of protein. Because they are a vegetable, however, it is not a complete protein. That is to say lentils do not contain all of the amino acids that make up a complete protein. But if you take the lentils and combine them in a dish with nuts or grains like rice, you end up with a protein that is as complete as the protein you would find in meat, fish, or poultry. You don't even need to add the nuts and grains in the same recipe, or even the same meal. As long as it's in the same day, you're fine. Lentils are also low in fat and sodium. They are good stuff, easy to cook and perfect for soups, stews, sauces, stuffings, and salads.

The Bible says that Esau sold his birthright for a bowl of lentil stew. It might not have been a great deal from a financial point of view, but when it comes to good nutrition, he was clearly moving in the right direction.

◆

WHAT WE CAN LEARN
FROM GALLEY COOKS

During my late twenties I took all of my savings and a substantial bank loan and put the funds into the purchase of a boat. I learned quite a bit from the experience. I learned the truth of the old saying that a boat is a hole in the water into which you throw money. I also learned how wonderful it is to get away from everything and settle in to the real rhythm of nature—the sea and the sky. The sun wakes you up instead of an alarm clock, and the moon puts you to sleep instead of "The Tonight Show." I also learned a lot about how to make good food under bad conditions. Much of what I learned from my days at sea works just as well in a home kitchen. Here are a few examples of what I mean:

- *Breakfasts are our most important meal, but not everyone is ready to do much cooking first thing in the morning. So do a little the night before. Good old-style oatmeal is one of my favorite breakfasts and one of the healthiest too. Oats appear to have the ability to lower cholesterol levels. Instead of facing twenty minutes over a simmering saucepan in the morning, I put the oats and boiling water into a wide-mouth insulated bottle, close it up, and let it cook over night. In the morning my oatmeal is ready. It's a good start for the ocean or the office.*

- *When you're pouring something into a glass or a cup, do the job over the sink. If anything spills you save the cleanup work and the surface of your counter.*

- *Cookie dough freezes well, so mix up a batch of your favorite cookie dough, roll it out into portion-size balls, and freeze them. Then keep the balls frozen until you are ready to bake them.*

- *When you have dry-ingredient mixtures that are a regular part of your cooking, make those mixtures when you bring those ingredients back from the supermarket and keep them in an airtight container. For example, I have a standard pancake mix that I make. It requires equal amounts of whole-wheat flour, white flour, and cornmeal, plus a little baking soda. I mix that together ahead of time and when I want to make pancakes I combine one cup of that mixture with one cup of skim milk and an egg white. The result is a high-fiber pancake that's great. The cornmeal gives them a nice crunch.*

SHRIMP ASOPAO (SHRIMP STEW)
EL SAN JUAN HOTEL ◆ SAN JUAN, PUERTO RICO

Asopao is a stew made with rice and seafood or chicken. It is as traditional a Puerto Rican specialty as you can find. The following recipe is how it is prepared by Chef John Carey of the El San Juan Hotel.

1. In a large saucepan over medium-high heat, heat the vegetable oil until hot. Add the onion and sauté until translucent, 3 to 4 minutes.

2. Add the tomatoes and sauté until softened, 2 to 3 minutes. Add the shrimp and sauté until opaque, about 3 minutes. Stir in the recaito. Add the remaining ingredients, and stir well. Bring the stew almost to a boil, then serve at once.

NOTE: If recaito is not available, combine equal parts of chopped onion, chopped jalapeño peppers, and cilantro, and add a little olive oil.

MAKES 6 SERVINGS

2 tablespoons vegetable oil
1 cup chopped onion
2½ cups chopped, seeded tomatoes
16 large uncooked shrimp, peeled, cleaned, and deveined
¼ cup recaito (see Note)
5 cups warm chicken stock
3 cups cooked white rice
1 cup cooked asparagus tips
1 cup cooked peas, fresh or frozen
½ cup chopped stuffed olives

RECAITO

Recaito is a seasoning mixture. In Puerto Rico most cooks buy it ready-made in a jar, but you can make a fairly close duplication by mixing together equal amounts of chopped onions, chopped jalepeño peppers, and chopped cilantro with a little bit of olive oil.

◆

◆

ABOUT PUERTO RICAN CULINARY TRADITION

The recipes and kitchen techniques that make up today's Puerto Rican cooking result from the blending together of three major culinary traditions. The oldest is that of the original Taino tribe whose residence in Puerto Rico dates back to A.D. 300. Superimposed on that are the gastronomic influences of the Spanish, who came during the early 1500s. Finally, the dishes of the Africans, who began arriving in Puerto Rico over four hundred years ago, were yet another influence. The chili peppers, root vegetables, corn, local fruits, and fish were on the island with the Tainos. The Spanish brought beef cattle, goats, sheep, pigs, olive oil, and some new fruits, and vegetables, including coconuts, bananas, plantains, and citrus fruits. They also brought sugar and coffee. The West Africans introduced an entire cooking style based on the slow cooking of one-pot dishes. Many of the great soups and stews of Puerto Rico have their origins in the pots of West Africa. The Africans also brought to Puerto Rico okra, a vegetable that has become a part of many Southern stews. The African word for okra is gumbo. So, every time you see a dish described as a gumbo, you are looking at a recipe that has a West African heritage and was originally made with okra.

◆

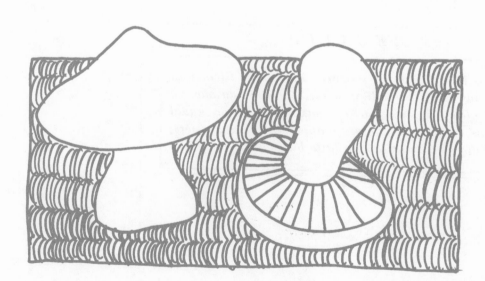

SOFRITO
LUQUILLO KIOSKOS, PUERTO RICO

Of all the elements in Puerto Rican cooking none is more Puerto Rican than sofrito. Sofrito is a seasoning sauce that is incorporated into stews, soups, rice dishes, and anything else the cook feels is appropriate. It has a subtle and delicate flavor and deserves its reputation. It's traditionally made with pork fat, but I tested the recipe with vegetable oil and it worked fine. It's important to remember that the lower your diet is in saturated fat, the better off you are. The following is a healthful adaptation of the classic sofrito.

1. In a large stockpot, heat the oil. Add the prosciutto and sauté until golden over medium heat. Reduce the heat to low and add the remaining ingredients. Simmer for about 10 minutes, or until tender, stirring occasionally.

2. Cool thoroughly and spoon into freezer containers, filling three quarters full. Freeze. Transfer as needed to the refrigerator. A few tablespoons of this mixture is often added as seasoning to a Puerto Rican recipe.

MAKES 5 CUPS

1 cup vegetable oil
6 ounces prosciutto or lean cured ham, cut into ¼-inch pieces
2 medium onions, chopped
2 large green bell peppers, seeded, ribs removed, chopped
4 red Italian frying peppers, or 2 medium red bell peppers, seeded, ribs removed, chopped
6 cloves garlic, chopped
20 cilantro leaves, chopped
4 teaspoons dried oregano

PUERTO RICAN CHICKEN GUMBO
SANDS HOTEL ◆ SAN JUAN, PUERTO RICO

MAKES 6 SERVINGS

2 tablespoons vegetable oil
1½ cups diced carrots
1½ cups diced celery
1½ cups diced green bell
   peppers
1½ cups chopped onions
3 boneless, skinless chicken
   breasts, cut into bite-size
   pieces
1½ cups chopped fresh or
   frozen okra
½ cup chopped scallions
5 cups diced potatoes
10 cups chicken stock
2 teaspoons hot sauce
Pinch of saffron (optional)
¼ teaspoon white pepper
¼ teaspoon freshly ground
   black pepper
1 teaspoon salt
Cooked white rice, for
   serving

The faces of the people of San Juan tell the story of the major migrations to the island. The Taino tribes of South America, the Spanish, and the Africans can be seen on the streets of the city. The culinary traditions that each group brought can be seen in the town's pots and pans. Chef Ramon Rosario, the executive chef at the Sands Hotel in San Juan, prepares a Puerto Rican gumbo with a recipe that clearly started in West Africa. It uses okra which was brought to the Caribbean by West Africans and continues with chickens, olive oil, and carrots which came over with the Spanish.

1. In a large saucepan or stockpot over medium-high heat, warm the vegetable oil until hot. Add the carrots, celery, bell peppers, and onions, and sauté until the onions are translucent, about 5 minutes.

2. Add the chicken and sauté until almost cooked through, about 3 minutes. Stir in the okra, scallions, potatoes, chicken stock, hot sauce, and seasonings. Bring to a boil over high heat.

3. Reduce the heat to medium and simmer uncovered for 30 minutes, or until the potatoes are tender. Serve over hot, white rice.

◆

WALDORF LAMB STEW
WALDORF-ASTORIA ◆ NEW YORK, NEW YORK

The Irish peasant farmers of the 1800s led an extremely difficult life. The recurrent crop failures kept them on the edge. As a result, they developed many techniques for getting the most for the least, especially when it came to cooking. John Doherty, the executive chef at New York's Waldorf-Astoria Hotel, learned about Irish cooking in his mother's kitchen and prepares a home-style recipe for Irish lamb stew.

1. Place the cubed lamb in a stockpot. Add the cold water and bring to a rolling boil. Turn off the heat. Drain off all of the water, leaving the meat in the pot.

2. Pour in enough fresh water to just cover the meat. Add the onions, leeks, garlic, bay leaf, and thyme. Bring the mixture to a boil over moderate heat. Stir in the potatoes. Cover and cook for 30 minutes over low heat.

3. Taste and season well with salt and pepper. Remove the bay leaf and discard. Serve the stew in shallow bowls, garnished with chopped parsley.

MAKES 6 TO 8 SERVINGS

1 boneless leg of lamb
    (about 5 pounds),
    trimmed well and cut into
    cubes
4 cups cold water
4 cups thinly sliced onions,
    separated into rings
1 cup sliced leeks (the white
    and light green parts)
4 cloves garlic, sliced
1 bay leaf
1 teaspoon fresh thyme
    leaves, chopped
5 large potatoes, peeled and
    thinly sliced
Salt and freshly ground
    black pepper
Chopped parsley, for
    garnish

ABOUT LEEKS

The leek is a member of the Lily family and has an onionlike bulb at its base. Archaeologists tell us that we have been growing leeks for over four thousand years. The ancient Egyptians cultivated them. Records show that leeks were part of the rations for the workers who built the pyramids. The Assyrians believed that leeks had considerable medical value. They were recommended to prevent your hair from turning white—a bit of information that I could have put to good use about twenty-five years ago. Leeks were quite popular in the United States during the early years of this century but seem to have lost the limelight in the 1930s. They did not make their comeback until the last few years.

The one thing you must remember when you are using leeks is that they almost always have a great deal of soil between the leaves and you must clean them carefully. Trim off the roots from the bottom and any damaged ends at the top. The best technique for getting out the soil is to cut two slices down the center of the leaves so you've actually quartered them. Then open the leaves as you hold them under running water. When you've got out the grit, slice them into the size called for in your recipe, and you're ready to cook.

ABOUT THE IRISH AND THEIR FOOD

On New Year's Day of 1892, a fifteen-year-old girl named Annie Moore became the first immigrant to pass through the government station on Ellis Island in New York Harbor. She had come from County Cork in Ireland. Annie Moore was welcomed to her new home by millions of Irish men and women who had come to the United States to avoid starvation after the potato crops repeatedly failed during the 1800s. For many years, the potatoes had been the basis for almost every meal in the Irish peasant household. The Irish had developed an unending collection of recipes for potatoes. Three of the most popular dishes are colcannon, boxty, and Dublin coddle. Colcannon is mashed potatoes and vegetables, usually cabbage. Boxty is potato pastry filled with bacon. Dublin coddle is a casserole of bacon, sausages, onions, and potatoes. When the Irish arrived in North America, they immediately planted potatoes and single-handedly gave rise to the popularity of potatoes in the United States. Today, potatoes are becoming even more popular as people begin to use simple baked potatoes as snacks. Potatoes are low in fat, an excellent source of potassium and fiber, and contain only 150 calories.

FISH AND SEAFOOD

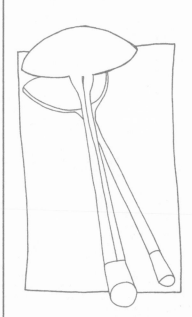

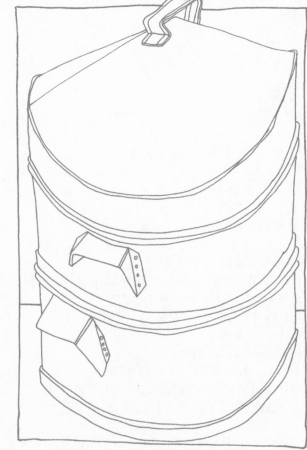

FISH WITH LIME SAUCE
SANDS HOTEL ◆ SAN JUAN, PUERTO RICO

Many of the chefs working in San Juan have come to Puerto Rico from other parts of the world. However, instead of trying to reproduce the cooking of their homelands, they quickly fall in love with the traditional dishes and ingredients of the island. For example, Peter Ivanovick of California prepares local specialties at the Reino Del Mar Restaurant in San Juan's Sands Hotel.

1. In a nonstick skillet over medium-high heat, combine the garlic, lime juice, vermouth or white wine, cilantro, capers, and vegetables. Stir-fry briefly, just until the carrot strips are limp, about 3 minutes. Remove from the heat.

2. In a large nonstick skillet over medium-high heat, heat the vegetable oil until it starts to shimmer.

3. Meanwhile, coat the fish fillets with the flour; then, dip into the beaten eggs. Add the fish to the skillet and sauté for 3 minutes on each side, until lightly browned and cooked through.

4. Place the fish fillets on the serving plates and top with the sauce. Serve at once.

MAKES 4 SERVINGS

2 tablespoons chopped garlic
¼ cup fresh lime juice
¼ cup vermouth or white wine
½ cup chopped cilantro leaves
2 tablespoons drained capers
1 small onion, cut into 2-×-¼-inch strips
2 small carrots, cut into 2-×-¼-inch strips
1 small green bell pepper, cut into 2-×-¼-inch strips
3 tablespoons vegetable oil
4 sole or flounder fillets
½ cup all-purpose flour
2 eggs, beaten

◆

PEANUT-CRUSTED FISH WITH RED PEPPER SAUCE

THE BUCCANEER RESORT ◆ ST. CROIX, U.S. VIRGIN ISLANDS

MAKES 4 SERVINGS

RED PEPPER SAUCE
1 tablespoon vegetable oil
4 medium red bell peppers,
  seeded and roughly
  chopped
1 small onion, roughly
  chopped
2 cloves garlic, crushed
2 tablespoons water

PEANUT-CRUSTED FISH
½ cup finely chopped
  unsalted peanuts
¼ cup finely ground coffee
  beans
¼ cup curry powder
½ cup all-purpose flour
1 egg
⅓ cup milk
4 flaky white fish fillets,
  such as scrod

There are a number of elements that give each regional cuisine its distinct flavors; the most important are the seasonings. When we think about the flavor of Louisiana what comes through most often is cayenne, in Italy it's oregano, and sesame is regularly associated with the tastes of China.

Mike Smith is the executive chef at the Brass Parrot Restaurant at The Buccaneer resort on the U.S. Virgin Island of St. Croix, and he has been studying the use of seasonings by world latitude. He sees a pattern of spice use based on the area's relationship to the equator, and he is testing his theory with this Peanut-Crusted Fish.

1. For the sauce: In a small saucepan over medium heat, warm the oil until hot. Add the bell peppers, onion, and garlic. Cover and cook for 7 minutes, or until the onion is translucent.

2. Stir in the water and mix well. Set aside to cool for 10 minutes. Puree the mixture in a blender until smooth. Set aside.

3. Preheat the oven to 350° F. Line a baking sheet or jelly-roll pan with parchment paper.

4. For the fish: On a shallow plate, combine the peanuts, ground coffee beans, and curry powder. Place the flour on another plate. In a shallow bowl, whisk together the egg and milk.

◆

5. Coat each fish fillet first in the flour, then in the egg wash, and finally in the peanut mixture. Place the fillets on the prepared baking sheet and bake for 20 minutes, or until the fish is cooked through and flaky.

6. Divide the sauce among 4 dinner plates and place a fish fillet on top. Serve at once.

Manny Centeno,
Director of the
Film Promotion Office,
who guided us through
the United States
Virgin Islands.

ABOUT THE ESTATE WHIM PLANTATION MUSEUM

The cone-shape towers that dot the landscape of the U.S. Virgin Island of St. Croix are monumental reminders of the island's agricultural past. They are the remains of windmills that were used to power grinders that crushed sugarcane. When the Danish bought St. Croix from the French, they turned it into one of the most important sugar-producing colonies in the Caribbean. Europe had developed an almost insatiable sweet tooth, and these sugar plantations became the source of its satisfaction. It also became the source of extraordinary wealth for the planters.

Today, on the west end of St. Croix, there is an excellent restoration of a plantation from the 1700s known as Estate Whim. The cane came in from the fields and went into the windmill to be crushed. If the wind wasn't blowing the crushing was done by horse power. The juices were drained out and transferred to kettles, where they were boiled down to molasses, and in some cases eventually dried out to sugar. The owner of the plantation lived in the "great house," which even by today's standards looks pretty great.

A BRIEF HISTORY OF ST. CROIX

During his second voyage in 1493, Columbus came upon a group of islands which he named the Virgin Islands after the legend of St. Ursula. The story is about the son of a powerful pagan prince who demanded the hand in marriage of Ursula, the beautiful daughter of the King of Britain. Ursula had pledged herself to a life of saintliness, but in order to save her father and his kingdom from the pagan prince she agreed to the marriage. There was, however, one condition. Eleven thousand of the most beautiful virgins in the two kingdoms had to become her companions for the next three years. At the end of that time she would marry the pagan prince. The deal was made and the eleven thousand virgins showed up for the three-year stint. During those three years Ursula trained the girls into an army of amazons and pledged their allegiance to God. When the pagan prince found out what was going on he flew into a rage, and in the year 238 took his army into battle against Ursula. During the battle, which is said to have taken place near the German city of Cologne, all of the virgins were martyred.

When Columbus saw the beauty of these islands they reminded him of the legend of St. Ursula, and he called them the Virgin Islands. There are actually dozens of islands in the group, but the three most famous are St. Thomas, St. John, and St. Croix. St. Croix is the largest of the U.S. Virgin Islands, with a surface of about eighty square miles. Most of those square miles are flat enough for farming, which is not true for St. Thomas and St. John. As a result, St. Croix developed as an agricultural base.

At first it was home to the Arawak, Taino, and Carib tribes that had arrived from South America. Then the Spanish stopped in. When they had trouble defending their widespread interests in the Caribbean, the French took over. After the French, came the Dutch. The Knights of Malta had a base there, and for almost two hundred years the Danish had control. The area was known as the Danish West Indies until 1917, when the United States government plunked down $25 million in gold and purchased the property from Denmark. Acre for acre it's the most money that the federal government has ever paid for land, but it was well worth it. At the time, the United States was involved in World War I, and people in Washington were concerned that Germany might use the Danish West Indies to set up a submarine base.

RED SNAPPER WITH BLACK BEAN SALSA
EL SAN JUAN HOTEL ◆ SAN JUAN, PUERTO RICO

The Taino tribes that came to Puerto Rico from South America were skilled farmers who had developed a series of planting methods that were ideal for their environment. A number of different crops were planted in the same mound of earth. Those that needed a lot of water went on the bottom. Those that required good drainage went on the top. The tribes grew a range of vegetables that included yams, corn, various squashes, and beans. They gathered fruits and nuts, made nets and fished the waters, and hunted with bows and arrows for small game. One of the old Taino recipes called for the frying of fish in corn oil. John Carey, chef at the El San Juan Hotel, prepares the dish much as it was done 1,000 years ago.

MAKES 4 SERVINGS

Two 16-ounce cans black
  beans, drained and rinsed
1 large tomato, seeded and
  roughly chopped
⅓ cup chopped scallions
2 tablespoons chopped
  fresh cilantro
2 tablespoons olive oil
1 tablespoon fresh lemon
  juice
Salt and black pepper, to
  taste
¼ cup vegetable oil
4 whole red snappers
  (about 12 ounces each),
  cleaned

1. In a large bowl, combine the beans, tomato, scallions, cilantro, olive oil, and lemon juice. Season with salt and black pepper. Cover and refrigerate for 1 hour.

2. In a large skillet over medium-high heat, heat the oil until hot. Add the fish and sauté for 5 minutes on each side, or until cooked through.

3. Drain the fish on paper towels. Serve hot, with the chilled black bean salsa.

FISH STEAKS WITH PAPAYA SALSA
HALEKULANI HOTEL ◆ HONOLULU, HAWAII

MAKES 4 SERVINGS

PAPAYA SALSA
¼ cup fresh lime juice
½ jalapeño pepper, seeded
  and finely chopped,
  (approximately 1 heaping
  teaspoon)
1 tablespoon finely chopped
  fresh ginger
½ cup vegetable oil
2 cloves garlic, minced
½ cup chopped onion
1 fresh ripe papaya, peeled,
  seeded, and cut into bite-
  size pieces
1 red bell pepper, seeded
  and coarsely chopped
1 tablespoon minced
  cilantro, leaves only
Salt and freshly ground
  black pepper, to taste

FISH
Four 3- to 4-ounce fish
  steaks (such as moonfish,
  salmon, tuna, swordfish,
  or monkfish), trimmed of
  all skin, excess fat, and
  bones

George Mavrothalassitis was born in the south of France on the shores of the Mediterranean Sea and trained with some of the great chefs of Paris. These days he is the executive chef at a magnificent restaurant called La Mer, which is French for "the sea." When I call him an artist, it's not just a figure of speech. George starts his recipes with a drawing, a precise vision of what he wants to present. The following is his recipe for Fish Steaks with Papaya Salsa.

1. To make the salsa: In a mixing bowl, gently combine all of the ingredients. Cover and let the mixture rest, at room temperature, for 1 hour, at which point it can be refrigerated for future use. The salsa should be brought back to room temperature before serving.

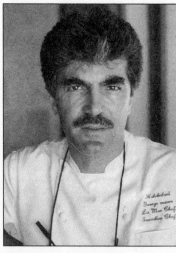

2. To make the fish: Baste the fish steaks with a little of the salsa juice and place them into the basket of a steamer. Steam them over hot water for 8 to 10 minutes, or until cooked to your preferred degree of doneness.

3. Transfer the fish to serving plates. Put some of the salsa on each piece of fish.

George Mavrothalassitis.

ABOUT PAPAYA

Shortly after Columbus landed in the Caribbean he noted in his log book that the natives were very strong and lived largely on a tree melon called "the fruit of the angels." The particular fruit that Columbus was actually talking about was the papaya.

European countries that had trading companies in the Caribbean, such as France, England, and Portugal, were also doing business in the South Pacific; they brought the papaya to Hawaii. If you see a fresh papaya in a U.S. market, the odds are a thousand to one that it was grown in Hawaii.

When you are picking out a papaya in your market, look for ones that have a smooth and unblemished skin. The green color should be gone and replaced with a golden yellow-orange. Half a papaya has almost 80 calories and is a good source of vitamins C and A, and potassium. Papayas can be served as a fruit with a spray of lemon or lime juice to enhance the flavor in salads, or as the container for seafood or chicken recipes. Hawaiian cooks use papayas to make jams, jellies, drinks, and sherbets. Perhaps the papaya's most unusual quality is its ability to tenderize meat. Its juice contains the enzyme which is used to make commercial tenderizers. Moisten tough meat with a few drops of papaya juice and you will see a magical effect.

◆

PAPAYA FOR THE GODS

When a volcano would erupt in Hawaii, an offering of meat was thrown into the fiery lava in order to quiet down Pele, the goddess of volcanoes. You always threw in a papaya to make sure that the meat offering would be tender. A small touch, but the kind of thing a goddess always appreciates.

◆

RED SNAPPER WITH HAWAIIAN PESTO SAUCE
KAHALA HILTON ◆ HONOLULU, HAWAII

MAKES 4 SERVINGS

PESTO SAUCE
4 tablespoons vegetable oil
½ cup fresh ginger, sliced
  into matchstick shapes
4 cloves garlic, peeled and
  minced
¼ cup nuts (macadamia,
  cashew, pine, or any
  combination)
¼ cup minced cilantro
  leaves
¼ cup minced basil leaves
Juice of 1 lemon
Tabasco sauce, to taste
1 tablespoon sesame oil

RED SNAPPER
Juice of 1 lemon
2 cups fish stock (or
  chicken stock or water)
1 pound red snapper fillets,
  cut into four 4-ounce
  portions

1. For the sauce: In a small saucepan over medium-high heat, heat 2 tablespoons of the vegetable oil. Add the ginger and garlic, reduce the heat to medium, and cook for 1 minute, stirring constantly.

2. Pour the cooked ginger and garlic into a blender, add all the other sauce ingredients, including the remaining oil, and process until smooth, about 2 minutes.

3. For the fish: Select a pan that will hold all of the fish in one compact layer. Pour in the lemon juice and stock or water and bring to a simmer. Place the fish into the simmering liquid and cook for 8 minutes, or until the fish is fully cooked to your taste. Remove the fish from the pan and hold aside on a covered plate.

4. Raise the heat to high and boil down the remaining cooking liquid until you have only a ½ cup of liquid left. Then add in the contents of the blender. Stir and cook for 2 minutes, until the sauce is heated.

5. Place the fish on a serving dish and pour the sauce over the fish.

◆

ABOUT HAWAIIAN GINGER

Ginger originated in southeast Asia and was transplanted to the warm growing areas of the planet thousands of years ago. Ancient documents show that ginger was being traded around the Mediterranean in the first century A.D. By the eleventh century it was showing up in English recipes, and the Spaniards started planting it in the Caribbean right after the arrival of Columbus.

Hawaii's early immigrants were from southern China, especially the district of Canton. It was only natural that the Cantonese style of Chinese cooking became an important part of Hawaiian cuisine. Stir-frying is a major technique in Cantonese food preparation and fresh ginger is a common ingredient in many stir-fried recipes. As a result, fresh ginger became an important crop in Hawaii.

The ginger that is grown in Hawaii has a rich, pungent, and peppery flavor. It's an ideal flavoring agent for appetizers, salads, soups, and the natural sauces that are made for meat, fish, and poultry. When you're picking out fresh ginger in the market, look for roots that are smooth and firm. At home, peel off the outer skin, and slice the ginger thinly or chop it according to the recipe. Remember, whenever you are using fresh ginger you want to chop it, not grate it. The grating takes out the moisture and reduces the flavor.

ABOUT TARO

For thousands of years, a tropical plant called taro has been the basic starch for many cultural groups living in the South Pacific. Taro was brought to Hawaii by the Polynesians about 1,500 years ago and quickly became a food of great importance. The root is baked and pounded into a puree called poi, which is served at every luau. It has a taste somewhere between artichoke hearts and chestnuts.

The islanders realized that poi could be wrapped in leaves and stored for months at a time without losing its nutritional value. That made it a perfect food to bring on long ocean voyages or to store as a secure food supply. These days taro is used in Hawaii to make the traditional poi, but you also find it in stuffings, cakes, breads, and stews. The leaves are used as if they were spinach.

Taro root and its leaves are a good source of protein, vitamins A and C, thiamin, riboflavin, niacin, calcium, and iron. Taro is very low in fat and high in complex carbohydrates. The actual starch grains are so small that they are easily digested by infants, the elderly, or people with restricted diets.

SWORDFISH WITH A WATERCRESS CRUST
HALEKULANI HOTEL ◆ HONOLULU, HAWAII

MAKES 4 SERVINGS

CRUST
1 bunch watercress, thick
  stems removed
  (approximately 3 cups
  lightly packed)
2 egg whites
1 tablespoon vegetable oil
Salt and freshly ground
  black pepper, to taste

FISH
Four 3- to 4-ounce
  swordfish steaks, about ¾
  inch thick, trimmed of all
  skin, fat, and dark areas
Salt and freshly ground
  black pepper, to taste
1 tablespoon vegetable oil

FOR SERVING:
Steamed carrots with fresh
  ginger
Steamed whole-grain rice

1. Preheat the oven to 350° F.

2. To make the crust: Place all of the ingredients into a food processor or a blender and process until you have a smooth puree, about 2 minutes.

3. To make the fish: Season with salt and pepper. In a saucepan with a heat-proof handle, heat the vegetable oil and cook the swordfish steaks for 1 minute on each side. The pan and the oil should be hot when the fish goes in, the objective is to slightly brown the surface of the swordfish.

4. Remove the pan from the heat. Coat the top of each fish steak with some of the watercress puree. Place the pan into the preheated oven for 5 minutes, or until the fish is cooked to your preferred degree of doneness.

5. The fish should be served immediately. Chef George Mavrothalassitis at the Halekulani Hotel serves the fish with steamed carrots flavored with fresh ginger and a side dish of whole-grain rice.

TRIM OFF THE DARK PARTS OF FISH

Wherever you have a piece of fish with a dark core, cut it out. If there are impurities in the fish, this is where they are most often stored.

THE POLYNESIAN FOOD OF HAWAII

About 1,500 years ago, the first people to immigrate to Hawaii were from Polynesia, particularly Tahiti. They sailed in with a cargo of pigs, chickens, coconuts, bananas, ginger, sugarcane, and a starchy root called taro. Their major food festival was called a "luau." The luau was a way of bringing all members of a family together for a shared experience. Today, authentic luaus are presented from time to time as charity events.

Preparation for a luau centers around an imu, an ancient form of oven dug into the ground. The base and walls of the pit are lined with fragrant wood and lava stones. A pig is surrounded with tea and banana leaves, covered, and placed in the imu. The fire heats up and the meat is cooked in the steam. Ten to twelve hours later, you are ready for the ultimate pig-out.

ABOUT WATERCRESS

Watercress has been part of the human diet for thousands of years. The ancient Greeks were great lovers of watercress and recommended it as a health food. They would feed it to their soldiers before a battle. About two thousand years later, the English navy had a similar approach. They used it to prevent scurvy, a disease caused by a shortage of vitamin C. Both the Greeks and the English knew what they were talking about. Watercress is packed with vitamin C as well as carotene, a building block for vitamin A, which may turn out to be a cancer blocker. Watercress also contains a collection of minerals which are important to good health.

PICKEREL WITH TOMATO AND BASIL
CANADA'S VIA RAIL TRAIN

MAKES 4 SERVINGS

4 tablespoons vegetable oil
1 cup finely chopped onions
2 cups roughly chopped
   tomatoes
2 tablespoons drained
   capers
¼ cup chopped fresh basil
1 tablespoon Pernod
   (optional)
Salt and freshly ground
   black pepper, to taste
¼ cup all-purpose flour
4 boneless, skinless pickerel
   or any firm white fish
   fillets

As Via Rail's transcontinental express train rolls through the Canadian province of Saskatchewan, it passes some of the best fishing areas in North America . . . a fact which is regularly honored by the chefs on board. You will often see local fish, such as this pickerel dish, on the menu.

1. In a large skillet over medium-high heat, heat 2 tablespoons of the oil. Add the onions and sauté until translucent, 3 to 5 minutes.

2. Stir in the tomatoes, capers, basil, and Pernod (if used), and cook until heated through, about 5 minutes. Season with salt and pepper. Cover the skillet and let stand over very low heat.

3. Meanwhile, place the flour in a shallow plate. Coat the fish fillets lightly with the flour.

4. In a large skillet over medium-high heat, heat the remaining 2 tablespoons of vegetable oil. Add the fish fillets and cook for 1 to 2 minutes on each side, or until the fish is cooked through.

5. Drain the fish on paper towels. Place each fillet on a dinner plate and cover with a quarter of the sauce.

ABOUT CAPERS

Capers are the buds of an unopened flower that have been pickled. They are picked from a bush which we think originated in North Africa but now grows throughout the countries that border on the Mediterranean Sea. Recently we have begun to grow them in the southern part of the United States.

As a general rule, the smaller the caper, the better the quality. The best are the tiny nonpareils. The larger capers are very tasty but stronger in flavor. It's usually a good idea to chop up the larger capers before you use them in a recipe.

It's also easy to change the flavoring put in by the pickling process. When you get the capers home from the market, just pour off the liquid that they are being held in, and pour in something with a flavor that you want. I often pour in some sherry wine. The alcohol in the sherry acts as a natural preservative and I much prefer the mild flavor of the wine to the intensity of the brine in which capers are usually shipped. Keep the jar in your refrigerator, and after a few days you will have an interesting flavor added to the capers. You will have also flavored the sherry which can be used as a flavoring agent all by itself.

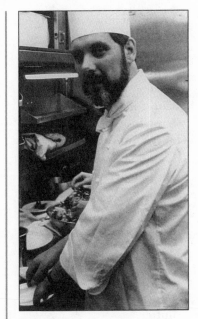

Dave Kissack.

FISH PROVENÇALE
HOTEL PLAZA ATHÉNÉE ◆ PARIS, FRANCE

MAKES 4 SERVINGS

6 large tomatoes, roughly chopped, with the juices reserved

1 cup roughly chopped onions

¼ cup finely chopped fennel

One 10-ounce package frozen spinach

½ cup dry vermouth or fish stock, or ¼ cup clam juice combined with ¼ cup water

8 small firm, white fish fillets such as scrod (about 3 ounces each)

2 tablespoons unsalted butter

One 10-ounce can lima beans, drained

Salt and freshly ground black pepper, to taste

A dish from Executive Chef Gérard Sallé of the Plaza Athénée in Paris, France, is Fish Provençale. Provence is an area in the south of France which is famous for the use of tomatoes in its recipes.

1. Preheat the oven to 350° F.

2. In a large skillet over medium-high heat, combine two thirds of the tomatoes, all of the tomato juices, the onions and the fennel. Cook, stirring frequently, until the onions are translucent and the juices have almost evaporated, 5 to 7 minutes. Cover and keep warm.

3. Meanwhile, cook the spinach according to the package directions. Drain and keep warm.

4. Pour the vermouth, fish stock, or diluted clam juice into a large oven-proof skillet. Arrange the fish fillets side by side. Cover and bake for 10 to 15 minutes, or until the fish is thoroughly cooked.

5. Remove the fish fillets from the skillet and set aside. Place the skillet over medium-high heat and add the butter, lima beans, and salt and pepper. Heat thoroughly, stirring constantly, for about 3 minutes.

6. Place 4 of the fish fillets onto a serving plate, top each one with a quarter of the spinach and an eighth of the tomato sauce. Place the remaining fish fillets on top and coat with the remaining tomato sauce.

7. Pour the lima bean sauce over the fish fillets. Sprinkle on the remaining chopped tomatoes and serve.

A B O U T   T H E   T O M A T O

Tomatoes have not always been one of the world's most popular foods. They got their start in the Andes mountains of South America and spread to ancient Mexico where they became very popular. But when Spanish conquistadors brought them back to Europe during the 1500s, tomatoes were thought of as only a decorative plant. That continued for hundreds of years. Fortunately, the Italians, who have always had a gift for good eating, realized that the tomato was an excellent food. It was the Italians immigrating to the United States who brought the tomato to its present state of acclaim.

Americans eat about twenty pounds of tomatoes per person annually. The tomato is our third most popular produce item in the vegetable area of the market, right behind potatoes and lettuce. A series of medical research programs indicate that many fruits and vegetables that are red in color contain an element that is a cancer blocker; the tomato is a good example. A medium tomato, about five and a half ounces, contains about 35 calories, almost no fat, and quite a bit of potassium. The tomato, in spite of a Supreme Court ruling in 1893, is a fruit . . . not a vegetable.

FISH BAKED WITH ONIONS AND BELL PEPPERS
WYNDHAM'S ELBOW BEACH RESORT ◆ BERMUDA

MAKES 4 SERVINGS

6 tablespoons vegetable oil
2 tablespoons butter
2 cups sliced onion
2 tablespoons sliced fresh
  ginger
½ cup dry white wine
2 fish fillets, about 8 ounces
  each, red snapper or
  other firm-fleshed fish,
  cut into 4-ounce pieces
½ tablespoon paprika
½ tablespoon cayenne
  pepper
Salt, to taste
2 green bell peppers,
  seeded, cored, and sliced
  into thin strips
2 yellow bell peppers,
  seeded, cored, and sliced
  into thin strips
2 red bell peppers, seeded,
  cored, and sliced into thin
  strips

About 70 million years ago, a three-mile-high volcanic cone of rock came shooting up off the floor of the Atlantic Ocean. The action took place about 600 miles off the coast of what is now North Carolina. The very tip of the projection eventually broke through the surface of the water. The water was warm and attracted millions of tiny sea animals whose skeletons compressed together to form what is now the island of Bermuda. And being an island, well out in the Atlantic Ocean, it's a great place for fish recipes.

1. Preheat oven to 375° F.

2. Place 2 tablespoons of the oil and all the butter in a heatproof sauté pan, over a medium heat. Melt the butter. Add the onion, the ginger, and the wine and sauté for 4 minutes or until the onions are milky white and translucent. Hold this pan aside.

3. Give each fish fillet a *very* light sprinkling of the paprika and cayenne pepper and salt to taste.

4. In a second sauté pan, over medium heat, heat 2 tablespoons of the oil. Add the fish fillets and cook for 4 minutes on each side. When the fillets are cooked, remove them from the pan they were cooked in and place them on top of the onions in the first pan.

5. Add the final 2 tablespoons of the oil to the pan the fish was cooked in, and over medium heat, heat the oil. Scrape any pan drippings from the fish into the oil. Add the slices of peppers and sauté for 3 minutes or until the peppers begin to soften. Spoon the peppers onto the fish. Place the sauté pan with the fish and onions and peppers into the oven for 5 minutes, or until heated through. Transfer the fish to serving plates and serve immediately.

NOTE: The chef used butter in this recipe because he wanted its rich flavor, but butter tends to burn at low temperatures. Oil has a much higher burning point. By mixing the two together, he got the rich flavor of the butter along with the higher cooking temperature of the oil. The dish will also work well using only the oil.

Royal Naval Dockyard, Bermuda.

ABOUT BERMUDA'S ROYAL NAVAL DOCKYARD

The success of the revolutionary forces during the American War of Independence against England deprived the British Navy of its ports on the east coast of North America and placed the British fleet in a somewhat insecure position. The young American Navy was quite aggressive and England feared that their centuries-old position as ruler of the seas might soon be challenged. So, in the late 1700s England devised a plan to construct a naval fortress on Bermuda, and by 1807 the work was well under way.

The most interesting structure is the Clock Tower Building. It was meant to be a dull Navy warehouse; however, the wrong plans were sent from London. Bermuda by mistake got the architectural renderings for the British Embassy in Khartoum and they were used in error to produce a magnificent building. It does make you wonder what the British Embassy looks like in Khartoum. The building has two towers, and each tower has a four-faced clock, known locally as the Four-Faced Liar because no one face can keep time with the others. It appears to be quite useful to people who are late for work or want to leave early. The towers are 101 feet high and have become one of Bermuda's most recognizable landmarks.

The U.S. Navy never gave the Royal Naval Dockyard any trouble, but the Docks were a real source of aggravation to the U.S. It was from this yard that a large British invasion force crossed over and entered Washington D.C. during the War of 1812. They actually burned down part of the White House. It was the only time the United States was ever invaded, assuming you exclude British rock bands and Japanese investment bankers.

When the First World War started in 1914, the Bermuda Dockyard became a key element in Great Britain's defense. That role was repeated for both the English and U.S. forces during the Second World War. The yard was a major port for ship repairs and antisubmarine patrols. But in 1950 the British Navy closed the Dockyard and it fell into a state of neglect. Fortunately a group of local citizens realized that the Dockyard was a valuable historic property and started bringing it back to life.

The Keep Yard has become the setting for the Maritime Museum, where Bermuda's maritime history is on display. The old cooperage, where storage barrels were once made, is now the Frog and Onion Pub. The name is a somewhat rude reference to the fact that the establishment is owned by a Frenchman, "the frog," and a Bermudan, "the onion." It seems rather unfair, though, that onions are on the menu but no frogs are served.

The Dockyard hosts the Island Pottery, where potters pot jugs, bowls, teapots, and vases to your order. The husband's rocking chair is a somewhat sexist element but clearly quite functional. There is also a craft market that sells works made by Bermudan craftsmen and women, as well as a complete selection of locally produced foods and beverages for tourists to take home.

◆

BAKED SALMON FILLETS OVER BUCKWHEAT NOODLES
QANTAS JET BASE ◆ SYDNEY, AUSTRALIA

1. Preheat the oven to 375° F.

2. Brush the inside surface of an oven-proof casserole with 1 tablespoon of the oil. Place the salmon in one layer. Brush the salmon with the remaining oil. Sprinkle with the lemon juice, salt, pepper, minced scallions, parsley, carrots, and chicken broth. Place in the oven and cook for 8 to 10 minutes, or until the salmon is just cooked through.

3. Meanwhile, bring a large pot of water to a boil. When boiling, add the buckwheat noodles and cook for 8 minutes, or until just limp. Drain in a colander and rinse under warm water. Remove the cooked salmon from the oven. Sprinkle the julienned scallions over them.

4. Serve the salmon over the buckwheat noodles and spoon carrots and the sauce from the pan over all.

MAKES 6 SERVINGS

3 tablespoons vegetable oil
1½ pounds skinless,
   boneless salmon fillets,
   cut into 6 portions
1 tablespoon freshly
   squeezed lemon juice
¼ teaspoon salt
¼ teaspoon freshly ground
   black pepper
4 scallions, finely minced,
   plus 2 scallions, cut in
   fine julienne
2 tablespoons chopped
   parsley
4 medium carrots,
   julienned
½ cup chicken broth
4 ounces buckwheat
   noodles

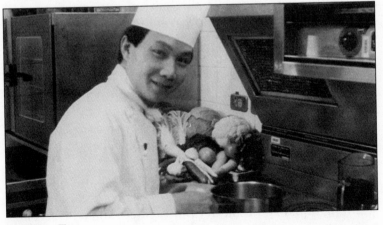

Y. Cheong Tse.

STEAMED FISH OVER CORN CAKES
ROCKPOOL RESTAURANT ◆ SYDNEY, AUSTRALIA

MAKES 4 SERVINGS

THE FISH

¼ cup peanut oil

¼ cup sesame oil

½ cup dry sherry

½ cup reduced-sodium soy
sauce

2 teaspoons granulated
sugar

Four 6-ounce white-fleshed
fish fillets, such as scrod,
halibut, or orange roughy

1 bunch scallions, green
part only, cut in fine
julienne strips

½ pound asparagus or snow
peas, cut in julienne
strips (optional)

THE CORN CAKES

3 cups fresh or frozen corn
kernels

1 clove garlic

2 tablespoons chopped
cilantro

½ teaspoon salt

2 eggs

1 cup all-purpose flour

Vegetable oil, for frying

We usually think of Australia in its historic roll as part of the British Empire, and with a gastronomic tradition that is more English than anything else. Until very recently that was true. But these days Australia is very much aware that it is geographically closer to Asia than anywhere else, and that is having an enormous effect on the country's eating and drinking. The result is a style of cooking called "East Meets West." A perfect example is this dish of steamed fish and corn cakes as prepared by one of Sydney's top chefs, Neil Perry.

1. To make the fish: In a high-sided sauté pan, combine peanut and sesame oils, sherry, soy sauce, and sugar. Heat until just simmering. Add the fish fillets in one layer and cover pan. Cook over medium heat, until fish is opaque, about 3 to 5 minutes, depending on the size of the fillet.

2. For the corn cakes: In the bowl of a food processor or blender, combine 2 cups of the corn, the garlic, cilantro, salt, and eggs. Process until the mixture is smooth. Transfer to a medium bowl, stir in the remaining cup of corn and the flour.

3. In a large skillet, add the frying oil to a depth of ½ inch. Warm over high heat. When hot, add ¼ cup of the corn batter and flatten slightly. Fry for 1 to 2 minutes on each side, or until golden brown. Drain the corn cakes on paper towels.

4. Place 1 or 2 cakes on each plate. Place the fish fillets over the cakes. Add the scallions and snow peas or asparagus to the steaming liquid and cook until just wilted, about 30 seconds. Spoon the sauce and vegetables equally over each dish.

THE SYDNEY FISH MARKET

One way to think of Australia is as the world's largest island. The vast majority of the population lives on the coasts, and so almost every Australian has an appreciation of the sea. This is particularly true in Sydney. The city was built around a huge natural harbor which gives the town about 150 miles of waterfront. Sydneysiders, as the residents call themselves, use the water as much as possible. They get to work and home again on ferries; they swim, they surf, and they sail. They also eat some of the world's best seafood.

Every weekday morning local distributors and retailers come to the Sydney Fish Market to take part in the seafood auction. The auction is run on what is called the "Dutch System," which is being used more and more as it is proving to be the fairest system for fishermen and farmers throughout the world. The day's catch is displayed in the inspection area by batch. The prospective purchasers walk through and note the lots that interest them. The buyers sit like spectators in a sports arena. The auctioneers are set up on a podium with a huge scoreboard above. The number of the individual batch of fish lights up on the board with the opening price. A clocklike device shows the price going down. The first bid to come in gets the fish.

This is quite a sport. Everyone sitting in the stands has come to buy fish for their restaurant, market, or orders for export that need to be filled. They must leave with the seafood that they need for the day. If you bid early, you will get the fish but at a higher price. If you wait until the price goes down, someone else may make a bid and you will be left without the fish you need for your business. Tough sport.

The market also has a wonderful retail area. The spot I liked the best is called Pete's. There are hundreds of different types of seafood, and the quality is absolutely topnotch. You can purchase what you want and take it home to cook. Or for a few dollars, the chefs at Pete's will do the cooking for you.

The Australians are in the enviable position of being able to select their seafood suppers from over three thousand types of seafood. Some of the most interesting species are now being exported to North America. Because Australia is off in its own part of the world, thousands of ocean miles from the highly industrialized areas, its local fish comes from some of the cleanest waters on the planet. The southern coast and the island-state of Tasmania get their weather from the Antarctic, which is about as clean as it gets. Consequently, they have taken advantage of that pollution-free environment to develop a fish-farming industry.

◆

FISH WITH MANGO SAUCE
HALEKULANI HOTEL ◆ HONOLULU, HAWAII

MAKES 4 SERVINGS

2 large ripe mangoes
1 teaspoon plus ¼ cup
  vegetable oil
¼ cup chopped shallots
3 to 6 tablespoons balsamic
  vinegar (depending on
  tartness desired)
Juice of 2 lemons
Tabasco sauce, to taste
1 to 1¼ pounds fresh tuna
  or salmon fillet, cut into 4
  narrow, thick portions
Salt and freshly ground
  black pepper, to taste

1.   Peel the mangoes. Cut the flesh away from the large pits; cut the flesh into rough cubes. Place the mango in a blender or food processor.

2.   Warm the teaspoon of oil in a small saucepan over moderately high heat. Add the shallots and vinegar and bring to a boil. Cook until the liquid is reduced by half, 3 to 5 minutes.

3.   Pour the shallot mixture into the blender and add the lemon juice, Tabasco, and remaining ¼ cup of oil. Process to a smooth puree.

4.   Place a nonstick skillet over moderately high heat. Meanwhile, lightly brush the fish with vegetable oil and season with salt and pepper. Place the fish in the hot pan and cook for 30 seconds on each side, until the fillet exterior is cooked, and then cook the interior to the degree of doneness you prefer.

5.   Serve the fish in a pool of the mango sauce.

◆

THE HAWAIIAN PLATE LUNCH

One of the truly unique aspects of Hawaiian food is the plate lunch. During the last century when large numbers of sugarcane workers started showing up in the fields, feeding them lunch became a major problem. The growers decided that the best way to get the job done was to put a kitchen into a truck and drive into the fields. That way, the workers could eat a full lunch with the least loss of time.

You can no longer find the trucks in the cane fields, but plate lunches are still a basic part of Hawaiian food. These days the trucks drive around town and set up shop in the business districts. Workers come out of their office, pick up their plate lunch, and head off to a park or back to their office to eat. A plate lunch is one of the best food values in town, and no matter what else is on the plate, there are always two scoops of rice and one scoop of macaroni salad. It's a throwback to the original menu that was served in the fields. The cooks of the time believed it was essential to get as much starch onto the plate as possible in order to help the workers keep up their strength. It's an early form of carbo-loading and not a bad idea. A midday meal that is high in complex carbohydrates, but low in fat, can go a long way to keeping up your energy.

FISH WITH PAPAYA
GRAND PALAZZO HOTEL ♦ ST. THOMAS, U.S. VIRGIN ISLANDS

MAKES 4 SERVINGS

FISH

1 tablespoon curry powder
½ teaspoon salt
¼ teaspoon freshly ground
 black pepper
½ cup all-purpose flour
1½ pounds snapper,
 halibut, or grouper fillets
1 teaspoon butter
1 tablespoon vegetable oil
1 large ripe papaya, peeled,
 seeded, and thinly sliced

TOPPING

1 tablespoon vegetable oil
½ onion, finely minced
2 cloves garlic, minced
1 tablespoon minced fresh
 ginger
¼ teaspoon hot red pepper
 flakes
¼ cup chopped parsley
2 tablespoons chopped
 cilantro

The Caribbean island of St. Thomas was purchased by the United States in 1917 from Denmark. You would think that the Danish gastronomic influence would be all over the place. But if you look into the local pots, the strongest influence comes from the Africans, who were brought there to work the sugarcane. There is also an echo from the East Indians who came there to work the fields after emancipation. Patrick Pinon, the chef at St. Thomas's Grand Palazzo Hotel, makes the point with this fish recipe that uses traditional Indian ingredients like papaya, ginger, and curry.

1. To make the fish: In a shallow glass dish, combine the curry powder, salt, pepper, and flour. Lightly dredge the fish fillets in the flour mixture.

2. In a large sauté pan over high heat, heat the butter and oil. Add the papaya and cook, stirring, for 1 minute, or until heated through. Remove from the pan and keep warm.

3. Add the fish to the same pan, flesh side down, and cook for 3 to 5 minutes. Turn to the second side and continue to cook for an additional 3 minutes, or until the fish flakes nicely with a fork. Transfer to a platter with the papaya to keep warm.

4. For the topping: Heat the oil in a small sauté pan over high heat. Add the onion. Cook for 2 to 3 minutes, or until slightly wilted. Add the garlic, ginger, and hot pepper and cook for 1 to 2 minutes longer. Remove from heat and stir in the parsley and cilantro. Reserve.

5. For the sauce: Heat the oil in a saucepan over medium heat. Add the curry powder and cook for 2 minutes. Add the chicken broth. Bring to a boil over high heat. Reduce heat to simmer and cook until the liquid reduces by half. Add the heavy cream and tomato puree and continue to simmer until the sauce coats the back of a spoon, about 5 minutes longer. Season with salt and pepper.

6. To serve, place a small amount of curry sauce on each plate. Place the fish over the sauce and surround the fish with papaya.

SAUCE
1 tablespoon oil
2 tablespoons curry powder
1½ cups chicken broth
½ cup heavy cream
¼ cup tomato puree
Salt and freshly ground
    black pepper, to taste

ABOUT THE U.S. VIRGIN ISLANDS

The islands of the Caribbean form a chain that starts just off the southern tip of Florida and continues down to the northern coast of South America. About midway through the group are the U.S. Virgin Islands. There are actually about fifty islands, but the most important are St. Thomas, St. Croix, and St. John, each having its own unique quality.

When Columbus bumped into the islands of the Caribbean he claimed them for the King and Queen of Spain. Nice try, but no cigar. As soon as the other kings and queens of Europe heard about what was going on, they immediately began to challenge the Spanish. France, England, Holland, and Denmark sent their ships across the Atlantic and began battling for a piece of the pie. For three hundred years European monarchs fought over the islands of the Caribbean. And the only reason for all the action was money. The European powers realized that the islands of the Caribbean were ideal locations for trade and profit. For Denmark, the prized possessions were three parcels of land known as the Virgin Islands. Two of them, St. John and St. Croix, became agricultural centers covered with plantations. The third, St. Thomas, became a duty-free trading port.

MONKFISH WITH LIME SAUCE AND CRANBERRIES
AIR FRANCE CONCORDE KITCHENS

MAKES 6 SERVINGS

FISH
1½ pounds monkfish fillets
2 tablespoons butter
3 tablespoons minced
   shallots or onions
¼ cup white wine
Zest of 1 lime
½ cup heavy cream
¼ cup fresh lime juice
2 tablespoons plain yogurt
Salt and freshly ground
   black pepper, to taste

CRANBERRIES
½ cup sugar
½ cup water
1 cup cranberries

I recently flew to Paris on the Air France Concorde. It took three hours and forty-five minutes from New York. The head chef of Air France is Michel Martin, and not only did he prepare a great meal for my flight but he let my camera crew come in and get the recipe. A noble man.

1. Preheat the oven to 375° F.

2. To make the fish: Cut the monkfish on the bias into ½-inch slices. Butter a high-sided oven-proof sauté pan. Place the monkfish in the pan. Sprinkle with the shallots or onions and white wine. Bake the fish for 5 to 7 minutes.

3. Meanwhile, add water to a small saucepan and bring to boil over high heat. Blanch the lime zest for 1 to 2 minutes. Strain and reserve.

4. To make the cranberries: In another small saucepan, combine the sugar and water. Bring to a boil over high heat and cook for 5 to 7 minutes, until syrupy in consistency. Remove from heat and stir in the cranberries; let sit for 5 minutes, or until cranberries are tender.

5. When the fish is fully cooked, remove the pan from the oven. Transfer the fish to a platter, and cover to keep warm.

6. Return the pan with cooking liquid to the top of the stove. Over high heat bring the liquid in the pot to a boil and allow the liquid to reduce by a quarter, or until it is syrupy in consistency, 5 to 7 minutes. Stir the cream into the cooking liquid and allow the sauce to reduce until it coats the back of a spoon. Remove the sauce from heat and stir in the lime juice and yogurt. Adjust seasonings with salt and pepper.

7. To serve, spoon the sauce over the fish and garnish with the blanched lime zest and candied cranberries.

GETTING THE MOST FROM YOUR LIME

Before you cut a lime, squeeze it or roll it on a hard surface. If you do that, you will get about twice as much juice out of it. Also, when you're zesting a lime, you want just the green outside surface. If you get the white connective tissue right under the skin, it will be bitter.

Michel Martin.

HALIBUT WITH ORZO AND FENNEL
PENINSULA HOTEL ◆ NEW YORK, NEW YORK

MAKES 6 SERVINGS

2 teaspoons butter
2 tablespoons olive oil
1 clove garlic, minced
1 teaspoon fennel seeds
1 fresh fennel bulb,
    julienned
1 ounce Pernod
1¼ cups chicken broth
1½ pounds halibut steak
2 cups cooked orzo pasta
Zest of 1 lemon
1 tablespoon chopped fresh
    mint

The Peninsula Hotel in New York City is situated in one of the city's most beautiful old buildings, but beneath its traditional facade is state-of-the-art technology. The hotel's main restaurant is called Adrienne and it has become well known throughout the New York area for its excellent food. The following recipe represents one of the restaurant's specialties.

1. In a medium saucepan over medium heat, warm the butter and oil. Add the garlic, fennel seeds, and fennel. Cook for 3 to 5 minutes, stirring occasionally, until the fennel is tender. Add the Pernod, turn the heat to high, and let reduce for 2 to 3 minutes. Add 1 cup chicken broth and continue to cook for 5 minutes. Remove from heat and adjust the seasonings.

2. In a large sauté pan heat about an inch of water. Place the halibut in the pan. Bring the water to boil over high heat and reduce to a simmer. Cover the pan and let the fish simmer for about 5 minutes, or until it is opaque and just cooked through.

3. In a small saucepan, combine the remaining ¼ cup of chicken broth, cooked orzo, lemon zest, and mint. Warm over low heat.

4. Place some of the warmed orzo on each plate. Top with the fish and spoon fennel sauce over all.

THE KRANENBORG TWO-PLATE TECHNIQUE FOR FISH COOKERY

During the 1980s North America saw an enormous increase in the consumption of seafood. Scientific reports indicated that there were elements in fish that could help protect against heart disease, and fish that were generally low in fat and calorie content were heavily promoted by the industry. But the marketers of fish ran into one very serious problem. Millions of home cooks felt they didn't know how to cook fish properly. Robert Kranenborg is well-known for his work as executive chef at the Amstel Inter-Continental hotel in Amsterdam, but he is also a respected author with a book on fish cookery. In his book Kranenborg provides a simple fish-cooking technique.

A little water is brought to a boil in a saucepan. A heat-proof plate goes on top of the pan with a little oil on the plate. The fish—tuna, snapper, scallops, whatever you like—is cut into similar-size pieces so they will take about the same time to cook, and put on the plate. Then, a second plate is placed on top, and everything cooks for five minutes.

BERMUDA FISHCAKES
ONCE UPON A TABLE ◆ HAMILTON, BERMUDA

MAKES ABOUT 15
FISHCAKES

1 pound new potatoes
1 pound dried codfish,
   soaked for 8 hours, then
   drained of the soaking
   water, or 1 pound of fresh
   cod fillets that have been
   cooked until they flake
   easily
¼ cup chopped onion
¼ cup chopped parsley
1 tablespoon dried basil
2 tablespoons Outerbridge's
   Sherry Pepper Sauce
   (optional)
2 tablespoons
   Worcestershire Sauce
Salt and freshly ground
   pepper
2 egg whites
¼ cup vegetable oil
1 cup flour

A private home that is over a century old has been restored and transformed into one of Bermuda's finest restaurants. It is called Once Upon A Table and it is run by Lew Harvey.

The interior of the building has been decorated in the Victorian style of the 1800s and the food is basically French with a Bermudan influence. If you are in Bermuda and you give Lew thirty-six hours' notice, he will produce a traditional Bermudan meal. The following fishcake recipe is from one of Lew's Bermudan menus.

1. Boil the potatoes until they are fully cooked. Drain them, and while they are still warm, slice them into quarters and place them in a mixing bowl. Add the fish and mash these ingredients together until they are well mixed.

2. Add the onion, parsley, basil, Sherry Pepper Sauce, Worcestershire, salt and pepper to taste, and egg whites and continue mixing. Form the fish mixture into patties that are about 3 inches in diameter and ½-inch thick.

3. In a sauté pan, over medium heat, heat the oil until shimmering. Spread the flour out on a flat dish. Dip the fishcakes into the flour to give them a light dusting on each side. Sauté the fishcakes in the hot oil for 3 to 4 minutes on each side or until they develop a golden crust. Remove the fishcakes and drain them on paper toweling.

4. Make the sauce by mixing the mustard into the mayonnaise and then blending in the honey and the water.

5. Serve the fishcakes with a few thin slices of the banana on top, and the sauce on the side.

NOTE: These fishcakes were used in three different presentations. The first was as a main course with two vegetables, the second was on a bun with lettuce and tomato, and in the third they were only 1 inch in diameter and served as a first-course appetizer.

try

THE SAUCE
1 tablespoon dry mustard
1 cup mayonnaise (regular or low fat)
¼ cup honey
3 tablespoons water

THE GARNISH
1 banana

Yeaton Outerbridge,
creator of Outerbridge's
Sherry Pepper Sauce.

ABOUT BERMUDA'S ARROWROOT

The first colonists to arrive in Bermuda were English, and they have left their mark politically, militarily, linguistically, and culturally. Queen Victoria ruled from 1837 to 1901 and set the standards for behavior in all things, including gastronomy.

Victorian ladies made a public display of being very delicate, and that was particularly evident in things that had to do with cooking. Victorians developed the little covers that are put on the legs of roasted meat and poultry because it was offensive for a lady to see "legs" in any setting. They also began to thicken their sauces with arrowroot instead of flour because arrowroot was easier to digest and produced a more limpid sauce, which was therefore more ladylike. During the 1800s Bermuda became the source for the world's best arrowroot.

GRILLED JUMBO SHRIMP WITH CITRUS SAUCE
GRAND BAY HOTEL ✦ COCONUT GROVE, FLORIDA

MAKES 6 SERVINGS

MARINADE
½ cup vegetable oil
Grated zest of 1 orange
Grated zest of 1 lime
1 tablespoon minced fresh
  basil, or ½ tablespoon
  dried
1 teaspoon minced fresh
  thyme, or ½ teaspoon
  dried
1 teaspoon minced fresh
  parsley, or ½ teaspoon
  dried
1 pound uncooked extra-
  large shrimp (about 18),
  shells removed, cleaned

Coconut Grove was once the site of Miami's first hotel. These days it's the site of Miami's most elegant hotel, the Grand Bay. It's the first of the CIGA hotels in the United States. CIGA stands for the Italian Company of Grand Hotels, which is a good description. It operates some of the grandest hotels in Europe, including The Danieli in Venice, which was built in the 1300s. After seven hundred years you pick up those little tips that make your hotels special.

The Grand Bay in Coconut Grove is true to the tradition. It's the only Mobil five-star hotel in Florida. Shaped like a Mayan temple, it looks out on beautiful Biscayne Bay. The public rooms are decorated with a collection of art and antiques and the staff has been trained to the top European standards of CIGA.

For me, one of the Grand Bay's most valuable works was Katsu Sugura, nicknamed Suki. He was chosen by Food and Wine magazine as one of America's top-ten new chefs. Born in Japan and trained throughout Europe and the United States, Suki makes art to eat. This is his recipe for grilled Florida shrimp.

1. To make the marinade: Combine all of the ingredients in a mixing bowl. Add the shrimp, and marinate at room temperature for 3 hours.

2. When the marinating time is over make the vegetable sauté: In a sauté pan over medium heat, warm the oil. Add the vegetables and garlic; sauté for 4 minutes, stirring constantly. Season with salt and pepper. Add the balsamic vinegar and continue cooking for 1 minute more.

3. To make the citrus vinaigrette: Combine all of the ingredients in a mixing bowl. Whisk to dissolve the honey.

4. Remove the shrimp from the marinade and grill or broil for 2 minutes on each side.

5. Divide the sautéed vegetables among 6 salad plates, put 3 shrimp on top of each, and pour on the citrus vinaigrette.

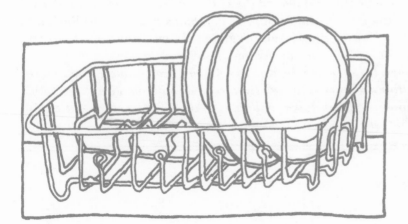

VEGETABLE SAUTÉ
1 tablespoon vegetable oil
3 cups vegetables,
  (zucchini, hearts of
  artichokes, fennel, red
  bell pepper), cut into
  ½-inch-wide sticks about
  2 inches long
1 clove garlic, minced
Salt and freshly ground
  black pepper, to taste
3 tablespoons balsamic
  vinegar

CITRUS SAUCE
1 tablespoon orange juice
1 tablespoon grapefruit
  juice
1 tablespoon lime juice
2 tablespoons honey
1 tablespoon Dijon-style
  mustard

ABOUT MIAMI

During the early years of this century, the extraordinary piece of property known as Miami Beach was owned by one man; he was a New Jersey Quaker named John Collins. But there wasn't much he could do with the property until he could connect it to the mainland. Carl Graham Fisher, who made a fortune by inventing the first bright automobile head lamp, lent Collins the money to build the connecting causeway. Miami Beach was then on its way to becoming the playground of the Western world. In 1915, the beach elected its first mayor and began building hotels, swimming pools, and a very colorful reputation.

I first saw Miami Beach in the 1940s and it was quite a piece of work. Hotels faced out onto beaches lined with palm trees, and the Atlantic Ocean was right at my front door. I was swimming while my classmates up north were bundling up against the cold. My uncle Maxwell had taken me there for a Christmas vacation and I loved it.

During the 1950s, Miami Beach became one of the world's great centers of excess. Hotels turned up their air conditioning so guests could wear their mink jackets to dinner; the biggest names in the entertainment world played the clubs; Arthur Godfrey broadcast his show from a local hotel on the beach. But in the 1970s, things began to decline and Miami Beach fell into a state of tragic deterioration. Miami Beach, however, has had more comebacks than Peggy Lee . . . and it's in the middle of one right now.

Today, South Miami Beach is known as So-Be. Developers are calling it the American Riviera, and the celebrities are coming back. Hundreds of millions of dollars have been spent to renovate the hotels and apartment buildings in the area. Oceanfront cafés are packed, and the restaurants are the hottest on the United States East Coast.

◆

JAMAICAN SHRIMP
THE ENCHANTED GARDEN RESORT ◆ OCHO RIOS, JAMAICA

1. Shell and clean the shrimp, saving the shells.

2. In a sauté pan large enough to hold all of the ingredients, over medium heat, warm the oil. Add the shrimp and pepper, cook and stir for 2 minutes. As soon as the shrimp are pink, remove them to a holding dish.

3. Put the shrimp shells into the pan; stir for 1 minute. Then add the onion, garlic, celery, thyme, bay leaf, tomato paste, wine, and water. Bring to a boil, then lower heat and simmer for 20 minutes. Strain the stock and discard the solids.

4. Pour the stock back into the pan and add the potatoes and carrots and cook over a low heat for 2 minutes.

5. Add the shrimp, heat through, and serve over the rice with a garnish of parsley.

MAKES 4 SERVINGS

1 pound uncooked medium
   shrimp, in their shells
2 tablespoons vegetable oil
Freshly ground black
   pepper, to taste
1 onion, minced
2 cloves garlic, minced
1 cup celery, sliced into
   ½-inch lengths
½ tablespoon dried thyme
1 bay leaf
2 tablespoons tomato paste
½ cup white wine
2 cups water
1 cup diced potatoes,
   parboiled for 10 minutes
   or until almost tender
1 cup diced carrots,
   parboiled for 10 minutes
   or until almost tender
3 cups cooked rice
Parsley sprigs, for garnish

◆

PORTUGUESE SPICY SHRIMP
FOUR SEASONS HOTEL ◆ TORONTO, CANADA

MAKES 6 SERVINGS

3 tablespoons vegetable oil
¼ cup minced garlic
2 cups thinly sliced red onions
2 cups thinly sliced yellow or white onions
½ cup seeded and diced fresh red chili peppers
8 tomatoes, each cut into 6 wedges
Salt and freshly ground black pepper, to taste
2 pounds uncooked large shrimp, peeled, cleaned, and deveined
2 cups tomato juice
½ cup chopped scallions
¼ cup chopped parsley
¼ cup chopped cilantro

The history of Portugal is the history of men and the sea. For hundreds of years the best ocean navigators came from Portugal. Even Columbus went there when he was planning his voyage. Portugal is a great place to learn about the sea and that goes for cooks as well as explorers. Portugal has some of the world's greatest seafood recipes. Chef Susan Weaver at Toronto's Four Seasons Hotel prepares a classic Portuguese spicy shrimp that she learned from Toronto's Portuguese community.

1. In a stockpot, warm the oil over moderately high heat. Add the garlic and onions and sauté for 5 minutes.

2. Stir in the chilies, tomatoes, salt and pepper, and the shrimp. Cook, stirring and tossing, for 5 minutes.

3. Add the tomato juice and scallions and bring the mixture to a simmer. Stir in the parsley and cilantro and cook for 1 minute. Serve hot.

Susan Weaver and student.

ABOUT PORTUGUESE FOOD TRADITIONS IN TORONTO

A number of historians believe that the Portuguese knew about North America long before Columbus arrived. For hundreds of years Portuguese fishing fleets had been following Atlantic codfish across the ocean to the Grand Banks off the coast of Canada. There is evidence that these fishermen came ashore quite regularly. But they never said anything about it; they considered the information a trade secret.

Today, Canada has a large Portuguese community with over 100,000 Portuguese living in Toronto. The central Portuguese area of the city even has street signs that read "Portugal Village." Because many Portuguese hold dual citizenship, the politicians of Portugal regularly show up in Toronto looking for votes. When it comes to food they must feel very much at home. The neighborhood is packed with Portuguese restaurants and take-out stores serving their traditional dishes. The bakeries are in a class by themselves, as the Portuguese have a highly developed sweet tooth. Finally, the dried codfish that originally brought the Portuguese to this part of the world can be found everywhere.

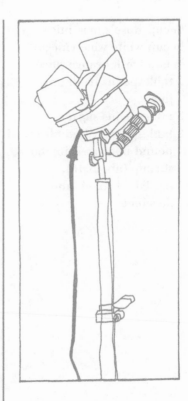

Shrimp with Orange Sauce
THE GRAND FORMOSA REGENT HOTEL ◆ TAIPEI, TAIWAN

MAKES 4 SERVINGS

¼ cup Rose's lime juice
¼ cup white wine vinegar
½ cup fresh orange juice
2 tablespoons fresh lime juice
3 tablespoons sugar
2 tablespoons vegetable oil
1 pound uncooked jumbo shrimp (about 16), peeled, cleaned, and deveined

The waters around the island of Taiwan have been an ongoing source of seafood for thousands of years. As a result, seafood cookery has been a hallmark of Taiwanese cuisine since as far back as the aborigines, who were the island's original inhabitants. The Chinese chefs who do the cooking of the island these days have continued the tradition. Chef Kow of the Grand Formosa Regent Hotel in Taipei prepares a classic, Shrimp with Orange Sauce.

1. In a nonreactive* small saucepan over high heat, bring the lime juice, vinegar, orange juice, fresh lime juice, and sugar to a boil, stirring constantly to dissolve the sugar. Remove the sauce from the heat.

2. In a wok over high heat, warm the oil until it shimmers. Add the shrimp, and stir-fry until they are opaque on the outside and cooked through, about 4 minutes.

3. Remove the shrimp and drain on paper towels. Place the shrimp on a serving platter and drizzle the sauce over them. Serve at once.

*A nonreactive saucepan is made of a material that will not interact with the acid in the food. Stainless steel, ceramic, glass, and anodized aluminum are fine.

◆

THE FOOD OF TAIWAN

Today the Taiwanese capital city of Taipei is the epicenter of Chinese gastronomy. More than any other city, Taipei offers a resident or a visitor the largest and most varied collection of Chinese foods, foods that represent all of the regional cuisine of this ancient society. There are, however, a few things that a visitor should not miss, for they are unique to the food of China.

My favorite offering is Peking duck, an exceptional dish that is made by inflating the duck with air between the meat and the skin. That produces a space for the fat to drip out. At that point, the skin is tightened with boiling water, coated with sugar water, and then roasted. The duck is served with a sweet sauce, green onions, and fresh pancakes.

Another must is dim sum. The words mean "point to your heart," and the suggestion is to eat to your heart's content. When you sit down to a dim sum meal, tea is brought to your table. All around you there are rolling carts filled with small portions of food—steamed buns with various fillings, baked dishes, and fried specialties. You point to what you want and eat until you've had enough. You might also include a taste of shark fin soup. It is said to have the ability to revive a man's youthful strength. You also owe yourself a bowl of tan tan noodles. It's reminiscent of a perfect noodle soup topped off with a spicy marinara sauce.

◆

ABOUT BALANCING COOKING TECHNIQUES

The idea of cooking a food with two or three different types of heating is a specialty of Chinese chefs. In the West we usually decide to heat the food with one system, and that's it. We'll roast it, fry it, or sauté it, but normally only one cooking method is used. The Chinese, using several techniques, can vary the taste and textures. It's a little more work, but not much, and the results are quite interesting. And even though many of the recipes start out with deep-frying, you can contain your general fear of frying to some extent. These dishes don't cover the foods with batters or coatings, which is normally where many of the extra fat calories are held when deep-frying.

◆

ABOUT CHOPSTICKS AND CHINESE TABLE MANNERS

Chinese children, like children all over the world, start eating by using their fingers. After a while, the spoon is introduced. At about the age of four, chopsticks training begins. Chopsticks appear to have been developed specifically for use with the type of rice prepared by the Chinese. The words for chopsticks in Chinese mean something like "fast helpers," which is quite descriptive.

The meal at a Chinese home begins with each person getting a bowl of rice. You receive the bowl of rice with two hands as a mark of respect. Rice is the real food of China. The fish, meat, poultry, vegetables, and fruits are considered almost a relish for the rice. The other foods come to the table in family-style serving dishes. You transfer the morsel you want to eat from the serving bowl to your rice bowl. It is impolite to poke around in the serving dish. Pick your target carefully. If you touch it, you must take it. If the piece is too big to eat in one bite, you may eat some of it and return the rest to your rice bowl and finish it later. The rice bowl is held up near your mouth and the food helped along the short distance by the chopsticks. To leave any rice in your bowl at the end of a meal is a disaster. It means you don't know how to choose the amount of food you need and it translates into waste. Waste is unacceptable in Chinese culture.

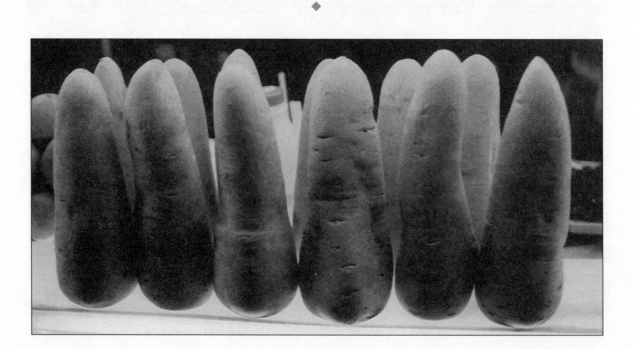

SHRIMP WITH VEGETABLES, FORMOSA STYLE
THE GRAND FORMOSA REGENT HOTEL ◆ TAIPEI, TAIWAN

Seafood has always been an important part of Chinese cooking, but of all the seafood available, none is more popular than shrimp. The following recipe is a simple combination of shrimp and vegetables that stands in the perfect balance of Yin and Yang that is recommended in the ancient gastronomic instructions of the Taoists. The green leafy spinach is one of the cool female foods in the Yin group. The high protein shrimp is a male food from the Yang group.

1. In a mixing bowl, combine the egg whites, 1 teaspoon of the cornstarch, and the shrimp. Let the shrimp marinate in this mixture for 15 minutes. In a second bowl, mix together the remaining teaspoon of cornstarch and the warm water and hold aside until Step 4.

2. In a wok or high-sided sauté pan, heat 1 cup of the oil until shimmering. Add the shrimp and cook for 1 minute. Remove the shrimp from the oil and hold aside. Drain the oil from the wok except for 2 tablespoons.

3. Over high heat, heat the oil remaining in the wok. Add the spinach and stir-fry for 1 minute. Remove the spinach from the wok and arrange it around the edges of a serving plate.

4. Over high heat, heat the wok and the remaining 2 tablespoons of the vegetable oil. As soon as the oil is hot, add the garlic, red pepper, and scallions and stir-fry for 2 minutes. Return the shrimp to the wok and add the sugar, the cornstarch-water mixture, and the soy sauce and stir-fry for 2 minutes more. Place the shrimp and vegetable mixture in the center of the spinach.

MAKES 4 SERVINGS

2 egg whites
2 teaspoons cornstarch
20 medium shrimp, shelled
  and cleaned
¼ cup warm water
1 cup plus 2 tablespoons
  vegetable oil
2 cups fresh spinach
1 clove garlic, minced
1 red bell pepper, cut into
  bite-size pieces
1 cup scallions, cut into
  1-inch pieces
1 teaspoon sugar
2 tablespoons soy sauce

SAUTÉED SHRIMP WITH PAPRIKA
CANADA'S VIA RAIL TRAIN

MAKES 4 SERVINGS

2 tablespoons vegetable oil
1 cup roughly chopped
  onions
1 cup sliced mushrooms
2 tablespoons minced garlic
1 cup roughly chopped
  tomatoes
20 uncooked large shrimp
  (about 1¼ pounds),
  peeled and deveined
2 tablespoons paprika
½ cup dry white wine
2 tablespoons chopped
  fresh cilantro, plus 4
  sprigs, for garnish
Salt and freshly ground
  black pepper, to taste
4 cups cooked white rice
  that has been boiled with
  1 teaspoon turmeric

The Canadian is the name of the train that takes passengers across Canada from Toronto in the east to Vancouver in the west, or vice versa. It passes through some of the most beautiful scenery on our planet— snow-covered mountains, unspoiled forests. It's the kind of scenery that gives you a real appreciation of North America.

During the past few years Via Rail, which is directed by the Canadian government, has made a great effort to bring back the good old days of railroad food. An example of what the company is doing is this dish of Sautéed Shrimp with Paprika.

1. In a large sauté pan over medium-high heat, warm the oil until almost shimmering. Add the onions and mushrooms and sauté for 3 to 5 minutes. Stir in the garlic and tomatoes, and cook for 3 to 5 minutes.

2. Add the shrimp, paprika, wine, and chopped cilantro and cook, stirring, until the shrimp turn opaque, 3 to 5 minutes. Season with salt and pepper.

3. Divide the rice among 4 dinner plates. Top each serving with some of the shrimp and sauce. Garnish each plate with a cilantro sprig.

ABOUT PAPRIKA

The simplest description of paprika is that it is a spice made by grinding red peppers into a powder. It appears that paprika was first brought to Europe by Spanish explorers shortly after Columbus's explorations. It traveled from Spain to Italy, and then the Turks brought the spice from Italy to what is now Hungary. That was very important because even though paprika began in Latin America, it didn't hit the big time until it got to Hungary. Hungary appears to have just the right blend of soil and climate to produce the finest paprika. For the first two hundred years or so it was all hot stuff. Then in the middle of the 1800s, two brothers developed a technique for removing the veins and seeds of the pepper before the milling. The result was a mild paprika with lots of flavor but much less heat. It quickly became a popular spice throughout Europe.

Paprika has had a long-standing reputation as being healthful, and starting in 1873 Hungarian medical researchers began producing reports explaining why. The first material dealt with the discovery that paprika contained large amounts of vitamin A. Additional information showed that paprika was an excellent source of vitamin C. Vitamins A and C are now described as antioxidants. They may work to retard cancer and reduce the effects of aging; I really should say, the negative effects of aging. As I grow older and encounter the effects of aging, I see that there are a lot of wonderful effects, as well as some not so wonderful ones.

ABOUT FRYING PANS

One of our earliest pieces of cooking equipment was the griddle, a flat surface heated from below and the food cooked on top. At some point in history someone decided that holding a little more moisture around the food was a good idea. The edges on the cooking surface got turned up and the first frying pan went into action.

It is very similar to the sauté pan. The only design difference is in the sides. Frying pans curve out. Sauté pans are straight sided. The theory is that the sauté pan is used for flipping the food around. The word sauté *is French and actually means "to jump." The straight sides help keep the food in the pan. The frying pan is used for foods that take a turn and depart.*

When you are buying a frying pan, look for one that is made of materials that are highly heat conductive—cast iron, anodized aluminum, lined copper. You want the heat to reach the food as fast and as intensely as possible. Also make sure the handle is securely fitted to the pan; this is the point that takes the most use. It's also nice to have a handle that is made out of a material that will go into the oven.

HUMMUS (CHICK-PEA SAUCE) WITH SHRIMP
ROCKPOOL RESTAURANT ◆ SYDNEY, AUSTRALIA

MAKES 4 SERVINGS

6 cups cooked chick-peas
2 tablespoons hot water
⅛ teaspoon ground cumin
Juice of ½ lemon
4 tablespoons olive oil
1 red onion, sliced
1 clove garlic, thinly sliced
Salt and freshly ground
  black pepper, to taste
12 uncooked large shrimp,
  shells removed, cleaned

Neil Perry.

Rockpool is one of the great restaurants of Australia. For two years in a row it has been voted as the best restaurant in the Australian state of New South Wales. That is like being picked as the best restaurant in California; it's a big deal. The owner and chef, Neil Perry, is clearly one of the country's most talented cooks. He prepares a dish of Australian prawns, which North Americans call "Australian shrimp." They are quite wonderful, and he serves them over a bed of chick-pea puree.

1. Put 4 cups of the cooked chick-peas into a food processor or blender, along with the hot water, cumin, lemon juice, and 1 tablespoon of the olive oil, and process until you have a smooth puree.

2. In a frying pan that has been heated over medium heat, warm 1 tablespoon of the olive oil until just hot. Add the onion and garlic, and cook for 2 minutes. Then add the remaining 2 cups of cooked chick-peas, salt, and pepper, and cook for 3 minutes more.

3. In a second frying pan that has been heated over medium heat, warm the remaining 2 tablespoons of olive oil until it is just hot. Add the shrimp and cook for 2 minutes on each side.

4. Place about ½ cup of the pureed chick-peas onto the center of each of 4 plates. Place about ½ cup of the whole chick-pea and red onion sauce on top of the puree. Place 3 shrimp on top of the sauce.

SQUID WITH SESAME OIL, FUKIENESE STYLE
THE GRAND FORMOSA REGENT HOTEL ◆ TAIPEI, TAIWAN

Most of the original Chinese immigrants to the island of Taiwan came over from the mainland province of Fukien. They started arriving over 400 years ago and they have come to represent a major portion of the present population. Their ancestral province is famous for its seafood cookery, and this dish of Squid with Sesame Oil is an example of the Fukienese influence in Taiwanese cooking.

MAKES 4 SERVINGS

¼ cup soy sauce

¼ cup rice wine vinegar

2 tablespoons sugar

1 cup vegetable oil

2 cups squid, cleaned and cut into bite-size rounds

2 tablespoons Chinese sesame oil

½ cup fresh or canned bamboo shoots, cut into bite-size pieces

4 cloves garlic, minced

1 tablespoon minced fresh ginger

1 cup basil leaves, lightly packed, or spinach leaves

1. In a small mixing bowl, blend together the soy sauce, vinegar, and sugar and set aside.

2. Over high heat, warm a wok or deep-sided sauté pan. Add the oil and heat until just shimmering. Add the squid and fry for 2 minutes. Drain the squid from the oil and set aside. Pour the vegetable oil out of the wok.

3. Over high heat, rewarm the wok and add the sesame oil. As soon as the oil is hot, add the bamboo shoots, garlic, and ginger and stir-fry for 1 minute. Return the squid to the wok. Add the mixture of soy sauce, vinegar, and sugar and stir-fry for 1 minute. Add the basil and stir-fry for 1 minute. Empty the wok into a serving bowl.

Angela Chang of the Grand Formosa Regent.

ABOUT CONFUCIUS

Of all the philosophies and teachings that have been developed in China, none has been more powerful than the work of Confucius. He was born in 551 B.C., during a period of political and moral chaos. The ruling dynasty was crumbling and petty factions were at war throughout the country. Confucius wanted to reestablish the ethical principles that had guided much of China during an earlier time. He spent his life trying to teach people that true happiness could only be found in acts of generosity and the promotion of peace and friendship. By the time he died at the age of seventy-two, over three thousand students had been trained in his teachings.

Confucius wrote a series of books that outlined the proper behavior for every situation that one might face. He advised his students: "Be strict with yourself, but benevolent toward others." He believed that the government should work for the good of the people, not for the good of government officials. What an amazing concept.

From the second century B.C. until 1905, the teachings of Confucius were literally the official body of moral and intellectual information for China. He established what is known as the "Five Cardinal Relationships" and explained how each should be handled. They cover the relations between the individual and the government, husband and wife, parent and child, older and younger siblings, and among friends. Today, some 2,500 years after he lived, the people of Taiwan still follow his teachings, and hold a giant birthday party for him each September 28. That celebration is of particular interest to me because my birthday is also on September 28. Plus, my Chinese name, Wu Bor Der, is associated with traveling teachers—two fortuitous facts that get me a lot of extra mileage and make it easier for me to work in China. I must admit, though, off the record, that I first heard of Confucius when he was quoted in the old Charlie Chan movies. At a key point in the mystery, Detective Chan would turn to one of his sons and say something like, "Ancient Chinese philosopher Confucius say, 'To hide stone, place stone with other stones; to hide man, place man with other men.' We must look for killer in crowd."

Charlie Chan movies aside, Confucius was clearly one of the world's great thinkers when it came to morals. But he was also a big deal when it came to meals. Many of the works associated with him have large sections of material that deal with the proper preparation and consumption of various foods. He was an expert on the gastronomic hygiene of the time and particularly interested in the relationship of good food to good health. Historians have even given credit to Confucius for the devotion of Chinese cooks to fresh ingredients.

◆

CRABS OVER STEAMED FRIED RICE
THE GRAND FORMOSA REGENT HOTEL ◆ TAIPEI, TAIWAN

There are over 4,000 species of crab, all edible, and Chinese cooks have known this for over 4,000 years. The crab's succulent taste has attracted the Chinese cook, but he is also drawn by its visual beauty. The crab is often presented whole for its dramatic effect. This recipe steams the crab over fried rice, and the dish is sent to the table in the steamer basket.

1. Over high heat in a wok or high-sided sauté pan, warm the oil until shimmering. Add the mushrooms, shrimp, pork, soy sauce, pepper, and sugar, and stir-fry for 2 minutes, or until the pork is fully cooked. Add the chicken stock and the rice and stir-fry for 2 minutes.

2. Take 4 saucepans that have a diameter that is slightly smaller than the diameter of the steamer baskets described below, and put 1 inch of water into each saucepan. Bring the water to a boil.

3. Line 4 Chinese steamer baskets (each 6 inches in diameter) with cheesecloth and divide the rice equally among the steamers. Place 1 crab on top of the rice in each basket. Put the cover on the steamers and place the steamers over the sauce pans of boiling water. Steam the crab for 10 minutes.

NOTES: The crabs are held in the freezer for 15 minutes so they will be easier to handle as you place them in the steamer baskets.

The recipe works as well when 3 jumbo shrimp are substituted for each crab. The shells are left on, but the veins are removed.

MAKES 4 SERVINGS

3 tablespoons vegetable oil
½ cup mushrooms, sliced
12 medium shrimp, shelled and cleaned, cut into small pieces
½ pound lean ground pork
¼ cup soy sauce
½ teaspoon freshly ground pepper
2 tablespoons sugar
½ cup chicken stock
6 cups precooked glutinous rice

4 live whole crabs, held in the freezer for 15 minutes before cooking (see Notes)

ABOUT TEA IN TAIWAN

The mountains of Taiwan are wrapped in mist and gently heated by the sun. The result is a warm and moist climate that is perfect for growing tea. Tea is a basic part of Chinese culture and goes back in Chinese history for hundreds of years. There are a number of Chinese folk legends that tell the story of the origins of tea. They all describe it as an accident in which a tea leaf dropped into someone's boiling water. They seem to date the drinking of tea back some four thousand years. There are documents that tell of ancient emperors tasting hundreds of different leaves in order to decide which make the best tea, and it was a Chinese scholar who first developed the tea ceremony that was later picked up and made famous by the Japanese.

After the Chinese scholar Lu Yu published his book on tea in the year 780, tea became the most important beverage in Asia. Lu told his readers that tea would "temper the spirit, calm and harmonize the mind, arouse thought, prevent drowsiness, and enlighten and refresh the body." Obviously, in those days there was no Chinese equivalent of the Food and Drug Administration requiring scientific proof for all medical claims. Had there been, it might have been a very short book with one page that read, "Good to the last drop."

Tea reflects the cosmic balance and is produced and brewed with great care. The tea fields of Taiwan are in production for nine months out of every year. There are actually five different harvest periods, but the best leaves are taken from the plants during the spring and early winter. Tea to the Chinese is very much like wine to the French; it is very serious stuff. They want to know what variety of bush was used, where on the island it was planted, what time of year the leaf was plucked, and how long the leaf was allowed to dry in the sun after harvest; did it go inside for fermentation and for what period of time; was it crumbled by hand or by machine; was it baked? To think that there was a time in my life when the only question I had about tea was, "Is it loose or in a bag?"

Taiwan specializes in three types of tea leaves. The first is called green tea. It has not been fermented at all and the tea that results is very light in color and has a delicate flavor. Semifermented tea has a slightly darker color and a more robust flavor. The tea normally drunk in North America and Europe is 100 percent fermented tea. In Asia it is called "red tea," or "black tea," and it produces the deep color and stronger taste that is associated with tea in the West.

The Chinese never add milk or sugar to their tea. They look for each of the complex and subtle flavors that they have learned to enjoy. There are tea experimental stations that are very much like our agricultural stations in North America, only the crop being studied is tea. There are regular classes throughout the country that teach young people the proper way to select and brew tea. There are teahouses in the countryside and throughout the major metropolitan areas which have become sanctuaries for people looking for a quiet place to sit and talk, relax, and find their psychic center.

The Chinese attribute a number of medical benefits to tea. Drinking it at the end of a meal helps the digestion of food by breaking down fats and easing the metabolic strain on the liver. I have never come to the table in a restaurant in Taiwan without having tea offered to me at the very start of the meal. It usually comes along with the menu. The Chinese believe that the vitamin C content of green tea helps to prevent illness and increases one's mental and physical energies. Tea also appears to have the ability to remove stains and grease from various surfaces. And that is why in an old traditional Chinese restaurant you may see a waiter pour the remaining tea out of a teapot onto the surface of the table before he wipes it off. Waste not, want not.

Sunpoling is the tea-producing area of Taiwan. Although Sunpoling translates into English as "Pine Bluff," there are no pine trees in the district. There are just rolling hills covered with bamboo groves and giant palm trees that were planted to shade acre after acre of tea plants. Sunpoling produces some of the finest tea in the world. Part of its success comes from the unique climate in the region and part from the unusual soil. But there is also an ancient tradition of exceptional craftsmanship that follows the techniques that have always resulted in the highest grades of tea. Each day teams of women come into the fields to pick the tea leaves one by one. The choicest teas are hand-harvested when the leaves are still quite small. The yield of the harvest will be less but the leaves will have been taken from the bush before they develop the heavy tannins that can make tea bitter. The pickers move through the fields selecting only those leaves that are at the perfect point of growth.

In the center of the district is the village of Sunpoling. The main street of the town is literally lined with shops selling tea that was grown in the nearby fields. Shop after shop. Street after street. And each one offering an hour-long service that is called "Old Folks Tea." It's called this because these days it seems that only old folks, and television food reporters, have the time to enjoy it. Actually, I could qualify for the service based on my chronological age, but I'm going to use my press credentials instead.

Taiwan's finest teas come from very young leaves grown on the top of the mountains. They have a rich and fragrant flavor that is virtually free of any bitter aftertaste. If you are interested in trying it, you can probably buy some in a good tea shop in any Chinatown. The tea producers of Taiwan do a big export business with their fellow tea lovers in Chinese neighborhoods all over the world.

ABOUT FLORIDA SEAFOOD

Seafood is a billion-dollar business in Florida with fishermen bringing in over a hundred different species. Each area along the state's coast has a different "seafood character" and each is worked to the advantage of the seafood lover. Commercial fishing is actually Florida's oldest industry. The original Spanish settlers who arrived in the 1500s started the practice. They caught the seafood in Florida waters, then salted, dried, and sold it to Havana and other Spanish settlements in the West Indies. Their biggest season was Lent when Spanish colonists gave up eating meat.

However, the most important breakthrough for Florida fishermen didn't occur until 1950. That was the year when they discovered deep-water pink shrimp in the Tortugas grounds. The quality of the product is excellent and it's a good choice for a heart-healthy diet. Shrimp are low in overall fat as well as saturated fat. They have some cholesterol, but, remember, scientists are telling us it is the fat, and particularly the saturated fat in our diets, that's the real problem. Prepare your shrimp with a low-fat recipe and you'll be in good shape.

*P*OULTRY

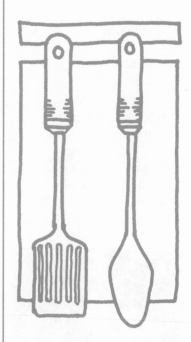

ALMOND CHICKEN WITH LEMON SAUCE
THE GRAND FORMOSA REGENT HOTEL ◆ TAIPEI, TAIWAN

MAKES 4 SERVINGS

2 boneless, skinless chicken
   breasts, halved
½ cup cornstarch
2 eggs, beaten
1 cup sliced almonds
½ cup fresh lemon juice
1 tablespoon rice vinegar
1½ tablespoons sugar
2 teaspoons cornstarch
   dissolved in 1 tablespoon
   cold water
2 tablespoons vegetable oil

Almond-coated chicken with lemon sauce is another classic of Chinese cooking. It is a combination of different textures, shapes, and flavors that meet all the requirements for a formal Chinese recipe.

1.   Dredge the chicken breasts thoroughly in the cornstarch. Dip each one into the eggs, then in the almonds, coating well. Chill until needed.

2.   In a nonreactive* small saucepan over medium-high heat, combine the lemon juice, vinegar, sugar, and dissolved cornstarch. Cook, stirring constantly, until the mixture thickens, about 3 minutes. Remove from the heat and set the dipping sauce aside.

3.   In a large nonstick skillet over medium heat, heat the vegetable oil until hot. Add the chicken breasts and sauté for 5 minutes on each side, or until cooked through.

4.   Cut the chicken breasts into bite-size pieces. Serve at once, with the lemon dipping sauce.

*A nonreactive saucepan is made of a material that will not interact with the acid in the food. Stainless steel, ceramic, glass, and anodized aluminum are fine.

THE DEITIES HAVE A DIFFERENT DIET

The Chinese folk religions of Taiwan believe that the human world and the supernatural world exist next to each other. The people who live in the human world are responsible for sending the supernatural beings what they need in the form of offerings. When it comes to food, you can tell a lot about the being in the supernatural world by the type of food that is offered. The closer the personal relationship between the human being and the spirit, the more the offering is similar to food as it is eaten by the living. If you are making an offering to a deceased relative that you know, you would send along foods that are fully prepared and ready to eat. If it is a processed food it might still be in the manufacturer's package. The common food shows the closeness of the relationship.

If you are making an offering to a very important god, the food will be totally unprocessed, such as a whole pig or a vegetable pulled out of the ground with its roots still on. Not the stuff you would find on your dinner table. The food is offered in an inedible state to symbolize the distance between the person offering the food and the deity on the receiving end. It illustrates the power of the god. Moo shu and McDonald's are for mortals. Deities have a different diet.

◆

ABOUT HUNGRY GHOSTS

According to Chinese folk religion, the world that one goes to after life is very similar to the world one lives in during life. Many of the same needs exist—food, money, clothing. All of these are required in the afterlife and it is the responsibility of the remaining family members to send these things to the deceased. Fortunately, they can be delivered in symbolic form. There is special spirit money that is transferred by burning and there are similar substitutes for everything else. Every year during the seventh lunar month, which usually falls in August and September, there is the Festival of the Hungry Ghosts. It is your last chance to properly feed and care for your deceased family members. Miss this and you will let a "hungry ghost" loose in the world. And the fewer the hungry ghosts in your town, the better off you are. During the festival period, everyone makes an effort to take care of their own ancestors, plus any loose souls who have come back. These characters are thought to form bands of ghosts that can cause great damage as they go in search of sustenance. This time of year you can find plates of food left out in front of homes and businesses to keep the spirits happy and well fed. A properly nourished ghost will go home without causing any trouble, and that sounds like a good thing to me.

◆

AMSTEL CHICKEN CURRY ✓
AMSTEL INTER-CONTINENTAL ◆ AMSTERDAM, HOLLAND

MAKES 4 TO 6 SERVINGS

¼ cup vegetable oil
2 whole boneless, skinless
    chicken breasts, cut into
    bite-size pieces
1 eggplant, peeled, cut into
    ¼-inch sticks about 1½
    inches long
1½ tablespoons curry
    powder, or more, to taste
1 cup chicken broth
2 sprigs fresh thyme, or ½
    teaspoon dried thyme
½ cup unsweetened coconut
    milk
½ cup sour cream or plain
    low-fat yogurt
Salt and freshly ground
    black pepper, to taste
1 tomato, seeded and diced

Holland's four-hundred-year-old history of trading with the East Indies has influenced the way the chefs of Holland do their work. Marcel Driessen, the sous chef at Amsterdam's Amstel Inter-Continental hotel, illustrates the point with his choice of seasonings for his Chicken Curry.

1.   In a wok or large sauté pan over high heat, heat the oil until it shimmers. Add the chicken and stir-fry until it's white on all sides, about 2 minutes. Remove the chicken with a slotted spoon and set aside. Pour off all but 2 tablespoons of the oil.

2.   Add the eggplant to the wok and sprinkle on the curry powder. Pour in the chicken broth and add the thyme. Bring the broth to a boil, and cook for 2 minutes. Add the coconut milk and sour cream or yogurt and mix well. Season with salt and pepper.

3.   Add the chicken back into the wok and sauté, stirring, until the chicken is cooked through. Do not allow the sauce to boil. Stir in the tomato and heat through. Discard the thyme sprigs, if sprigs were used. Serve at once.

Burt Wolf, Robert Kranenborg, and Marcel Driessen.

Sometime during the 1100s, a group of herring fishermen settled along the banks of the Amstel River. That small community eventually became the city of Amsterdam. Those ancient fishing families were also the people who figured out how to build dikes to keep the sea from flooding their land. During the 1500s Amsterdam made a deal with Portugal for salt, which the herring fishermen used to preserve their catch. The salt allowed them to stay at sea longer and make everyone wealthier. At the same time, the local beer brewers had become so skilled that they were actually exporting their beers to other parts of Europe. But the real golden age of Amsterdam was the 1600s.

Amsterdam was Europe's center for business as well as its cultural capital. It started in 1595 when a Dutch trading ship landed in what was then called the East Indies, and is now Indonesia. Bali, Java, Borneo, and Sumatra were lands which produced some of the world's most valuable spices and the places that Columbus was really looking for. When the Dutch got there they took control of a spice trade that made many people rich. In 1602, the Dutch East India Company was formed and, in an unusual move for the time, sold shares to the general public. Within ten years, Holland became the largest importer of spices to Europe. The wealth made from the trade with the East Indies was used to build houses along Amsterdam's canals. The wealth was also used to buy art for those houses from neighborhood painters like Rembrandt. So much money was being made by so many people that for just about the first time in Western history, middle-class citizens were purchasing art. Painters were no longer under the control of the nobles or the church. The commercial middle class was the most powerful group. If a farmer wanted a painting of himself and he had the money, he was on his way to becoming a patron of the arts.

The Dutch also established coffee plantations in Indonesia. The coffee was shipped out of a port in Java that became so important that the word "java" is now a synonym for coffee. The four-hundred-year-old relationship between the East Indies and Holland has also left the Dutch with some of the world's finest Indonesian restaurants serving the traditional dishes of places like Borneo and Bali. The Dutch adopted the flavors of the East Indies as part of their national cuisine.

Amsterdam was actually put together by connecting ninety islands with about five hundred bridges. You could, if you want, get from place to place by boat. Most citizens, however, get around on bicycles. The town has only 750,000 people but a million bikes.

BARBECUED CHICKEN X
THE BUCCANEER RESORT ◆ ST. CROIX, U.S. VIRGIN ISLANDS

MAKES 4 SERVINGS

¾ cup fresh lime juice
   (about 4 limes)
1 cup ketchup
½ cup molasses
¼ cup vegetable oil
1 teaspoon ground allspice
2 teaspoons chili powder
1 teaspoon salt
1 teaspoon freshly ground
   black pepper
4 chicken breast halves,
   bone in

The great agricultural estates of the Caribbean had only one objective, and that was to grow and process as much sugarcane as possible. The first commercially valuable product of the procedure was molasses, a valuable ingredient on its own. Michael Smith, the executive chef at the Brass Parrot Restaurant in The Buccaneer resort on the U.S. Virgin Island of St. Croix, uses molasses to make a basting and barbecue sauce that adds a rich flavor to just about anything.

1. In a large mixing bowl, whisk together the lime juice, ketchup, molasses, oil, and seasonings.

2. Divide the sauce into 2 equal portions. Marinate the chicken breasts in one portion for 30 minutes.

3. Meanwhile, prepare a barbecue grill or preheat the oven to 375° F.

4. Arrange the chicken breasts on the grill rack or in a large roasting pan. Brush generously with the remaining barbecue sauce. Grill or bake until the chicken is thoroughly cooked through, basting it with the sauce.

ABOUT THE BUCCANEERS AND BBQ

The first Europeans to set foot on the beautiful shores of the Caribbean carried the flag of Spain. For many years Spain controlled all the wealth in this part of the world. When the other European countries found out what was going on, they wanted a cut. One of the ways they moved toward that goal—or should I say, gold—was to encourage the local tough guys to steal from the Spanish. The agents of England were extraordinarily successful. They were known as "the Buccaneers" and were basically pirates with a note from their doctor. Actually, the notes were from the King or Queen of England and generally said, "To whom it may concern: Please excuse my friend Henry Morgan from killing, looting, burning, stealing, and other inhuman acts. Cordially, your friend, the King." The Buccaneers appear to have been a ruthless, daring, and lawless bunch but were extremely well organized. They even had little sayings to help them through their work day: "No prey, no pay!" was always a favorite. But I shouldn't be so hard on the Buccaneers because they gave many of the people of North America a very important gastronomic gift.

The Buccaneers had a favorite way of cooking. They liked to dig a pit, fill it with wood chips, light a fire, make a frame of moist wood that wouldn't burn, and cook their food on the frame. The Carib word for this cooking method was barbacoa, which has become BBQ to us. So, next time you are in front of the old grill, remember that we may owe our favorite cooking technique to outstanding historical figures like Blue Beard.

CHICKEN IN MANGO SAUCE X
SANDS HOTEL ◆ SAN JUAN, PUERTO RICO

MAKES 4 SERVINGS

3 large mangoes, peeled,
   pitted, and the flesh
   cubed
4 skinless, boneless chicken
   breast halves
¼ cup all-purpose flour
2 tablespoons vegetable oil
¼ cup light rum
2 tablespoons sugar

*The mango is basic to the gastronomy of Puerto Rico.
Chef Ramon Rosario of San Juan's Sands Hotel has a
favorite recipe for chicken breasts in a mango sauce.*

1. In a blender, puree two thirds of the mango cubes until
smooth. Set aside.

2. Dredge the chicken breast halves lightly in the flour;
shake off any excess.

3. In a large sauté pan over medium-high heat, warm the oil
until hot. Add the chicken breasts and sauté until brown on
one side, 5 to 7 minutes. Turn and sauté the other side until
cooked through, 5 to 7 minutes more.

4. While the chicken cooks, combine the remaining mango
cubes, the rum, and sugar in a small saucepan. Place over
medium heat and stir with a wooden spoon until the sugar dissolves. Add the mango puree and cook, stirring, until the mixture is hot. Reduce the heat to low and keep warm until the
chicken is ready to serve.

5. Arrange the chicken on a serving dish and coat with the
mango sauce. Serve at once.

ABOUT MANGOES

The tree that produces the mango fruit is quite tall and often reaches sixty feet. It's highly productive until the age of forty, when it begins to slow down. The mango has been called the "apple of the tropics" and it is certainly as widely appreciated in the warm parts of the planet as the apple is in the cooler zones. Mangoes have been cultivated by man for so long that no one is quite sure where they got their start. In general, though, they appear to have begun to grow in Asia, probably in eastern India.

All mangoes start out green, but as they ripen they change colors. A ripe mango can range in color from green to rose red. The best way to tell if a mango is ripe is to press the outside skin; it should yield to gentle pressure. Mangoes range in weight from about ten ounces to over four pounds. Considering the fact that they are not the easiest fruit in the world to peel and to clean off the inside stone, I always feel that bigger is easier. Ripe mangoes are eaten as a fresh fruit and used in drinks, pies, ice creams, and uncooked relishes and salsas. The unripe mango is usually cooked into a chutney. Puerto Ricans often call the mango the "king of fruits," and it certainly deserves its royal treatment.

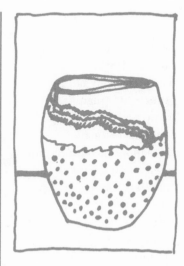

DATE-STUFFED CHICKEN
GRAND PALAZZO HOTEL ◆ ST. THOMAS, U.S. VIRGIN ISLANDS

MAKES 4 SERVINGS

1 cup coarsely chopped
  pitted dates
¼ cup coarsely chopped
  pine nuts (pignoli nuts)
¼ cup coarsely chopped
  shelled pistachios
½ teaspoon ground cumin
½ teaspoon ground
  cardamom
½ teaspoon ground
  cinnamon
1 teaspoon cayenne pepper
4 skinless, boneless chicken
  breast halves
2 tablespoons vegetable oil
½ cup dry white wine

During the 1930s, Sir Edward Cunard of the famous Cunard Steamship Company built himself a magnificent beach house in the Caribbean. He modeled it on his family's Renaissance palace in Venice. It was that piece of architecture that became the inspiration for St. Thomas's Grand Palazzo Hotel. The chef at the Grand Palazzo is the classically trained Patrick Pinon. For a number of years Patrick was the personal chef to the Crown Prince of Oman in the Middle East. One of the recipes he brought with him from Oman is this Date-Stuffed Chicken.

1. In a medium bowl, mix together the dates, pine nuts, pistachios, and seasonings.

2. Cut a pocket in the side of each chicken breast half to make room for the stuffing. Divide the stuffing among the pockets and press firmly to flatten and compress.

3. In a large skillet or sauté pan over medium-high heat, warm the oil until hot. Add the chicken breast halves and sauté on one side, until browned, 5 to 7 minutes. Turn the breasts and sauté the second side, until cooked through and browned, 5 to 7 minutes more, depending on the thickness.

4. Remove the chicken to 4 dinner plates. Pour off all but 1 tablespoon of the oil remaining in the pan. Add the wine and bring to a boil over high heat, whisking briskly to scrape up the browned bits that cling to the bottom of the pan. Drizzle the pan juices over each portion and serve at once.

◆

ABOUT DATES

The date may be the world's oldest cultivated fruit. Seven-thousand-year-old Egyptian sculptures clearly show the date palm. It has been a basic part of Middle Eastern agriculture for centuries, and our earliest photographs of the area show date palm trees growing throughout the region. The Arabs brought the date to Spain, and Spanish missionaries transported the trees to California. The first date palms planted in California were planted in a town called Mecca. Today, California produces almost all of the dates grown in North America.

A date palm has been described as living with its feet in the water and its head in the sun. It's perfect for the desert oasis and the Coachella Valley of California. There is dry air above and irrigation below. Date palms come in male and female forms, but that doesn't work too well for farmers. It means that much of their land would be given over to male trees that don't bear fruit. As a result, date growers do the pollinating by hand.

Dates are often called "Nature's candy" because of their sweet taste and caramel flavor. They also contain some valuable nutrients. Dates are a very good source of potassium, which may turn out to be a valuable tool in controlling high blood pressure. The best way to store your dates is in an airtight container in the refrigerator. They'll hold their flavor for at least eight months. Though the date harvests take place in the fall, dates are actually available all year round.

◆

Grand Palazzo Hotel, St. Thomas.

CHICKEN WITH MINT (CHICKEN ADOBO)
EL SAN JUAN HOTEL ♦ SAN JUAN, PUERTO RICO

MAKES 4 SERVINGS

1 tablespoon freshly ground
  black pepper
2 tablespoons salt
4 cloves garlic, crushed
2 teaspoons dried oregano
2 tablespoons olive oil
3 tablespoons coarsely
  chopped fresh mint leaves
4 tablespoons fresh lime
  juice
4 skinless, boneless chicken
  breast halves
2 tablespoons vegetable oil

John Carey is the executive chef at the El San Juan Hotel in San Juan. When he first arrived in Puerto Rico from the United States he recognized that there was an extraordinary local cuisine. Working with his wife, Ainslie, he has begun to collect the traditional recipes of Puerto Rico. His chicken with mint sauce is a good example.

1.   In a mortar or sturdy bowl, use a pestle or heavy spoon to mash together the pepper, salt, garlic, oregano, olive oil, mint leaves, and 1 tablespoon of the lime juice. Work the mixture until it forms a paste.

2.   Rub one quarter of the spice paste over the outside of each chicken breast, covering evenly.

3.   Place a large sauté pan that will hold all the chicken over medium-high heat, and heat the vegetable oil. When the oil is hot, place the chicken breasts, coated side down, into the pan. Cook the breasts for 5 minutes.

4.   Turn the chicken breasts, coated sides up, and sprinkle with the remaining 3 tablespoons of lime juice. Sauté for 5 minutes more, or until the chicken is cooked through. Serve hot or cold.

♦

FELIDIA'S CHICKEN
FELIDIA RISTORANTE ◆ NEW YORK, NEW YORK

Lidia Bastianich was born in a part of the world called Istria. It is in the northeast corner of Italy, and at various periods has been part of Italy, Austria, Germany, and Yugoslavia. At the end of the Second World War, her family moved to New York City. Today, Lidia and her husband own and run one of Manhattan's finest restaurants, Felidia. It offers an extraordinary collection of great dishes, many of which were chosen from Lidia's own cookbook, La Cucina di Lidia. The following was a family favorite.

1. Warm the oil in a large sauté pan over moderately high heat. Add the chicken pieces and cook for about 8 minutes on each side, or until lightly browned all over. Remove the chicken and drain on paper towels. Spoon off all but 2 tablespoons of the fat in the sauté pan.

2. Return the sauté pan to moderate heat and add the onion, bacon, bay leaves, rosemary, chicken livers (if desired), mushrooms, and cloves. Sauté for 5 minutes.

3. Add the tomato paste and stock or broth and stir to mix well. Return the chicken pieces to the pan and bring the mixture to a boil. Reduce the heat to moderate and cook for 5 minutes. Turn the chicken pieces and cook for an additional 5 minutes. Season with salt and pepper.

4. Divide the chicken among 4 dinner plates. Strain the sauce and remove and discard the bay leaves. Spoon the sauce over the chicken, or if you'd rather have a chunky sauce, skip the straining and spoon the sauce over each serving of chicken.

MAKES 4 SERVINGS

¼ cup vegetable oil
4 chicken breasts, halved, bone in, all skin removed
1 large onion, minced
3 strips bacon, minced
2 bay leaves
2 teaspoons chopped fresh rosemary
½ cup chopped chicken livers (optional)
1½ cups sliced mushrooms
½ teaspoon ground cloves
¼ cup tomato paste
1½ cups chicken stock or broth
Salt and freshly ground black pepper, to taste

◆

ABOUT EQUALITY AND THE
AMERICAN "FOOD" WAY

We are a nation of immigrants and the children and grandchildren of immigrants. As a result, we love the idea of the equality of opportunity. We may not end up with what we want, but we like the feeling that we at least have a fair shot at getting it. Equal opportunity was very important to the people who passed through Ellis Island and even more important to their descendants. The desire for equality of opportunity has had an enormous impact on our nation's food.

In past centuries you could always tell who the most important people were at a dinner table. They were the ones who got to eat the most important parts of the meat, fish, or poultry. The life-giving protein in that flesh was the most significant part of a meal and it was usually cooked whole and brought to the table in one piece. As it was carved, the most valued parts went to the most valued people. The person who got the breast was more important than the person who got the neck.

Today, we are attracted to systems that appear to be free of hierarchy. The old approach was clearly unacceptable for our equality-seeking hearts. One result of this is that more and more of our food is precut, premeasured, and preprocessed into a form where one piece is indistinguishable from the next. The success of hamburgers, fish sticks, and chicken nuggets is to a large extent the result of our love of democracy.

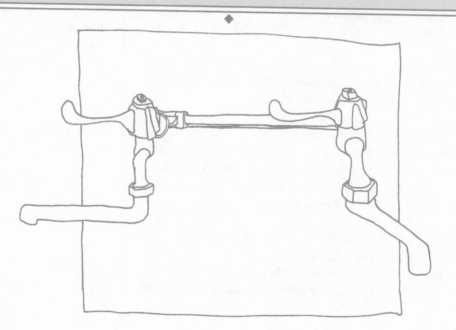

JAMAICAN CHICKEN ✓
THE ENCHANTED GARDEN RESORT ◆ OCHO RIOS, JAMAICA

1. In a saucepan over low heat, heat 2 tablespoons of the oil. Add the spices and stir for 1 minute (see Notes).

2. Add the chicken stock. Raise the heat and bring the stock to a boil. Boil for 2 minutes. Add the coconut milk, garlic, ginger, cornstarch mixture, and salt and pepper. Reduce the heat and simmer for 2 minutes to thicken. Remove the cinnamon stick. Set the sauce aside.

3. In a nonstick sauté pan over medium-high heat, warm the remaining tablespoon of oil. Add the chicken to the pan and cook for 2 minutes. Turn the chicken and cook for 3 minutes more, or until cooked through. Serve the chicken with the reheated sauce on top.

NOTES: The technique of heating the spices in a little oil at the beginning of a recipe is a traditional Indian method for increasing and blending the flavors.

Fresh ginger should be minced rather than grated. Grating removes moisture from the ginger and reduces the flavor.

MAKES 4 SERVINGS

3 tablespoons vegetable oil
2 teaspoons ground cumin
2 teaspoons ground turmeric
2 teaspoons coriander seeds
1 cinnamon stick
1 cup chicken stock
2 tablespoons coconut milk
1 clove garlic, minced
1 tablespoon minced fresh ginger (see Notes)
1 teaspoon cornstarch dissolved in 1½ teaspoons cold water
Salt and freshly ground black pepper, to taste
2 skinless, boneless chicken breasts, fat removed, halved

The first people to inhabit the island of Jamaica were a group of Arawak tribes that sailed over in their canoes from South America sometime in the mid-600s. The Arawaks were seafarers who made their homes near the shore and lived on seafood, fruits, and roots. Because the island came up out of the sea in a volcanic eruption, everything that grows on Jamaica was brought by human travelers or dropped off by birds. After the Arawaks came the Carib tribes. The Caribs were followed by the Europeans, first the Spanish and then the English. The Europeans brought the Africans. There were also large immigrations of Arabic communities—Chinese and East Indians. The national motto is "Out of many; one people."

While it may be one people, there are many pots. Each of these ethnic groups brought their traditional foods to Jamaica. They kept their basic cooking style but adapted it to the local ingredients. However, there are a number of foods that stand out as particularly Jamaican. Probably the most famous is ackee. Ackee is a fruit, red on the outside and yellow on the inside. It has three large black seeds set between the yellow meat. The meat is used to make the national Sunday morning breakfast dish, ackee and salt fish. The ackee tastes a little like well-done scrambled eggs. Ackee can only be eaten after the skin opens by itself. When an ackee is closed and you can't clearly see the black seeds, it's poisonous. There's also a Jamaican fruit that looks like a red pear and tastes like an apple; it's called an Otaheite. The first time a European saw it he said, "Oh, Tahiti! I saw a fruit like that in Tahiti." So now everyone calls it Otaheite. That story was told to me by one of Jamaica's leading authorities on the island's history. I did not make it up.

Someone did make up the ortanigue. It's a cross between an orange and a tanger- ine that was developed by a local grower. Jamaica is also famous for its Blue Mountain coffee, which is made from the beans on a small estate in the mountains. The beans are often thought of as the finest on the planet. The supply of these beans, however, is very small, and last I heard, most of them were going to Japan, which is rapidly becoming a nation of coffee lovers.

One of my favorite Jamaican foods is the jackfruit. I was told that when you buy a jackfruit it's important to have the seller cut it open. If you don't, a "Duppy" ghost will follow you home. And if you're using a car or a bike, the ghost will give you a flat tire. It's an interesting custom because the only way to make sure that a jackfruit is ready to eat is to open it; the superstition forces the seller to do the right thing.

◆

REGENT CHICKEN WITH PINEAPPLE ✓
THE GRAND FORMOSA REGENT HOTEL ◆ TAIPEI, TAIWAN

The idea of putting meat and fruit together in the same recipe is rather uncommon in today's Western cooking. But in earlier times it was standard operational procedure. Recipes from ancient Roman times to the Renaissance regularly combined meat, fish, and poultry with fruit. This is also a regular part of cooking in China. Chef Kow at the Grand Formosa Regent Hotel in Taipei, Taiwan, makes this point with wok-fried chicken with pineapple.

MAKES 4 SERVINGS

½ cup pineapple juice from canned pineapple chunks
½ cup ketchup
1 tablespoon vinegar
1½ tablespoons sugar
1 teaspoon soy sauce
¼ cup vegetable oil
1 whole boneless, skinless chicken breast, cut into bite-size pieces
1 egg yolk, beaten with 2 teaspoons cornstarch
1 cup drained canned pineapple chunks
1 cup green bell pepper strips or triangles
⅓ cup chopped scallions
⅓ cup red bell pepper strips

1.   In a wok or large sauté pan over medium-high heat, combine the pineapple juice, ketchup, vinegar, sugar, and soy sauce. Bring the mixture to a boil and cook until the sugar dissolves and the mixture is reduced to about ½ cup. Pour the sauce into a bowl and set aside. Rinse out the wok.

2.   Set the wok over high heat and warm the oil until it shimmers. Meanwhile, dip the chicken pieces in the egg yolk mixture to coat well. Add the coated chicken to the wok and stir-fry for 2 minutes, until the chicken is opaque on all sides. Using a slotted spoon, remove the chicken to a plate, leaving any oil in the wok.

3.   Set the wok over medium-high heat and add the pineapple chunks and green bell pepper. Stir-fry for 30 seconds. Add the scallions and red bell pepper, and stir-fry for 30 seconds. Return the chicken and the reduced sauce to the wok and stir-fry with the vegetables for 1 minute, until the chicken is cooked through and the sauce is hot. Serve at once.

◆

STIR-FRY CHICKEN WITH CASHEWS ✗
THE GRAND FORMOSA REGENT HOTEL ◆ TAIPEI, TAIWAN

MAKES 4 SERVINGS

2 cups vegetable oil
1 cup cashews
1 whole boneless, skinless
  chicken breast, cut into
  bite-size pieces
3 cloves garlic, chopped
½ cup chopped scallions
½ cup red bell pepper
  strips
1 tablespoon soy sauce
1 tablespoon Chinese chili
  paste (optional)
1 cup celery, sliced on the
  diagonal
1 cup carrots, very thinly
  sliced on the diagonal
1 cup drained bamboo
  shoots
1 cup sliced mushrooms
1 teaspoon Oriental sesame
  oil
1 teaspoon cornstarch
  dissolved in 1 tablespoon
  cold water

The rules for a proper Chinese recipe go back thousands of years and deal with a search for balance and contrast. In the area of texture the Chinese are the absolute masters. A good example is this recipe for Chicken with Cashews.

1. In a wok or large sauté pan, heat the oil until the oil begins to shimmer. Add the cashews and deep-fry for 20 seconds. Remove the cashews with a slotted spoon. Add the chicken pieces and deep-fry for about 1 minute, or until opaque on all sides. Remove the chicken with a slotted spoon. Pour off all but 2 tablespoons of the oil.

2. Set the wok over high heat. Add the garlic and stir-fry for 10 seconds. Add the scallions and red bell pepper and stir-fry for 30 seconds. Stir in the soy sauce and chili paste, if using, and mix well. Add the vegetables and stir-fry for 2 minutes.

3. Return the chicken to the wok and cook briefly, until just heated through. Stir in the sesame oil. Add the cornstarch mixture and stir-fry for 1 minute. Add the cashews, toss to blend thoroughly and cook for 1 minute. Serve hot.

◆

ABOUT BAMBOO SHOOTS

Bamboo shoots are a grass that is native to southern China. They are the leading vegetable crop in Taiwan, and over 380,000 metric tons are produced each year. It is kind of difficult to find fresh bamboo shoots in the average North American supermarket, but canned bamboo shoots are readily available in any market that has a section for Asian food. They come as chunks, slices, or prediced. When a can of bamboo shoots is opened, the shoots should be drained of the water they came in and given a quick rinse. Any remaining shoots that you don't use in the recipe should be stored in fresh water, in a glass jar, in the refrigerator. If you change the water every other day, the shoots will last for about two weeks. Cooks peel and slice the shoots, and put them into just about any dish. Bamboo shoots are especially good with meat and are often used to lighten a dish. They are high in fiber and low in fat, and the stalks are used to make chopsticks.

WHY THERE ARE SO MANY CHINESE RESTAURANTS IN NORTH AMERICA

During the mid-1800s, tens of thousands of Chinese laborers left China to find work in the United States and Canada. Their primary task was the construction of the transcontinental railroads that stretched across each country. The Chinese workmen had their own camps and their own cooks who did their best to reproduce the recipes of their homeland. Very often, as a section of construction concluded in a part of the country that a worker liked, he would drop out of the construction crew and find work in a local town. Frequently that work was as a cook in a restaurant. Eventually, he would save up enough money to open his own restaurant and would return to the cooking of the region of China from which he came. Since most of the Chinese workers who came to North America during this period had come from the area of Canton, most of those original Chinese restaurants served or tried to serve traditional Cantonese dishes. They did not have most of the ingredients that they were accustomed to using in China. Nor did they have the real equipment that they used back home. Yet their skill levels were high enough to develop a local following. That is why almost every town in the United States and Canada has ended up with at least one Chinese restaurant.

STUFFED CHICKEN BREASTS
THE RUSSIAN TEA ROOM ◆ NEW YORK, NEW YORK

MAKES 4 SERVINGS

STUFFING
2 tablespoons vegetable oil
1½ cups thinly sliced onions
1½ cups thinly sliced
  mushrooms
Salt and freshly ground
  black pepper, to taste
1 tablespoon flour
½ cup red wine
1 tablespoon chopped fresh
  parsley

2 whole chicken breasts,
  halved, skin and bones
  removed, then sliced
  almost in half through
  thickness and pounded
  thin
Salt and freshly ground
  black pepper, to taste
½ cup flour, for dredging,
  placed in a shallow bowl
2 eggs beaten with 2
  tablespoons milk, with
  salt and freshly ground
  black pepper to taste,
  placed in a shallow bowl

Russian cuisine is rich and varied, having drawn its material from the many geographic areas and cultures that have influenced its history. The most elegant Russian food was produced in the kitchens of the noble families, like the De Beausobres of St. Petersburg, who regularly imported the techniques of great French chefs. But there was also an enormous amount of plain good cooking in the homes of the farmers and peasants, like my great-grandmother's house.

Today, however, much of the best Russian cooking takes place in restaurants. Unfortunately, those restaurants are not in Russia. A good example of what I mean is the following recipe from the Russian Tea Room.

1. To make the stuffing: Place the oil in a sauté pan and sauté the onions over medium heat for 2 to 3 minutes, until softened. Add the mushrooms and sauté for another 3 minutes. Add the salt and pepper and cook for 2 minutes more. Sprinkle the tablespoon of flour over the entire mixture and stir to distribute evenly. Add the wine and continue stirring and cooking for 3 minutes. Add the parsley, combine, and remove from the heat.

2. Season the chicken breasts with salt and pepper. Lay each breast out flat and place one quarter of the stuffing mixture down the center of each. Fold each breast into thirds to enclose the stuffing. Carefully roll each breast into the flour first, tap off the excess, then dip each into the egg mixture. And lastly, dip each into the bread cubes. Press firmly so that the cubes adhere.

3. Preheat the oven to 350° F.

4. Heat the oil in a large sauté pan until very hot. Gently slip in the chicken breasts, seam side down. Sauté on each side until brown. Remove the chicken breasts carefully and place into an oven-proof baking dish or roasting pan. Bake for 20 to 25 minutes, until the chicken is cooked through. Allow to remain at room temperature for 5 minutes before serving.

NOTE: It is important to use the homemade bread cubes; do not substitute croutons, as they are too crunchy and overseasoned. If you prefer, roll the chicken breasts into some *unseasoned* breadcrumbs and continue as instructed above.

6 cups ½-inch-square fresh bread cubes made from coarsely textured bread with the crust removed (don't use white bread—see Note)

3 tablespoons vegetable oil

♦

ABOUT THE RUSSIANS AND THEIR FOOD

As the 1800s came to an end, Russia found itself in constant turmoil—crops failing, agonizing poverty throughout a majority of the population, religious persecution. It is no surprise that during the fifty-year period starting in 1875 over 2 million Russians left their homeland and took passage to New York City.

When you talk about the food of Russia you are actually talking about the food of more than 170 individual ethnic groups, each one clinging to their own particular customs. There are, however, a number of food ways that have become a part of almost all of those groups. These were the gastronomic habits that the Russian immigrants brought to the United States at the beginning of the twentieth century.

The Russians loved rich whole-grain breads, which were much healthier than the other processed white breads. They chose water as their favorite drink and liked to have it infused with bubbles. They were responsible for the development of the New York seltzer business and called seltzer the "workman's champagne." They were masters at smoking fish and meat and responsible for the introduction of pastrami to the East Coast delicatessens. They loved cooked fruit and did much to popularize the drinking of tea.

♦

Van Gogh Chicken with Chives
AMSTERDAM, HOLLAND

MAKES 8 SERVINGS

3 tablespoons vegetable oil

1 medium onion, roughly chopped

4 cloves garlic, crushed

8 skinless, boneless chicken breast halves, cut into bite-size pieces

2 tablespoons chopped fresh rosemary leaves

1 pound mushrooms, washed and roughly chopped

3 large tomatoes, roughly chopped, with seeds and juices reserved

1 cup dry white wine

⅔ cup heavy cream

6 tablespoons chopped fresh chives, or more to taste

Salt and freshly ground black pepper, to taste

When Van Gogh lived in Paris during the 1880s, he would often pay for his meals at the local café by giving the owner a painting of flowers or food, which was then used to decorate the café. One of my favorite paintings of food by Van Gogh is the Flower Pot with Chives, *which he painted in Paris during the spring of 1887. KLM Chef Paolo-Arpa Sanna was inspired by this work and responded by creating a chicken recipe with chives.*

1.   In a large sauté pan over medium-high heat, warm the oil until hot. Add the onion and garlic and sauté for 1 minute. Add the chicken and rosemary and stir-fry until the chicken is browned on all sides, 2 to 3 minutes. Remove the chicken pieces with tongs or a slotted spoon and set aside.

2.   Add the mushrooms, tomatoes, and wine to the onion and cook until slightly tender, 3 to 5 minutes. Stir in the cream and 4 tablespoons of the chives. Return the chicken and any juices that have collected to the pan and bring the mixture almost to a boil. Reduce the heat to medium and simmer uncovered, stirring occasionally, until the chicken is cooked through, 8 to 12 minutes.

3.   Check the seasonings, adding salt and pepper, as necessary. Serve hot, sprinkled with the remaining 2 tablespoons of chives.

ABOUT ART IN
HOLLAND'S GOLDEN AGE

Holland's Golden Age of the 1600s was the time of Rembrandt, Van Dyck, Frans Hals, and Vermeer. Their works give us a detailed picture of what Dutch life was like at the time. The Dutch masters have left us a picture of the period's menu—cheese, fresh fruit and vegetables, milk, fish, beer. They are the same foods and drinks that make up the traditional meals of today's Dutch family.

Very often, the way a food was shown was meant to tell a story. The Merry Family by Jan Steen looks like a great Sunday afternoon lunch with the kids. But when you look closely, you see that the children are following the habits of their parents—drinking, smoking, overeating. The painting is actually a warning against weak morals and a seventeenth-century cry for improved family values.

Amstel Inter-Continental,
Amsterdam.

CHICKEN WITH TOMATOES
QANTAS JET BASE ◆ SYDNEY, AUSTRALIA

MAKES 4 SERVINGS

6 tablespoons plus 1
teaspoon vegetable oil
1 red onion, thinly sliced
3 teaspoons chopped garlic
1 tablespoon chopped sun-
dried tomatoes
One 14½-ounce can chicken
broth
Salt and freshly ground
black pepper, to taste
2 boneless, skinless chicken
breasts, split
2 teaspoons freshly ground
white pepper
2 teaspoons freshly ground
black pepper
1 teaspoon ground
coriander
1 tablespoon chopped fresh
basil leaves
¼ cup finely chopped
scallions
2 cups string beans,
topped, tailed, and
blanched
8 small new potatoes,
peeled, left whole, and
boiled until tender
4 cherry tomatoes, stemmed
and peeled

Cheong Tse is the executive chef of Qantas Airlines in its hometown of Sydney, Australia. He has been interested in art since he was a child and uses his drawing skills to plan the look of his finished dishes.

1. In a medium saucepan over medium-high heat, warm 2 tablespoons of the vegetable oil until the oil is hot. Add the red onion and 2 teaspoons of the garlic and sauté until the onion is translucent, about 5 minutes. Stir in the sun-dried tomatoes and chicken broth, and bring to a boil. Add the salt and pepper. Reduce heat to low, cover the pan, and simmer while you prepare the chicken.

2. Using a sharp knife, slice each chicken breast half through its thickness, cutting almost, but not quite, in half. Coat a sheet of plastic wrap with 1 teaspoon of the vegetable oil and place a chicken breast onto half of it. Fold the other half of the plastic wrap over the top. Pound the breast until almost flat. Remove from the plastic and set aside. Repeat with the remaining chicken breasts, using the same sheet of oiled plastic wrap.

3. Combine the white and black peppers, coriander, and basil. Sprinkle the mixture evenly over both sides of each chicken breast.

4. In a large skillet over medium-high heat, heat 2 tablespoons of vegetable oil until the oil is hot. Cook the chicken breasts for 1 to 2 minutes on each side, until the chicken is golden brown and cooked through. Drain on paper towels and keep warm.

◆

5. Using the same skillet over medium-high heat, warm 1 tablespoon of the vegetable oil until the oil is hot. Sauté the remaining teaspoon of garlic and the scallions for 2 minutes. Add the string beans and toss for 1 to 2 minutes, or until the beans are heated through. Set aside with the chicken and keep warm.

6. Using the same skillet over medium-high heat, warm the remaining tablespoon of vegetable oil until the oil is hot. Cook the potatoes for about 5 minutes, or until evenly browned on all sides. Drain on paper towels and keep warm.

7. Add the cherry tomatoes to the red onion–chicken stock sauce and turn up the heat to medium-high. Cook for 2 minutes.

8. Place each chicken breast on a dinner plate and spoon some of the cherry tomato sauce over each serving. Arrange the green beans and potatoes on each side of the chicken and serve hot.

CHICKEN IN PORT WINE SAUCE
CANADA'S VIA RAIL TRAIN

MAKES 4 SERVINGS

¼ cup all-purpose flour
Salt and pepper, to taste
4 skinless, boneless chicken
   breast halves
2 tablespoons vegetable oil
1 cup milk
¼ cup low-fat cream cheese
¼ cup sun-dried tomatoes
¼ cup port wine

Although the kitchens on Canada's Via Rail trains are not the easiest kitchens that I have ever worked in, they do have two distinct advantages: They make the cooks select recipes that give you the most taste for the least work; and, the scenery outside the window is always changing. One of the most popular dishes on the menu, that also gives you lots of taste for very little effort, is this chicken breast in a port wine sauce.

1.   Place the flour in a shallow plate. Lightly dredge the chicken breasts with the flour. Salt and pepper.

2.   In a large skillet over medium heat, warm the oil. Add the chicken breasts and cook for 4 to 6 minutes on each side, or until cooked through. Remove the chicken and drain on paper towels.

3.   Add the milk, cream cheese, sun-dried tomatoes, and port to the skillet. Stir well and bring the sauce to a boil. Reduce the heat to medium and simmer for 2 minutes.

4.   Place each breast on a plate. Top each serving with some of the sauce.

MEALS ON TRAIN WHEELS

The earliest meals for train passengers were offered by track-side vendors. The vendors would wait for the trains at the stations. As soon as the train came in they would sell the food to the passengers through the train windows. Unfortunately, the coal-burning engines passed into the station first and deposited a layer of soot on all of the food just as it was about to be offered to the travelers.

The station-vendor period was followed by the era of the news butcher. News butchers were characters who came on board the train and walked through the cars selling newspapers, magazines, and food. Skilled practitioners of this craft always offered salted peanuts on their first pass to insure better beverage sales during their second tour.

News butchers were still around when I made my first train trip during the 1940s. They would walk through the cars with big trays hanging from their necks. I can still remember their pitch: "Life, Look, Collier's, Reader's Digest, Atlantic Monthly, Harper's Bazaar, Time magazine. Hershey bars, Milky Ways, Jujubes, Baby Ruths. Sandwiches, milk, coffee, tea, Coca-Cola, bonbons. What'll ya have, kid?" I was about six years old and my mother was sending me from New York to Boston to visit my aunt. The high point of my trip was always the food vendor.

The next major development in the history of meals on wheels was the introduction of eating houses in the existing train stations. The train would come to a stop and the passengers would rush out to the eating area. They would bolt down their food and rush back onto the train. The stop was scheduled for twenty minutes and was officially called a meal stop. The passengers usually described it as an "indigestion stop." As railroad technology improved and greater and greater distances were being covered in shorter and shorter amounts of time, it became impractical to stop three times each day for meals. So, the first on-board food service was offered. Often it was a buffet set up in the baggage car. Sometimes it was an official service set up by the company, and sometimes it was a little free-lance operation set up by the train crew to earn some extra money. There was actually a long tradition of independent entrepreneurial operations on the part of the train crews. The first restaurants in the railway stations had been set up by the wives of the conductors. The conductor would go through the train and find out how many people would like to have a meal at a station down the line. Then he would telegraph ahead and tell his wife how many people would be coming into their little restaurant when the train arrived.

In 1867, George Pullman introduced his "hotel car." It was the first car built specifically for cooking and serving meals while the train was in motion. It changed the way both the railroad companies and the passengers thought about their meals.

◆

CHICKEN FRICASSEE
HOTEL PLAZA ATHÉNÉE ◆ PARIS, FRANCE

MAKES 4 SERVINGS

1 chicken (about 3½ pounds), cut into 12 pieces
Salt and freshly ground black pepper, to taste
¼ cup vegetable oil
2 cups button mushrooms (about 10 ounces)
1 cup heavy cream
1 tablespoon fresh thyme leaves
2 cups peeled baby onions or pearl onions
2 tablespoons unsalted butter

Paris street vendor.

Gérard Sallé is the executive chef at the Plaza Athénée in Paris, France. We talked about the differences between the recipes used in home cooking and those that are used in most restaurants. I asked him about the traditional Sunday chicken dinners that were served in his childhood. In response, he cooked the following chicken fricassee.

1.   Liberally season the chicken pieces with salt and pepper.

2.   In a large sauté pan over medium-high heat, warm the oil. Add half of the chicken pieces, skin side down, and reduce the heat to medium. Cook the chicken, turning frequently, for 10 to 15 minutes, or until almost cooked throughout and golden brown. Remove the chicken and drain on paper towels. Cook the remaining chicken pieces in the remaining oil. Remove and drain.

3.   Add the mushrooms to the sauté pan and cook, stirring frequently, for 3 to 5 minutes. Add the cream and thyme and stir well. Return the chicken to the pan, cover, and simmer for 10 to 15 minutes, or until cooked through.

4.   Meanwhile, in a small saucepan over medium-high heat, combine the onions, just enough water to barely cover them, and the butter. Cover and cook until the onions are tender, 10 to 15 minutes.

5.   Remove the chicken pieces from the pan and divide among 4 dinner plates. Add a quarter of the onions to each plate and pour the mushroom cream sauce over the top. Serve immediately.

◆

CHICKEN WITH A PUNGENT SAUCE χ
TOPNOTCH INN ♦ STOWE, VERMONT

1.   Heat the sesame oil in a skillet. Add the garlic and ginger. Sauté for 30 seconds, then add the vinegar and sherry. Boil for 1 minute to reduce the liquid. Add the ketchup and pineapple juice. Simmer uncovered over a low flame for 5 to 7 minutes.

2.   In a second skillet, heat the vegetable oil and add the chicken breasts, being careful not to crowd them. Add salt and pepper and sauté for 1½ minutes on each side, until breasts are browned. Remove the chicken from the pan and set aside.

3.   Strain the sauce and return to the skillet. Place the chicken in the sauce. Cover and cook over a low flame for 5 minutes. Uncover and add the walnuts and pineapple. Cook just long enough to heat through.

4.   Remove the chicken to a serving dish and place the pineapple and walnuts around the chicken.

MAKES 4 SERVINGS

¼ cup sesame oil
6 cloves garlic, minced
¼ cup minced fresh ginger
¼ cup rice vinegar
¼ cup dry sherry
1⅓ cups ketchup
1 cup pineapple juice
3 tablespoons vegetable oil
4 skinless, boneless chicken
   breast halves
Salt and freshly ground
   pepper, to taste
1 cup chopped walnuts
6 pineapple rings, cut into
   quarters

MORE ABOUT GINGER

Ginger is one of the most common ingredients in Chinese cooking. However, it is important to remember that Chinese recipes are talking about fresh gingerroot. You can't substitute powdered or dried ginger for fresh gingerroot. Fortunately, these days you can get fresh ginger in many standard North American supermarkets. When you are picking it out, make sure that it is smooth, free of soft spots, and generally firm to the touch.

A little fresh ginger goes a long way. In general, the circumference of a gingerroot is about the same as that of a U.S. quarter. If you cut off two slices of fresh ginger, each about the same thickness as the coin, and you mince them, they will yield about one teaspoon of chopped ginger. It's a nice little tip that can help you judge the amount of ginger you need for a recipe. Two quarters' worth will give you a teaspoon.

Apprentice street vendor, Lukang.

Chinese food is probably the world's most well-traveled cuisine. In fact, it has been so easy for so many people in so many cities to eat in Chinese restaurants, that until recently there has been very little interest in Chinese home cooking outside of the Chinese communities. That began to change in the 1960s, and today there is a constant and ever-increasing curiosity about Chinese cooking in the home kitchens of the West.

Virtually every significant piece of Chinese cooking equipment is easily available, and our supermarkets offer all of the basics in terms of Chinese ingredients. The selection can get pretty elaborate, but in reality there are only a few items that are really needed in the area of condiments and seasonings.

Oyster sauce is one of the common condiments in Chinese cooking. It is a thick brown liquid that is produced by grinding oysters together with an assortment of flavorings. It was developed in the area of Canton and is used to give a dish color and a slight "meaty" flavor. Despite the fact that it is made from a shellfish, oyster sauce should never have a fishy smell. That's the first sign of a poor-quality product.

Sesame oil is made from toasted sesame seeds. It's rather thick and has a light brown color and a wonderful rich smell. The thicker it is the better the flavor. Don't use the light cold-press American sesame oil for Chinese dishes. That form of oil is fine, but it doesn't have the Chinese flavor that you need in the dish. On the other hand, Chinese sesame oil will burn at very low temperatures, so you don't cook food in it. It is really just a seasoning.

Soy sauce is the most important of all the Chinese seasonings. It is made from fermented soybeans, wheat, yeast, and salt. There are two major types: light soy sauce and dark. The light sauce is thinner and used for delicate dishes and as a dipping sauce. The dark sauce is actually a bit darker in color and has a slightly sweeter smell, but its major difference is that it is thicker. It is used for marinating and to give a dish a rich, deep, glowing color. Both forms of soy sauce have the ability to tenderize meat and poultry. Whichever type you use, it's important to remember that they should be kept in a glass container with a tightly closed lid. And as I have been told over and over again by the great chefs of Taiwan, don't substitute Japanese soy sauce for Chinese soy sauce. It won't give you the proper flavor and it's politically incorrect.

There is also chili sauce or paste, made from crushed fresh chili peppers, which will last for a year in the refrigerator; hoisin sauce made from soybeans, flour, sugar, salt, and garlic, and gives foods a sweet, peppery flavor and a reddish-brown color; sesame paste, which is a general flavoring agent; and, star anise, which has a licoricelike flavor. That's it. Seven different items that should be able to give most home cooked dishes their Chinese flavor. And all easily available. But remember . . . you're probably not going to use them everyday, so get them in small quantities.

◆

CHICKEN WITH SESAME OIL
THE GRAND FORMOSA REGENT HOTEL ◆ TAIPEI, TAIWAN

MAKES 4 SERVINGS

1 cup vegetable oil
1 boneless, skinless chicken
  breast, cut into bite-size
  pieces
½ cup scallions, cut into
  1-inch strips
1 tablespoon minced fresh
  ginger
2 cloves garlic, minced
1 red bell pepper, cut into
  bite-size pieces
1 tablespoon Chinese
  sesame oil
2 tablespoons soy sauce
2 cups basil leaves or fresh
  spinach

In Chinese cooking the chicken is a symbol of good luck, and has become a regular part of the offerings to the gods. For great and powerful gods who can easily do their own cooking, the chicken is offered raw. For gods of less strength and influence and for honored ancestors, the chicken is offered already cooked. This dish is a casserole of chicken with sesame oil. It has a rich and nutty flavor and is very simple to prepare.

1. Over high heat, heat a wok or high-sided sauté pan. Add the vegetable oil and heat until shimmering. Add the chicken and fry for 2 minutes. Drain the chicken from the oil and set aside. Remove all but 2 tablespoons of the oil from the wok.

2. Over high heat, warm the wok. Add the scallions, ginger, garlic, and red bell pepper and stir-fry for 2 minutes. Return the chicken to the wok and stir-fry for 1 minute. Add the sesame oil, soy sauce, and basil leaves and stir-fry for 1 minute more. Empty the wok into a warm serving dish.

Line chefs, Grand Formosa Regent Hotel.

THE TAO OF TRAFFIC

Each time I visit the Republic of China in Taiwan I spend a few hours with a friend of mine, Richard Vuylsteke. Richard has devoted the past thirty years to the study of Chinese culture, and his writings on the subject regularly appear in the Free China Review. *During my most recent trip I was talking to him about the traffic in Taiwan and my failure to understand what was going on in the streets.*

To me it was utter chaos. To Richard, however, Taipei's traffic is just another example of how Chinese thought patterns and their physical manifestations differ from those of the West. He pointed out that local traffic is totally understandable once you view it in the light of Taoist doctrine. Central to Taoist teaching is the idea of "flow," "free yet disciplined movement." A good metaphor would be a young and quickly flowing river, a rapid mountain stream. The water fills the space between the banks, racing over rocks, under fallen trees, and around any obstacle in its path. And as Richard points out, so does the traffic of Taipei. Just as a stream fills its banks, so do the vehicles fill the space between the curbs, and between other objects on the road. Instead of the Western idea of parallel streams of traffic clearly marked by lines that can only be crossed under rigidly defined rules, the Chinese draw upon different, less legalistic traditions. Anywhere there is room, there is a vehicle. This means faster flow, the more effective utilization of space, and a better chance at ultimately reaching your destination within a reasonable time.

The Taiwanese driver also has a different idea of what constitutes a "near miss." While the Western mind measures in feet, the Chinese mind measures in inches. What would send the average North American motorist into a fit, is totally ignored in Taiwan, or at the very worst, gets a honk of a horn.

The ancient Chinese concepts of flow and space have been adapted to modern traffic. But it is also an illustration of the Taoist idea of balance: the ability of two totally opposite forces to coexist in one object at the identical moment. Clearly, the drivers of Taipei are at the same time the best and the worst drivers in the world. And that's the yin and yang of it.

ABOUT TAOISM

Taoism had its beginnings in the ancient Chinese Shamanistic culture that goes back in history over four thousand years. Its formation into a philosophy appears to have taken place during the sixth century B.C.; it is attributed to a man called Lao-tzu, which literally translates as "The Old Master." He was the keeper of the royal archives in the court of the Chou Dynasty emperors. Eventually he got fed up with the government and decided to leave the country. When he came to the western border, the guards recognized him as one of the wise men of the court and would not let him pass until he wrote down the sum of his wisdom. So, "The Old Master" sat down, penned a five-thousand-word manuscript, handed it to the border patrol, and headed off, never to be heard of again. This story is similar to what's going on in the U.S. government. These days, when you are finished with your government service and want to leave Washington, you also get to write a book with the sum of your wisdom. But unlike Lao-tzu, before you get to head west, you have to cash a check from your publisher for a few million bucks.

The English title of the great Taoist work Tao-te Ching is "The Way Of Nature." It's not really a religious text in the Western sense, but much more a short poetic statement of moral philosophy. It talks about the natural "way" or "force" that is present in everything and yet greater than all things. It is very much concerned with balancing the powers of life, which it describes as yin and yang.

For thousands of years the Chinese have believed that the universe follows the principles of yin and yang. It has had an enormous effect on Chinese cooking. Yin is the feminine force; it is the earth; it is cool; it is shade. It is fruit; green vegetables; clear soups; and quite amazingly, in the light of modern medical information on diet, it is low-fat, low-calorie, complex carbohydrates. Yang is the masculine force. It is the sky; it is hot; it is bright light. It is red meat, saturated fats, peanuts, and beer. And keep in mind this information was compiled over 2,500 years ago. When the yin and yang powers within the body are thought to be out of balance, emotional and physical problems result. One way to bring these forces back into balance is to eat some yin foods to counteract too much yang; or, eat some yang foods if you're high in yin. Accordingly, there are extensive listings of foods with yin power and foods with yang power. Yin powers are found in cabbage, seafood, asparagus, and spinach. Yang foods include chicken, chilies, and ginger.

◆

Today's Chinese cooks, both in the professional kitchen and the home, are very much concerned with finding the right balance between yin and yang. This balance represents the Taoist "way" of nature. A recipe or meal that fails to find that balance is believed to cause illness. On any day, thousands of Chinese people who are feeling ill will consult with herbalists. The herbalists measure the balance of yin and yang forces in the body through the pulse, and then prescribe a diet that will bring things back into line with the "way." Our Western culture is very busy promoting the relationship of good food to good health as if it was a new discovery. The Chinese have been working with the relationship of food to health for centuries.

The desire to have a balance of forces is also echoed in the Chinese insistence on avoiding overindulgence. To eat more than you need, or to waste food, is a vice of major proportions. Empires have been destroyed by excessive food habits on the part of the monarchs. The Chinese believe that you should stop eating when you are only 70 percent full. I'm not sure how you tell when you are 70 percent full. So I'm implementing the program by reducing my portions by 30 percent. The math works, and the meal might, too. Most North American restaurants serve much larger portions than we need. Sharing or saving some for later makes great sense.

B&B Turkey Hash
OLD DROVERS INN ◆ DOVER PLAINS, NEW YORK

MAKES 4 SERVINGS

HASH
3 large red potatoes, boiled,
   peeled, and mashed
5 cups ground cooked
   turkey meat
1 teaspoon salt
¼ teaspoon freshly ground
   black pepper
4 tablespoons vegetable oil
1 onion, chopped
1 clove garlic, minced
2 eggs
¼ cup heavy cream
½ cup fresh breadcrumbs
¼ cup chopped fresh
   cilantro, plus whole
   leaves, for serving
   (optional)

SAUCE
One 10-ounce package
   frozen corn kernels,
   thawed
2 tablespoons fresh lemon
   juice
¼ cup corn oil
2 tablespoons B&B liqueur
Salt and pepper, to taste

1. To make the hash: In a large mixing bowl, combine the potatoes, turkey, salt, and pepper.

2. In a large skillet over high heat, warm 1 tablespoon of the oil. Add the onion. Cook, stirring constantly, until the onion is transparent, about 5 minutes. Add the garlic and cook, stirring, 30 seconds longer. Remove from the heat and let cool completely.

3. In a large mixing bowl, combine the cooled onion mixture with the ground turkey–potato mixture, the eggs, cream, breadcrumbs, and chopped cilantro. Blend well and shape into 8 patties.

4. In a large skillet over high heat, heat 3 tablespoons of the oil. Add the patties in one layer. Reduce heat to medium and cook for 3 to 5 minutes on each side, or until the patties are golden brown and cooked through. Remove to a platter and keep warm.

5. To make the sauce: Combine all the ingredients in a blender or the bowl of a food processor and blend until smooth. Strain the sauce through a fine meshed sieve into a small saucepan and heat over low heat until hot. Add salt and pepper.

6. Place a small amount of sauce on the bottom of a plate and top with two turkey hash patties. Garnish with fresh cilantro leaves, if desired.

◆

ABOUT BENEDICTINE

During the early 1500s a monk by the name of Dom Bernardo Vincelli began making an elixir. He made it in a Benedictine abbey in the French town of Fécamp. Bernardo had grown up with a great understanding of spices and how they were to be used, both for flavoring and medicinal effects. His secret formula for the distillation contains twenty-seven different exotic spices and local herbs.

For almost three hundred years the monastery produced Brother Bernardo's recipe. They felt that the drink helped them keep up their strength and good health. But the recipe and the process was lost during the French Revolution. Then in the mid-1800s, a gentleman by the name of Alexandre Le Grand was looking through some old books and came upon a volume that had belonged to the monks. It contained the recipe.

Le Grand started to experiment with the formula and was eventually able to produce an extraordinary drink which he began to offer the public under the name Benedictine. Le Grand was quite an amazing character. He built a fantastic replica of a Renaissance château to house his manufacturing facility and a museum of art. He was an early believer in advertising and commissioned artists to produce posters. He also asked them to design various other things with the Benedictine graphic. He was so successful in promoting his drink that hundreds of people began to make counterfeits. As a result, Le Grand was deeply involved in developing laws that protect brand identification. The name Alexandre Le Grand translates into English as Alexander the Great, and in the history of distilled spirits he sure was.

In 1937, a bartender at New York's "21" Club mixed some Benedictine together with some fine Brandy and created the drink called B&B. Shortly after, the company that made Benedictine decided to do the blending themselves and began to offer B&B in a bottle. Today these two products, Benedictine and B&B, are still made in the little French town of Fécamp.

ABOUT THE FORK

The fork is the most recent of our common table tools to arrive on the scene. The first mention of a fork came in the eleventh century and it wasn't a very nice mention at that. The bishop of Venice had seen a woman using a fork at a dinner party and it sent him into a fit of rage. He was sure that it was an invention of the devil. It took almost eight hundred years for the fork to come into general use. During most of those years, food came to the table in a big dish, and each diner took an individual portion onto a large piece of bread that sat in front of them like a plate. If you use a fork on a hunk of bread there's a good chance you'll make a hole in the bread allowing the moisture to drip out onto the table. Not good form. Eventually a hard wooden or pewter plate was introduced under the bread, and that gave the fork a chance to come into fashion. There was a three-pronged version and a four-pronged version. At one point, a five-pronged design was introduced based on the success of the five-fingered hand. In the end, however, the four-pointed plan became the most popular.

The fork has clearly become a fashionable part of Western ritual, but you never know what's going to happen. Most of the people on our planet eat with their hands. The next largest group eats with chopsticks. The knife, fork, and spoon gang is actually only a tiny minority, and as people migrate from one part of the planet to another, it's impossible to know which fashions will take hold and which will disappear.

MEATS

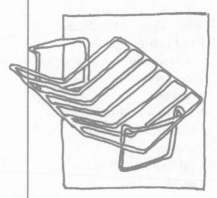

CHINESE BEEF WITH BROCCOLI
THE GRAND FORMOSA REGENT HOTEL ◆ TAIPEI, TAIWAN

MAKES 4 SERVINGS

2 cups water
2 cups broccoli florets
½ cup vegetable oil
1 pound boneless, lean
   beef, cut into strips
3 cloves garlic, chopped
1 tablespoon chopped fresh
   ginger (optional)
½ cup chopped scallions
1 red bell pepper, cored,
   seeded, and cut into strips
½ cup very thinly sliced
   carrots
1½ cups sliced mushrooms
1 cup drained bamboo
   shoots
3 tablespoons oyster sauce
   or black bean sauce
2 teaspoons soy sauce, or
   more to taste
White rice, for serving

It was during China's Tang dynasty in the A.D. 600s that a group of herbal pharmacologists decided what was good to eat in terms of health. The cosmic forces of yin and yang set the recipes, as well as when the food should be eaten and what was the proper amount in order to achieve internal harmony. Chef Kow at Taipei's Tsai Fung Restaurant demonstrates a recipe for Beef with Broccoli which is in perfect yin-yang balance.

1. In a wok or large sauté pan over high heat, bring the water to a boil. Add the broccoli and cook for 2 minutes. Drain the broccoli, discarding the water. Set the broccoli aside.

2. Return the wok to medium-high heat. Add the oil to the wok and heat until the oil begins to shimmer. Add the beef strips and stir-fry until the beef changes color, about 1 minute. Remove the beef with a slotted spoon. Pour off all but 2 tablespoons of the oil.

3. Add the garlic and ginger to the wok and stir-fry for 1 minute. Add the broccoli, scallions, bell pepper, and carrots and stir-fry for 1 minute. Add the mushrooms and bamboo shoots and stir-fry for 1 minute. Return the beef to the wok and add the oyster or black bean sauce and soy sauce. Stir-fry for 1 minute, or until the beef is cooked through. Serve at once, with white rice.

◆

ABOUT NAPKIN FOLDING

The idea of table napkins goes back at least as far as the ancient Romans. They used two napkins; one went around their neck and the other was held aside to clean their hands. When ancient Romans went to someone's home for a dinner party they would bring their own napkins. This was not because their hosts didn't have any but because they used their napkins to bring home some of the extra food that their host offered them at the end of the meal. It was a bit like showing up for a party with your own "doggy bag." During medieval times napkins were the size of towels and you hung them over your left shoulder as you ate. It was in the early 1800s that the napkin took up residence on the lap.

The fashion for fancy napkin folding started in the 1500s. It was considered an art form and the people who did it were paid big bucks. The more elaborate the folding, the more impressive the table. Napkins were folded into birds, flowers, and boats. For over three hundred years napkin folding was considered a respectable profession. However, in the late 1800s it fell out of fashion. It was considered too pretentious. The leading commentator on good manners said it was like wearing a ring over a glove. Well, excuse me. Today, at the annual Taipei Food Festival in Taiwan, napkin folding has been elevated to a competitive sport on the level of the Olympics.

ABOUT CHINESE WRITING

Anthropologists tell us that when a society starts to develop a written language, the first form is usually based on a picture of the thing being described. This is still true of Chinese writing. As the written language developed, the lines were modified so that the word would be easier to write. There are some fifty thousand images in the Chinese language, but only about five thousand are in common use. When they were first developed, they were written on thin strips of bamboo, which is why the Chinese got into the habit of writing from top to bottom. People who have mastered the technique of writing these images are considered major artists in Chinese society. Chinese is the only major writing system in the world that has continued its pictographic development without interruption. This means that the average Chinese student can read manuscripts that were written over three thousand years ago, and that includes cookbooks. While Chinese cursive script is thought of as a part of the mainstream of China's art, it is also a practical tool in everyday life. You will find examples of cursive script in major art collections, as well as on the menus of restaurants.

BEEF WITH SCALLIONS
THE GRAND FORMOSA REGENT HOTEL ◆ TAIPEI, TAIWAN

MAKES 4 SERVINGS

1 cup vegetable oil
1 pound lean beef, cut into
    bite-size pieces
1 cup scallions, cut into
    1-inch-long strips
1 red bell pepper, cut into
    bite-size pieces
2 tablespoons soy sauce
1 teaspoon cornstarch
    dissolved in 1 ounce warm
    water

It was the European explorers of the 1600s who brought cattle to the island of Taiwan. However, cattle raising requires large amounts of grassland, which was something that China never had. And the cooking of beef usually requires large amounts of cooking fuel, also something that China has never had. So when the Chinese chefs had their first contact with beef, they treated it with their traditional methods. No big steaks. No heat-intensive roasts. Just cut into small pieces and stir-fried. And that is precisely what this recipe does.

1.   In a wok or high-sided sauté pan over high heat, warm the oil until it is just shimmering. Add the beef and cook for 1 minute. Drain the beef from the oil and set aside. Remove all of the oil from the wok except for 2 tablespoons.

2.   Reheat the 2 tablespoons of oil. Add the scallions, and red bell pepper, and stir-fry for 2 minutes. Return the beef to the wok. Add the soy sauce and cornstarch mixture and stir-fry for 1 minute.

STIR-FRIED BEEF AND BROCCOLI
ROYAL YORK HOTEL ◆ TORONTO, CANADA

One of the largest and most important ethnic groups in British Columbia are the Chinese. They started arriving in the mid-1800s as part of a work force to build the transcontinental railroad. They stayed, expanded their numbers, and became a vital part of the community . . . especially when it comes to food. They have a significant number of great restaurants and have influenced cooking throughout Canada. A perfect example is this dish of Stir-Fried Beef and Broccoli.

1. In a large mixing bowl, mix the beef with the egg whites until well coated. Add the cornstarch and stir well.

2. In a wok over high heat, warm the vegetable and sesame oils until almost smoking. Add the ginger, onions, and beef and stir-fry until the beef is cooked to the desired doneness, 2 to 5 minutes.

3. Stir in the chicken broth, oyster sauce, and sesame seeds. Add the broccoli and stir-fry until crisp-tender, about 3 minutes. Serve with freshly cooked white rice.

MAKES 4 TO 6 SERVINGS

1½ pounds beef tenderloin,
  cut into bite-size pieces
2 egg whites, lightly beaten
2 tablespoons cornstarch
1 tablespoon vegetable oil
1 tablespoon Oriental
  sesame oil
2 tablespoons minced fresh
  ginger
1 cup finely chopped onions
1 cup chicken broth
2 tablespoons oyster sauce
2 tablespoons sesame seeds
2 cups broccoli florets,
  blanched and drained
Cooked white rice, for
  serving

George McNeill.

PAN-ROASTED BEEF
PENINSULA HOTEL ◆ NEW YORK, NEW YORK

MAKES 4 SERVINGS

3 tablespoons olive oil
1½ pounds filet mignon, tied
¼ cup diced carrot
¼ cup diced onion
¼ cup diced turnip
¼ cup diced celery
¼ cup diced potato
2 large cloves garlic, minced
1 tablespoon chopped rosemary
¼ cup port wine
¾ cup beef broth
Salt and freshly ground pepper, to taste

1. Preheat the oven to 350° F.

2. In a small oven-proof sauté pan over high heat, warm 2 tablespoons of the oil. When hot, add the beef and cook for 5 to 7 minutes on all sides, or until nicely browned. Place the pan in the oven and cook for 15 minutes.

3. In a medium saucepan over high heat, heat the remaining tablespoon of oil. When hot, add the vegetables, garlic, and rosemary. Add the port, scraping the bottom of the pan with a kitchen spoon. Add the beef broth and bring to a boil. Reduce heat to simmer, and cook until the vegetables are tender, about 10 minutes.

4. Remove the beef from the pan and let rest for 10 minutes before slicing. Thinly slice the tenderloin and spoon the vegetables and sauce over the top.

GRILLED MEDALLIONS OF BEEF
GRAND BAY HOTEL ◆ COCONUT GROVE, FLORIDA

When someone is described as a real Florida cracker, it usually means that they are country folk or that they were born in the state. But the real meaning of the term "cracker" goes back to the state's cowboys. Florida cow handlers moved their herds with the aid of 18-foot rawhide whips. They would snap their whips to make a loud cracking sound that would send stray cattle into line. That technique earned the Florida cowboys the nickname of "crackers." The cowboys of Florida have been raising cattle for almost 500 years, and the local chefs have the recipes and the skills to prove it.

1. To make the marinade: Place all of the ingredients into a shallow bowl or baking pan, mix together, add the beef medallions, and allow them to marinate at room temperature for 30 minutes.

2. While the beef is marinating, prepare the sauce: In a sauté pan over medium heat, warm the vegetable oil. Add the shallots and cook, stirring, for a minute. Add the white wine, sugar and water mixture, pureed mango, and beef stock. Reduce heat and simmer uncovered for 10 minutes.

3. Remove the beef medallions from the marinade and grill or sauté until they are cooked to the point of doneness that you prefer.

4. Place the medallions on serving plates and pour the warm sauce on top.

MAKES 4 SERVINGS

MARINADE
3 tablespoons vegetable oil
2 tablespoons minced onion
2 tablespoons minced fresh
  ginger
1 tablespoon curry powder
¼ cup lime juice
¼ cup honey
4 medallions beef
  tenderloin, 1½ inches
  thick

SAUCE
2 tablespoons vegetable oil
¼ cup chopped shallots
¼ cup white wine
1 tablespoon sugar
  dissolved in 2 tablespoons
  warm water
½ cup pureed mango
¼ cup beef stock

◆

BEEF TARRAGON
CANADA'S VIA RAIL TRAIN

MAKES 4 TO 6 SERVINGS

2 tablespoons vegetable oil
2 tablespoons unsalted
  butter
One 2-pound beef
  tenderloin, cut into
  ½-inch medallions
1 cup minced onions
1 tablespoon minced garlic
1 cup red wine
1 tablespoon Dijon mustard
2 tablespoons chopped
  fresh tarragon leaves
One 13¾-ounce beef broth
⅔ cup plain low-fat yogurt
Salt and freshly ground
  black pepper, to taste

The Canadian province of Alberta is true cattle country. You can see it in the land; you can see it in the culture; and, you can see it in the kitchens. If you still want to know "Where's the beef?" Alberta is a good place to look. An example is this Via Rail recipe for medallions of beef in a tarragon sauce.

1. In a large sauté pan over medium-high heat, warm the oil with the butter until bubbling. Add the beef medallions and sauté for 1 to 2 minutes on each side (longer if you desire the beef to be well done). Remove the beef to a serving platter and keep warm.

2. Using the same sauté pan, combine the onions and garlic and cook for 3 to 5 minutes. Add the wine, mustard, tarragon, beef broth, and stir thoroughly. Reduce the heat to medium, stir in the yogurt, and simmer the sauce for 5 to 7 minutes, until slightly thickened. Season with salt and pepper.

3. Spoon the sauce over the beef medallions and serve immediately.

ABOUT LEAN BEEF

Cattlemen are now using breeding and feeding techniques that produce animals that are lower in fat. Which cuts of beef you select in the market, however, can make a big difference in the fat content. A quick way to remember which cuts are lowest in fat is to keep in mind the words "round" and "loin." The butchers might mark the package round tip, eye of round, or top round. Loin could be marked top loin, sirloin, or tenderloin. As long as you see the words "round" or "loin," you are buying a lean cut of beef with about 180 calories in a 3-ounce serving.

ABOUT TARRAGON

The herb tarragon seems to have originated in Asia. It was brought to eastern Europe by the invading Mongols, and it was the Crusaders who spread it throughout western Europe. The first time we find anyone writing about tarragon was in the mid-1500s. A botanist of the time described tarragon as "one of the most agreeable of salads, which requires neither salt nor vinegar, for it possesses the taste of both these condiments." Good call. Tarragon is one of the best substitutes for salt, and anyone who is on a reduced-salt diet can put tarragon to good use as a flavor replacement.

Most herbs have a stronger flavor in their dried form than when they are fresh. Cooks usually use twice as much of a fresh herb in a recipe than they would if they were using the dried form. Tarragon is an exception. When tarragon is dried, it loses the essential oil that contains its flavor. So when you are substituting dried tarragon for fresh tarragon use two or three times the suggested amount.

Emily Aronson directs cameraman Bernard Couture and gaffer Blair Locke.

PUERTO RICAN STUFFED BEEF
EL SAN JUAN HOTEL ◆ SAN JUAN, PUERTO RICO

MAKES 6 TO 8 SERVINGS

One 2½-pound boneless eye
  of beef round, tied
1 cup cooked rice, white or
  brown
1 cup chopped walnuts
¼ cup vegetable oil
2 tomatoes, seeded and cut
  into strips
1 red bell pepper, cored,
  seeded, and cut into strips
1 large onion, halved
  lengthwise, cut into strips
2 cups beef stock or broth

Rice is one of the world's most important foods. It's also quite healthful. Rice is low in fat, has no cholesterol or salt, and is a good source of complex carbohydrates. The reason that rice is a basic part of many Spanish dishes comes from the fact that Spain was under Arab control for many years and it was the Arabs who brought rice to Spain from the Middle East.

Chef John Carey of Puerto Rico's El San Juan Hotel combines rice with fiber-filled crunchy walnuts to make a stuffing for a classic Puerto Rican dish of stuffed beef.

1. Preheat the oven to 350° F.

2. Using a long-bladed, sharp knife, poke a hole lengthwise through the center of the beef roast. Turn the knife to make a space for the stuffing.

3. In a bowl, combine the rice and walnuts and mix well. Stuff the mixture into the hole in the beef, pushing it in until firmly stuffed. Close the ends of the roast with toothpicks.

4. In an oven-proof sauté pan or casserole over medium-high heat, warm the oil. Make sure that the pan is large enough to hold the beef and vegetables snugly. When hot, add the roast and cook, turning as necessary, until browned on all sides. Scatter the vegetables around the sides of the roast and in a thin layer over the top. Pour the beef stock or broth over all and bring the stock to a boil.

5. Set the pan in the hot oven and cook until an instant thermometer inserted into the thickest part of the roast (not the rice stuffing) registers 150° F, about 1 hour.

6. Remove the roast from the oven and cut into rounds. Serve the roasted vegetables on the side.

◆

ABOUT THE FIRST PUERTO RICAN NATIVES AND CASSAVA

The first people to live on the island of Puerto Rico showed up about 4,500 years ago. They may have come down from Florida or over from Mexico; no one is quite sure. The second group to arrive, however, clearly came from the Orinoco valley of Venezuela in South America. They took up residence in Puerto Rico in about A.D. 300, settling along the coasts and rivers, and developed a rather advanced culture. The basis of their agriculture was the cassava plant. It was the basis for their bread and wine and the main staple of their diet, in much the same way the people of Asia use rice, or the farmers of Europe use wheat.

Cassava is a root vegetable about two inches in diameter and about ten inches long. It also goes by the names "manioc" and "yucca." There are two forms of the plant: One is bitter and the other is sweet. The bitter form is poisonous until it is cooked. The hard, white flesh inside can be prepared as a starchy vegetable or it can be grated and washed into a meal that is baked into a bread. Cassava in a ready-to-use meal form is also available in markets that have a Caribbean food section. It is often used to make tapioca. Cassava is still very much a part of the traditional cooking of Puerto Rico.

◆

A BRIEF HISTORY OF PUERTO RICO

Sometime during the first century A.D. *a tribal group from South America known as the Tainos settled down on the island of Puerto Rico. They appear to have been a rather peaceful group with a well-developed culture. Their biggest problems came from the aggressive Carib tribes that moved through the area attacking the native islanders. The Caribs considered the Tainos as a local delicacy. The word "cannibal" actually came into the language of Europe as a description of the Carib diet.*

On November 19, 1493, Columbus bumped into the island of Puerto Rico and claimed it for Spain. It was his second voyage and he had really gotten the knack of the "claiming thing." Like most visitors to the island he was interested in the local handicraft, especially the native jewelry; it was made of gold. In 1508, a shipmate of Columbus, Juan Ponce de Léon made a deal for the gold rights on Puerto Rico and moved in. There really wasn't enough gold on the island to make anyone very rich, but Ponce did well selling supplies to the prospectors. That, by the way, is a story that is continually repeated. I can't think of anyone who made big money in the California gold rush from gold and kept it. However, the guy who sold the miners their clothing—for example, Levi as in Levi's jeans—made a fortune.

When the little gold that was on Puerto Rico ran out, the settlers turned to farming. The children who were the products of intermarriages between the Spanish and the natives or the black slaves, were unable to get land by grants. They settled up in the hills and farmed on small plots. Thousands of their descendants are still there. Those colonists who were considered by the Spanish authorities to be "the right stuff" were given plantations. The cash crop of choice was sugar, which was worth big bucks back in Europe. Sugar was also processed into molasses and molasses into rum. The settlers also built up a trade in coffee and spices. For the next three hundred years or so, the Spanish crown, more or less, abused the economy of the island. Then in 1898, with the conclusion of the Spanish American War, Puerto Rico became a protectorate of the United States and today the island has Commonwealth status.

ABOUT HONEY

Florida is the top honey-producing state in the nation with beekeepers producing about 21 million pounds of honey each year. When you realize that one hive of bees has to fly over 55,000 miles and tap 2 million flowers just to produce a single pound of honey . . . you're talking about some serious activity. The average worker bee can make only one twelfth of a teaspoon of honey in her entire lifetime.

Flowers have always been a great source of beauty in man's environment, as well as the origin of many of our perfumes. But flowers have also been an important part of gastronomy. The different aroma of each flower has a culinary significance. It's the aroma-filled nectar of a flower that gives honey its flavor and color. There are over three hundred honeys available and each one comes from a different flower. The blossoms that the bees visit affect the color range. The range goes from nearly colorless to dark brown, and the flavors vary from light and mild to quite intense. In general, the lighter the color of the honey the milder the flavor. The most common floral source for honey in the United States is clover, but you'll also find orange blossom, tupelo, wildflower, alfalfa, and buckwheat.

In ancient myths milk and honey are often coupled together. The reason for their unusual status may be the fact that milk and honey appear to be the only two substances eaten by humans but produced by animals as food for their own species. They are also two foods we can eat without destroying other life forms. From fish to flowers, when we eat it we end its life. This is not the case with milk and honey.

◆

ABOUT HONEYMOONS

Bees have been producing honey for over 15 million years, and we have been eating it for at least 3 million. Paintings on the tombs of the ancient Egyptians show that they were skilled beekeepers. They treasured honey and actually used it to pay taxes. Egyptian bridegrooms were required to give large amounts of honey to their brides. The connection between marriages and honey has been carried on for thousands of years. The ancient Babylonians made a drink called "mead." It was produced from fermented honey and water and was the official drink at weddings. The bride's parents were required to supply it to the newlyweds for a month after the wedding . . . a period known as the "honeymoon."

◆

BEEF CASSEROLE
GRAND PALAZZO HOTEL ◆ ST. THOMAS, U.S. VIRGIN ISLANDS

MAKES 8 TO 10 SERVINGS

2 tablespoons vegetable oil
1 tablespoon butter
24 baby onions, peeled and
　trimmed
½ cup all-purpose flour
1 tablespoon salt
1 tablespoon freshly ground
　black pepper
5 pounds beef chuck,
　trimmed of all fat and cut
　into 1½-inch cubes
2 tablespoons tomato paste
1 cup dry red wine
2½ cups beef broth or stock
1 teaspoon dried basil
2 teaspoons dried thyme
Peel of 1 orange
3 medium carrots, peeled,
　cut into ¼-inch slices
Cooked hot noodles, for
　serving

Great views to dine by have always been considered a valuable asset to a restaurant. Certainly the vista from the Grand Palazzo on St. Thomas in the Virgin Islands is radiant. For me, however, the most important view in a restaurant is the one straight down to the plate in front of me. I have always felt that it's the cooking that really counts. Fortunately, the cooking here is in good hands.

The chef at the Grand Palazzo, Patrick Pinon, is a classically trained French chef. He was the head chef at Maxim's in Paris before he had the good sense to trade bistros for beaches. Pinon says that he started cooking because of his grandmother, and there was one dish that she made that he re-creates all over the world.

1. In a large saucepan or Dutch oven over medium-high heat, warm the oil with the butter until melted and almost sizzling. Add the onions and sauté, turning frequently, until browned on all sides, about 10 minutes. Remove the onions with tongs or a slotted spoon.

2. In a large bowl, mix together the flour, salt, and pepper. Add the beef and coat evenly with the seasoned flour.

3. Working in batches, if necessary, cook the beef in the fat that remains in the pan, stirring frequently, until the beef is browned evenly on all sides, about 5 minutes.

◆

4. Add the tomato paste and stir to coat the beef. Add the wine, broth, basil, thyme, orange peel, and carrots. Return the onions to the pan. Stir thoroughly and bring the mixture to a simmer. Reduce the heat to medium, cover, and simmer until the beef is tender, about 1 hour.

5. Taste and adjust the seasonings, if necessary. Remove and discard the orange peel. Serve the stew over the hot noodles.

WHY YOU SHOULDN'T SWIM AFTER YOU EAT

When I was a kid and lucky enough to spend a day at the beach, lunch always seemed to be an unnecessary interruption. However, the worst part was that after lunch my mother would not let me go back into the water. There was always a lecture about the dangers of swimming after eating. As I got older I found it harder and harder to believe that the weight of a bacon, lettuce, and tomato sandwich was enough to sink me, but I was too afraid to violate my mother's instructions.

Eventually I found out that there was a true scientific underpinning for her admonition. When you eat, your system sends blood to the center of your body to help with the digestion of the food. That blood is drawn from your body's extremities—your head, especially your brain, and your arms and legs. The reduction of the blood in your brain lessens your ability to think clearly. The diminished blood supply in your arms and legs increases the chances of getting muscle cramps. So there you are swimming along in the ocean, not thinking clearly and getting muscle cramps. It makes a good case for waiting about an hour between eating and swimming.

RUTH-ANNE'S MEAT LOAF
NORTHERN EXPOSURE

MAKES 6 SERVINGS

1 egg
1 teaspoon salt
½ teaspoon freshly ground
  black pepper
1 teaspoon dried thyme
2 tablespoons Dijon-style
  mustard
1 cup milk
½ cup chopped celery
½ cup chopped onion
¼ cup plus 2 tablespoons
  ketchup
1½ pounds ground chuck
1½ cups fresh breadcrumbs
3 strips bacon

"Northern Exposure."

"Northern Exposure" is a television series set in the fictitious town of Cicely, Alaska. It is actually filmed just outside of Seattle. Joel Fleischman, a classic New York kid (played by Rob Morrow), makes a deal with the state of Alaska to pay for his medical education in exchange for four years of practice after his graduation. The series traces his adjustment to his new and rather quirky environment. The show has great ratings, the critics love it, and it gets special attention from me because there's always something in the script that deals with food.

In confirmation of my theory that "Northern Exposure" is produced by people who have a deep interest in eating, they have gone and published the "Northern Exposure" Cookbook. It contains good recipes and a text that is cleverly written in the voice of the characters. The recipe I decided to try belongs to the character known as Ruth-Anne.

Ruth-Anne Miller, played by Peg Phillips, is the seventy-five-year-old owner of Cicely's General Store. The store also serves as the town library, video shop, and local post office. Ruth-Anne provides a soft strength and guides the other characters through their predicaments. She's the kind of person you can trust with a meat loaf.

1.   Preheat the oven to 350° F.

2.   In a large mixing bowl combine the egg, seasonings, mustard, milk, celery, onion, ¼ cup ketchup, ground chuck, and breadcrumbs. Mix well.

3.   Place the beef mixture in a standard 8-inch loaf pan. Spread the surface with the 2 tablespoons of ketchup. Layer the bacon over the top. Bake for 1 hour.

4.   Drain any excess fat from the pan. Remove the meat loaf and let cool at room temperature for 5 minutes. Cut into ½-inch-thick slices.

On the "Northern Exposure" set.

NUTRITIONAL INFORMATION ON BEEF

Beef is a good source of iron, which is the nutrient most often lacking in the diets of adult women and young children. Furthermore, the type of iron that you find in beef is the kind that is easier for your body to absorb. Beef is also a good source of vitamin B-12, niacin, and zinc. Zinc is important to your body in that it helps in the repairing of cells after a wound. For me, the most interesting thing about zinc is that it contributes to your ability to taste and smell. By eating beef, you get the zinc that helps you taste the beef.

SAUTÉED PORK LOIN WITH HONEY SAUCE
THE ENCHANTED GARDEN RESORT ◆ OCHO RIOS, JAMAICA

MAKES 6 SERVINGS

2 tablespoons vegetable oil
Salt and freshly ground
  black pepper, to taste
One 2-pound pork
  tenderloin, trimmed of all
  fat
2 tablespoons minced fresh
  ginger
2 cloves garlic, minced
¾ cup scallions, cut into
  ¼-inch rounds
2 tablespoons white wine or
  water
2 cups beef broth
3 tablespoons honey
½ cup minced carrot
1 teaspoon cornstarch
  dissolved in ½ teaspoon
  cold water

1.   In a deep sauté pan over medium heat, warm the vegetable oil.

2.   Salt and pepper the pork loin and place into the pan. Over medium-high heat, brown the pork for 2 to 4 minutes on each side. You want to brown all the surfaces of the meat. Then cover the pan, lower heat to medium, and cook until the pork is thoroughly cooked. The pork should have an internal temperature of 170° F. Remove the pork from the pan and hold aside.

3.   Remove any excess fat drippings from the pan. Add the ginger, garlic, ½ cup of the scallions, and the white wine or water. Cook over medium heat and scrape the surface until the wine or water boils down to about a tablespoon of liquid. Add the beef broth, honey, and carrots. Bring to a boil and boil for 10 minutes to produce a thick sauce. Add the cornstarch mixture and cook for another minute.

4.   The pork is sliced into thin rounds and served with the sauce on top and a garnish of the remaining ¼ cup of scallions.

◆

ABOUT PORK

During the 1980s there was a substantial decline in the amount of pork eaten in North America. The reduction was caused by the public's interest in a diet that was lower in fat, as medical researchers were discovering the importance of a low-fat diet. At the time, pork was very high in fat and so it quickly got on the "very limited consumption list."

The pork producers got the message, and today fresh pork is some 30 percent lower in fat than it was in 1983. This is not to say that pork has become a low-fat product. We're not talking poached haddock here, but there is clearly a place for pork in a healthful diet. I say it over and over again, mostly to remind myself. . . . There are no good foods and there are no bad foods; there are just inappropriate amounts. If almost all of the pork you eat is taken in lean cuts, served in a moderate portion of four ounces, and cooked to 170 degrees, it's fine.

The leanest cuts of pork come from the loin, and only about 25 percent of the calories in a pork loin come from fat. If you are looking for a lower-fat alternative to regular bacon, try Canadian bacon. It's a pork loin that has been smoked and cured. Only 41 percent of the calories in Canadian bacon come from fat. Regular bacon gets 74 percent of its calories from fat.

ABOUT JERK

In the middle of the 1600s an English fleet attacked the Spanish colony on Jamaica. The Spanish felt that they could not defend their position and withdrew to the safety of Cuba. As they were leaving Jamaica, they freed and then armed their slaves. The plan was to have these freed men wage a guerrilla war against the English until the Spanish could return with more troops. As it so happened, the Spanish never came back and the former slaves became such a powerful military force that they were eventually granted a form of self-government, which they still have. They were known as the Maroons, and to-day they represent a distinct community on Jamaica. For hundreds of years the Maroons lived in the central mountains of the island. When they would stop harassing the British troops for a few hours, which wasn't very often, they would hunt for wild boar. Some of the boar would be cooked and eaten on the spot. Most of it, however, would be preserved with hot spices and cooked between battles. The result was a dish that eventually became known as "jerked pork."

As you drive along the roads of Jamaica you are regularly confronted with the rich, pungent odor of outdoor cooking. It is like patches of aromatic fog that have settled on the highway. After a while, you realize that what you are smelling is a nearby jerk hut, a couple of simple shacks that form a gastronomic necklace around the island. The central structure is a circular counter with seats around the outside. Nearby is another building with the seasoning tables and the cooking pits.

Pork, chicken, fish, and sausage are the usual menu. The food is covered with a seasoning mixture and left to marinate. Each jerk chef believes that his or her seasoning is the best and keeps the recipe as a family secret. While the meat marinates, a pit dug into the earth is lined with the wood of an allspice tree and set aflame. When the wood has burned down to a bed of hot coals, the meat is put onto a grill about a foot and a half above the coals. The meat is protected from the direct heat by aluminum foil. As a result, the food is really cooked by the hot smoke. Sheets of zinc roofing go on top to help contain the smoke. At the end of the cooking time—which is about thirty minutes for a whole fish and three to six hours for large pieces of pork—the roofing is taken off and the meat receives some of the direct heat in order to give it a crisp outside surface. Moist on the inside, crisp on the outside, and great flavor.

◆

The quantities vary from chef to chef but the basic ingredients in the seasoning are usually the same. Chopped onion, chopped scallion, thyme, ground nutmeg, cinnamon, allspice, chopped jalapeño pepper, black pepper, salt, sugar, soy sauce, white vinegar, and vegetable oil. Mix that all together; rub it over the meat, fish, or poultry; let it sit in the refrigerator for four hours. When it comes out, you're ready to start the grilling.

The jerk is always served with things that are bland or sweet in order to cut down the impact of the spice. Most often it's a sweet donutlike dough called "festival." Also, there are always a few bottles of the local soft drink, which is a type of grapefruit soda known as Ting.

Some folks believe that the word "jerk" is a description of the constant turning of the meat as it is cooking. They say the pork is being jerked around. Others feel that jerk describes the process of pulling or jerking the meat apart before it is served. A third group says it's the name of the flavoring mixture. Personally, I think it is the word I would use to describe myself if I went to Jamaica and didn't eat some.

Video crew off the French coast.

ABOUT TAIWAN

The original inhabitants of the island of Taiwan arrived some ten thousand years ago. About 250,000 of their descendants remain on Taiwan and are called the "aborigines." They maintain their traditional music, dances, costumes, and customs.

Chinese contact with the island goes back to about A.D. 200 when the kingdom of Wu sent ten thousand men to check out the neighborhood. Since then, there have been a series of migrations from the mainland. Each migration brought a different ethnic group with a different set of objectives. Some came to escape persecution. Others came in search of economic opportunities.

During the 1500s, the Japanese tried to take over the island. Starting in the 1600s, European colonial powers made an effort to take control. During the late 1800s, foreign trade between Taiwan and British and American businesses became a major enterprise. European missionaries showed up and competed for areas of influence in the same way as the trading companies. Through it all, however, the Chinese managed to hold on to their culture and keep the island for themselves.

The most significant event in modern Taiwanese history took place in 1949 when Chiang Kai-shek and over 2 million of his followers left mainland China and moved to Taiwan in order to avoid Communist domination. They brought a high level of entrepreneurial skill and transformed the island into one of the world's most successful industrialized nations.

Today, Taiwan's standard of living is higher than any other Asian country with the exception of Japan. In two very interesting aspects of life, the people of Taiwan have a better existence than the Japanese—they have more living space, and they eat more food.

PORK IN SPICY GARLIC SAUCE
THE GRAND FORMOSA REGENT HOTEL ◆ TAIPEI, TAIWAN

In proportion to its size and population China has very little land available for farming and even less for grazing cattle. As a result, when Chinese cooks talk about meat they usually mean pork. Pork is found in many soups, main dishes, and as a stuffing for rolls and dumplings. One of its easiest presentations is in a recipe for pork with spicy garlic sauce. Chef Yeh of Taipei's Grand Formosa Regent Hotel starts the dish with a piece of lean pork that has been steamed, but you could just as easily make the dish with a loin that has been roasted. The most important point is that the pork should be free of all visible fat.

1. To make the dipping sauce: In a nonreactive* small saucepan over medium heat, combine the garlic, sugar, chili oil, chili paste, and soy sauce. Cook, stirring, until the sugar dissolves and the mixture is heated through, about 3 minutes. Remove from the heat and stir in the vinegar. Set the dipping sauce aside.

2. To prepare the pork: Trim off the sides of the roast pork to make a 5-x-2-inch rectangular block of pork. Working from one of the long sides, thinly slice the pork into long sheets. Roll up the sheets; place them on a serving plate. Top with some of the sauce and use the remaining sauce for dipping.

*A nonreactive saucepan is made of a material that will not interact with the acid in the food. Stainless steel, ceramic, glass, and anodized aluminum are fine.

MAKES 4 SERVINGS

1 tablespoon minced garlic
1 tablespoon sugar
4 teaspoons chili oil
4 teaspoons Chinese chili paste
¼ cup soy sauce
1 tablespoon red wine vinegar
1 rolled boneless pork loin, roasted and cooled, all fat removed

Steadi Berg, our cameraman in Taiwan.

◆

STUFFED CABBAGE
ROYAL YORK HOTEL ◆ TORONTO, CANADA

MAKES 4 SERVINGS

2 quarts water
8 whole large cabbage
  leaves, hard stems
  trimmed away
1 tablespoon vegetable oil
1 pound ground pork
1½ cups finely chopped
  onion
2 cups cooked white rice
1 teaspoon dried thyme
Salt and freshly ground
  black pepper, to taste
2 cups chicken broth
1 tablespoon unsalted
  butter
½ cup finely chopped
  mushrooms
1 cup heavy cream (see
  Note)

A massive immigration of Europeans to North America started in the mid-1800s. Millions of them came from eastern Europe. One of the largest groups of eastern Europeans to arrive came from Poland. Many Polish settled in the prairie provinces of Canada and put the fertile farmland to good use. Their cooking became a basic part of the ethnic cuisine of Canada. Chef George McNeill of Toronto's Royal York Hotel often uses typical Polish farm recipes like the following as part of his home cooking.

1. Preheat the oven to 350° F.

2. In a stockpot over high heat, bring the water to a boil. Place the cabbage leaves, one by one, into the water and boil for 3 minutes. Remove the leaves and set aside to drain and cool.

3. In a large skillet over medium-high heat, warm the oil. Add the pork and 1 cup of the onions. Cook, stirring frequently, for 5 to 8 minutes, or until the pork is no longer pink and the onions are translucent. Add the cooked rice, thyme, and salt and pepper. Stir thoroughly and allow to cool slightly.

4. Divide the pork mixture into 8 equal portions and place each portion in the center of a cabbage leaf. Fold the sides of each cabbage leaf over the pork mixture and roll up to enclose the filling in a cylinder. Place the rolls, seam side down, close together in a shallow baking dish. Add 1 cup of the chicken broth and cover the baking dish with foil or a lid. Bake for about 35 minutes, or until the cabbage is just tender.

5.   Meanwhile, in a large sauté pan over medium-high heat, melt the butter until bubbling. Add the remaining ½ cup of onions and the mushrooms. Cook, stirring frequently, for about 5 minutes, or until the onions are translucent.

6.   Add the remaining cup of chicken broth, the heavy cream, and salt and pepper to taste. Stir well and bring the sauce to a boil. Reduce the heat to medium-low and simmer for about 3 minutes, until slightly thickened.

7.   Place two stuffed cabbage rolls onto each of 4 dinner plates. Pour some of the sauce over each, and serve hot.

NOTE: In order to make a sauce without using heavy cream, add 1 cup roughly chopped tomatoes along with the onions and mushrooms in Step 5 and substitute an extra cup of chicken broth for the cream in Step 6.

Royal York Hotel, Toronto.

STUFFED PORK CHOPS
ROYAL YORK HOTEL ◆ TORONTO, CANADA

MAKES 4 SERVINGS

4 tablespoons vegetable oil
1 cup roughly chopped
    onions
½ cup diced carrots
½ cup diced celery
½ teaspoon ground nutmeg
1 teaspoon dried oregano
1 teaspoon dried thyme
½ cup chicken broth
1 egg, beaten
1 cup pumpernickel bread
    cubes
4 thick loin pork chops,
    about 10 ounces each
2 cups apple juice
1 cup beef broth
Freshly ground black
    pepper, to taste

The farms of Canada have been central to the nation's growth. These farms were settled in the 1800s by thousands of immigrants who came from all over Europe. One of the most important groups came from Germany. They reproduced the type of farm that they had worked on back in their original hometowns. They also tried to reproduce the cooking of their childhood memories. The meat that had been a part of German cooking for centuries—pork—was soon at their tables in sausages, hams, roasts, chops, and just about every other traditional form. The following recipe from Chef George McNeill is a classic example of German cooking.

1.   In a medium skillet over medium-high heat, warm 2 tablespoons of the vegetable oil. Add the vegetables and cook, stirring frequently, for 2 minutes. Reduce the heat to low, stir in the seasonings, and cook for 5 to 10 minutes, or until the carrots are tender.

2.   Scrape the vegetables into a large mixing bowl. Stir in the chicken broth, egg, and bread cubes and stir well. Cover the stuffing and refrigerate for at least 30 minutes.

3.   Preheat the oven to 375° F.

4.   Using a sharp knife, cut a pocket into the side of each pork chop. Stuff each chop with a quarter of the stuffing. Close the pocket with wooden toothpicks or wooden skewers.

◆

5. In a large skillet over medium-high heat, warm the remaining 2 tablespoons of vegetable oil. Add the pork chops and cook for about 2 minutes on each side, until they have browned. Transfer the chops to a shallow baking dish.

6. Add 1 cup of the apple juice to the sauté pan; whisk the pork juices into it. Pour the liquid over the pork chops. Cover the baking dish with aluminum foil. Bake for about 40 minutes, or until the chops and stuffing are cooked through.

7. Meanwhile, in the same sauté pan over medium-high heat, combine the remaining 1 cup of apple juice with the beef broth. Bring to a simmer and season with pepper. Reduce the heat to medium and simmer until reduced by half, about 10 minutes.

8. Serve the pork chops with the sauce.

PORK AND PRUNES
LE CORDON BLEU ◆ PARIS, FRANCE

MAKES 6 TO 8 SERVINGS

2 tablespoons vegetable oil
2 tablespoons unsalted
  butter
4 pork fillets about 12
  ounces each, sliced
2 cups roughly chopped
  onions
1 cup roughly chopped
  carrots
2 tablespoons all-purpose
  flour
1 bottle white wine
One 13¾-ounce can beef
  broth
½ cup heavy cream
1 cup pitted prunes

1. Preheat the oven to 375° F.

2. In a large sauté pan over medium-high heat, warm the oil and butter until bubbling. Add the pork fillets and cook for 10 to 12 minutes, turning the fillets until thoroughly browned on all sides. Remove the pork fillets to a large casserole.

3. Add the onions and carrots to the pan and sauté until the onions are translucent, 5 to 7 minutes. Stir in the flour and cook for 3 minutes.

4. Add the onion mixture to the casserole with the pork. Pour the wine into the sauté pan and boil, stirring constantly and scraping up the pan drippings. Boil until the liquid is reduced to about half of its original volume, 15 to 20 minutes.

5. Add the wine and the beef broth to the casserole. Cover and bake until the pork is thoroughly cooked, 30 to 45 minutes. The internal temperature should be 170° F.

6. Remove the pork fillets to a serving dish. Strain the onion, carrot, wine mixture through a fine sieve into a medium saucepan. Press down on the vegetables to extract their juices.

7. Place the pan of sauce over medium-high heat, add the cream and prunes, and cook, stirring constantly, for 5 to 7 minutes, or until the sauce thickens enough to lightly coat the back of a wooden spoon.

8. Cut the pork into slices, pour the sauce over the pork, and serve.

◆

ABOUT THE CORDON BLEU COOKING SCHOOL

She dropped her chicken on the floor and told us it was still okay to serve. She showed us that we could produce some quite acceptable French food in our average American kitchens. She came to us through the efforts of Public Broadcasting, and she changed the way millions of Americans cooked. She was . . . the French Chef.

But how did Julia Child get to be the French Chef? The proper preparation of *Rognons de Veau à la Graine de Moutarde* is not a skill you pick up on the way home from the supermarket. Julia Child learned to be the French Chef in Paris at Le Cordon Bleu Cooking School.

The history of Le Cordon Bleu goes back to the 1700s. At the time there was a centuries-old society of knights who wore blue ribbons to mark their membership. They also had a big-deal reputation for good eating. King Louis XV once told his girl friend, Madame du Barry, that he thought only men made great chefs. A while later, in what looked like a purely unrelated situation, Madame invited Louis over to her place for supper. It was a knock-out meal, and at the end the king commented that the new man she had cooking was as good as any cook in his own royal household. Du Barry told him that the cook was a woman and that he should honor her skill with a Cordon Bleu membership. From then on, the royal court, and, eventually, the populace, associated the idea of Le Cordon Bleu with great food.

Le Cordon Bleu Cooking School got started in Paris, in 1895. A lady named Marthe Distel was publishing a weekly magazine called The Blue Ribbon Cook. In each issue a famous chef taught a cooking course. The magazine gave cooking advice, helped readers exchange recipes, and discussed gastronomic topics of the time. Then one day Madame Distel realized that cooking should also be taught by live teachers in a classroom. She set up Le Cordon Bleu Cooking School and invited highly skilled professional chefs to teach. The classes were given free to subscribers. Now that is a gift with purchase.

This was the first school to set up a teaching system that starts with an instructor showing the students how to make the dish, then allows them to sample the proper taste, and finally, sends them off to their own individual cooking area to reproduce the recipe. It takes time to learn this way, and it takes money to give each student his or her own ingredients and cooking equipment, including a four-burner range and oven. But if you really want to learn to cook, the technique of watching, tasting, and cooking the recipe by yourself, under professional supervision, has proven to be the best method.

ROAST PORK WITH PAPAYA STUFFING
THE BERMUDA HOTEL AND CATERING COLLEGE ◆ BERMUDA

MAKES 6 SERVINGS

THE STUFFING
1 tablespoon vegetable oil
1 small onion, chopped
1 clove garlic, minced
½ cup sausage meat
½ teaspoon dried thyme
½ cup unseasoned bread
  crumbs
1 cup cubed papaya
2 egg whites
1 tablespoon minced fresh
  parsley
Salt and pepper, to taste

THE PORK
One 4-pound loin of pork,
  trimmed of fat, with 6
  bones in

The Bermuda Hotel and Catering College opened in 1965. Today it is part of Bermuda College and actually has its own hotel and restaurant built-in so the students can have a real working environment. It is called the Stonington Beach Hotel, and the food is top-notch.

Fred Ming is a professional chef who cooked at the famed Savoy Hotel in London, but while he was in England he also earned a degree as a teacher. These days he teaches culinary arts at Bermuda College. The following is a recipe he uses to teach his students about the pleasures of roast pork.

1. Preheat the oven to 375° F.

2. In a sauté pan, large enough to hold all the ingredients for the stuffing, over medium heat, heat the oil. As soon as the oil is hot, add the onion and sauté for 3 minutes. Add the garlic and sauté for 2 minutes more. Add the sausage meat and the thyme and cook for 5 minutes. Add the bread crumbs, papaya, egg whites, parsley, and salt and pepper. Cook for 2 minutes.

3. Slice an opening in the pork loin as shown below and fill the opening with the stuffing. Tie the loin together with kitchen string so the stuffing will remain in place during the roasting.

4. Place a piece of aluminum foil in a roasting pan and set the pork loin on top. Roast until the internal temperature of the pork reaches 165° F, about 2 hours.

5. While the pork is roasting, prepare the sauce. In a sauté pan, over medium heat, warm the vinegar and the brown sugar together for 1 minute. Add the crushed pineapple and a half cup of the pineapple juice. Add the beef broth and bring to a simmer. Add the cornstarch mixture and simmer for 2 minutes. Add the salt and pepper.

6. Place the pineapple rings onto a heat-proof dish. Mix the brown sugar and the cinnamon together and sprinkle on top of the pineapple rings. Place the pineapple under the broiler until the sugar begins to caramelize and the edges of the pineapple turn brown.

7. When the pork loin is removed from the oven, allow it to sit for 5 minutes before carving, then carve between each bone, as shown below.

8. The dish is presented by putting some of the pineapple sauce on the serving plate, a slice of the pork on top of the sauce, and a slice of pineapple on top of the pork.

THE SAUCE
1 tablespoon vinegar
2 tablespoons brown sugar
One 8-ounce can crushed
   pineapple with juices
2 cups beef broth
1 tablespoon cornstarch
   dissolved in 1 ounce water
Salt and pepper, to taste

THE GARNISH
6 canned pineapple rings
2 tablespoons brown sugar
1 tablespoon cinnamon

Fred Ming.

COLA-BASTED BAKED HAM
THE AMERICAN FESTIVAL CAFE ◆ NEW YORK CITY

MAKES 10 TO 12 SERVINGS

One 10-pound ham (not
  cured or aged)
4 to 8 cups cola, depending
  on the size of the roasting
  pan
1 cup brown sugar
1 cup bread crumbs
2 teaspoons dry mustard
1 teaspoon freshly ground
  black pepper

In 1608, three sows and a boar were brought from Great Britain to Jamestown, Virginia. Within two years, the pork population had increased to over sixty pigs. By 1625, Virginia, Maryland, and the Carolinas had become famous for their hams, and made pork the most popular meat in the colonies. Chef François Keller at the American Festival Cafe has a collection of traditional American ham recipes. The following is an example of a southern recipe which uses cola as the agent for basting moisture and sweetness.

1. Preheat the oven to 350° F.

2. Remove the skin from the ham. Place the ham, fat side down, in a roasting pan. Add about 1 inch of cola to the pan. Bake for about 2½ hours, allowing 15 minutes per pound. Baste the ham frequently with the cola. Add more cola to the roasting pan during the cooking to prevent burning. Turn the ham fat side up after 2 hours.

3. In a medium bowl, combine the brown sugar, bread crumbs, mustard, and pepper. After the ham has cooked a total of 2½ hours, remove the ham from the oven. Press the crumb coating onto the ham. Return the ham to the oven for 30 to 40 minutes more, until the coating is golden.

HERBED TENDERLOIN OF LAMB
THE OBSERVATORY HOTEL ◆ SYDNEY, AUSTRALIA

The executive chef at the Observatory Hotel is Kit Chan. She was born and raised in Hong Kong and studied her craft with some of the superstars of the European kitchen. The first time I experienced her skill was in London, when she was working in a kitchen headed by the master Swiss chef Anton Mosimann. She is the first woman to become the executive chef of a major deluxe hotel in Australia.

1. Preheat the oven to 375° F.

2. Season the lamb with salt and pepper. In a frying pan that has been heated over medium heat, warm the vegetable oil until it is just hot. Place the loin in the pan and brown each side for 1 minute. Then sprinkle on the rosemary, and cook in the oven for 1 hour, or until the meat has reached an internal temperature of 150° F. (medium).

3. In a small bowl, mix together the parsley, garlic, and lemon zest. Remove the lamb from the oven, place it on a serving plate, and sprinkle on the parsley mixture.

4. Place the pan that the loin was roasted in on top of the range over a medium heat. Put the butter in the pan and scrape the pan drippings into the melting butter to make a sauce. Pour the sauce over the lamb and serve.

NOTE: The pan sauce in Step 4 can be made using a cup of Madeira, red wine, or a fruit or vegetable juice like apple or tomato instead of the butter. Cook the liquid down until it is reduced by half.

MAKES 4 TO 6 SERVINGS

One 3- to 5-pound loin of lamb
Salt and freshly ground black pepper, to taste
2 tablespoons vegetable oil
2 tablespoons fresh rosemary, or 1 tablespoon dried
1 tablespoon chopped parsley
1 clove garlic, minced
Zest of 1 lemon
¼ cup butter

Kit Chan.

LAMB TORTILLAS
THE OBSERVATORY HOTEL ◆ SYDNEY, AUSTRALIA

MAKES 6 SERVINGS

LAMB
2 tablespoons soy sauce
2 teaspoons sesame oil
1 clove garlic, minced
1 hot fresh chili pepper,
   seeded and finely minced
2 teaspoons Dijon-style
   mustard
½ cup red wine vinegar
¼ cup vegetable oil plus 2
   tablespoons
1 tablespoon sugar
1 pound boneless lamb loin

SALSA
2 medium tomatoes,
   chopped
½ teaspoon salt
¼ teaspoon freshly ground
   black pepper
2 tablespoons red wine
   vinegar
½ cup olive oil

FOR SERVING
6 flour tortillas
½ cup chutney
4 cups shredded iceberg
   lettuce

Anthony Musarra is the sous chef at the Observatory Hotel. Anthony's father came to Australia in 1939, one of the early years of a major migration of Europeans to Australia. It was a migration that changed the way Australians eat. Quite frankly, they went from bland and totally uninteresting English food to the best of the European tradition. The Italians were at the forefront of that influence, and these days Anthony is carrying on that tradition, although not just with European dishes. He's interested in the foods of all nations, and he likes to take the common ingredients of Australia and use them in dishes from other countries. This recipe is for his Lamb Tortillas. Lamb is a traditional meat in Australia; tortillas are clearly Latin American.

1.   Preheat the oven to 350° F.

2.   To make the lamb: In a ceramic or glass dish combine the soy sauce, sesame oil, garlic, chili pepper, mustard, vinegar, ¼ cup oil, and sugar. Add the lamb and turn to coat. Cover and marinate for at least 1 hour and/or up to 24 hours in refrigerator.

3.   In a large oven-proof sauté pan over high heat, add the 2 tablespoons of oil. Drain the lamb from the marinade. Pat dry and cook in the pan on all sides for 5 minutes, or until the lamb is cooked to desired doneness.

4. Meanwhile, to make the salsa: Combine all the ingredients and let sit at room temperature to develop the flavors. Wrap the tortillas in aluminum foil and place in the oven for 5 minutes or until heated through.

5. To serve: Slice the lamb thinly. Spread 1 tablespoon of the chutney in the center of a warmed tortilla. Add a few slices of lamb, top with the tomato salsa and shredded lettuce, and roll into tubes.

HOW TO REMOVE THE HEAT FROM A HOT PEPPER

One of the simple ways to control the intensity of heat from the jalapeño, or any other hot pepper, is to remove some or all of the seeds inside, as well as the membrane that holds the seeds. The seeds and the membrane are the sources of heat. The more of those that are in the dish the hotter the flavor.

ABOUT AUSTRALIAN LAMB

When the first English fleet arrived in Australia in 1788, they brought over one bull, seven cows, and forty-four sheep and goats. The untouched pasture land made perfect grazing areas for the flocks and herds that developed from these original animals. The land was especially well suited to the sheep. They were able to roam freely in the meadows of clover and rye.

That is still going on. The result is range lamb that is tastier, leaner, and untainted by chemicals or additives. The Australians are also producing a lamb without the "gamy" taste that so many North Americans came to associate with this meat. The Australian cuts have as clean and clear a taste as you could want. The recent history of lamb production in Australia is a good example of how the public can use its purchasing power to influence producers.

The old style of lamb did not meet the taste or nutritional preference of the market. As a result, sales decreased. The industry, in self-defense, began to ask people what they wanted. The result is the fresh Australian Range Lamb Program that produces a meat that tastes the way North Americans want it to. It's lower in cholesterol and trimmed to result in a cut that is as low in fat as a piece of skinless chicken. They have also worked out a program that gets the lamb to North America within four days after it is processed. This is done with refrigeration, not freezing.

If you are roasting a leg, loin, or any cut of lamb, there is a little tip that always improves the final flavor. After the meat comes out of the oven, wrap it in a piece of aluminum foil. Then let it sit in a warm place for twenty minutes before you slice it. That resting period allows the juices in the meat to settle down after the cooking process, and the final slice will be more moist and more flavorful. It's a small thing to do, but it has a big impact on flavor.

In 1844, Dr. Christopher Rawson Penfold came to Australia from London in order to develop a medical practice. He brought along a few vine cuttings and planted them around his new home. His medical practice flourished and so did the vines. Within a few years, the wine that he produced from those vines became so popular that Dr. Penfold became more interested in healthy grapes than healthy patients. Today, Penfold's is probably the most famous winery in Australia, and its vintages have won some of the most important international awards.

Unlike many wine makers, Penfold's produces its product at a wide range of price points. It has bottles that sell for $9 and $90, and that is very much a part of the Australian love of democracy. Everyone should get a fair chance at the good stuff. One of the most appealing things about Australian wine makers is that they are not particularly interested in making wine to be stored in cellars and talked about for twenty years before it gets into a glass. Australian wine is made for drinking, which brings me to the question of the glass that the wine gets into.

Wine makers and glass makers have been in cahoots for centuries. You could spend a small fortune buying glasses if you wanted to. There is a glass for big red wines, and a glass for not so big red wines. There is a glass for white wines, and a glass for sweet wines, and on and on and on. A good wine deserves a good glass, and if you would like to have one glass that does a pretty good job for just about any wine, here is what you should look for. First, you want a glass that is slightly tapered at the top, like a tulip. That will concentrate the aroma at the tip of your nose. About 75 percent of what we call flavor is really smell. Second, only fill the glass halfway. You need the air above the wine to hold the aroma. We tend to have a four-ounce portion of wine, so you need a glass that will hold eight ounces or more. Select a glass that is clear. You want to appreciate the wine's color. Also, give the glass a wash with clean water before you use it. You don't want the taste of soap.

FROM SHEEPFOLD TO RESTAURANT

New York City's Central Park was constructed during the middle of the 1800s. It's two and a half miles long and a half mile wide. The designers wanted to give visitors a scene of nature but in a very controlled way. Central Park appears natural enough, but the whole place was very carefully thought out. Each year some 13 million people, and an assortment of animals, pay the park a visit.

On the west side of the grounds near Sixty-seventh Street stands an old building originally called the Sheepfold. When it was constructed in 1870 it was home to a sheepherder and his two hundred sheep. The sheep mowed and fertilized the nearby lawn, known today as Sheep Meadow. The sheep were shipped to Brooklyn in the 1930s, and the sheepfold building became the core of a restaurant called Tavern on the Green. Designed by Warner Le Roy, Tavern on the Green is quite a place. There are chandeliers with parts made for Indian princes in the late 1800s and an extensive collection of gold and copper weathervanes, to name just a few of its magnificent attractions. But in spite of its new and valuable exterior, the management of Tavern never forgets this building's humble beginnings. To prove this point, they always have a lamb dish on the menu.

BREADED VEAL CHOPS
TAVERN ON THE GREEN ◆ NEW YORK, NEW YORK

1. In a mixing bowl, beat the eggs lightly with a fork until the whites and yolks are mixed together.

2. Mix the breadcrumbs with the Pecorino Romano cheese. Spread the mixture onto a flat plate.

3. Flatten the veal chops with a meat pounder. Dredge each chop into the flour and shake off the excess.

4. Dip the chops, one at a time, into the eggs. Sprinkle with rosemary and season with salt and pepper. Coat the chops with the breadcrumb mixture.

5. In a sauté pan big enough to hold the chops in one layer, over moderate to high heat, warm the vegetable oil. Add the butter or margarine and the garlic. Sauté the chops until golden brown on both sides, about 3 minutes on each side. Drain on paper towels and serve with lemon wedges on the side.

MAKES 4 SERVINGS

2 eggs
1 cup dry breadcrumbs
¼ cup grated Pecorino
   Romano cheese
4 veal chops, ½ inch thick
Flour, for dredging
1 teaspoon finely chopped
   fresh rosemary, or ½
   teaspoon dried
Coarse salt and freshly
   ground black pepper, to
   taste
3 tablespoons vegetable oil
1 tablespoon unsalted
   butter or margarine
3 cloves garlic, lightly
   crushed
Lemon wedges

◆

STUFFED LAMB CHOPS
AIR FRANCE CONCORDE KITCHENS

MAKES 4 SERVINGS

LAMB CHOPS
2 tablespoons vegetable oil
8 rack lamb chops,
  trimmed

SAUSAGE STUFFING
1 tablespoon butter
1 tablespoon minced shallot
  or onion
1 cup chopped mushrooms
1 tablespoon fresh thyme,
  or 1 teaspoon dried
¾ pound loose sausage meat
¼ cup heavy cream
¼ cup chopped parsley
¼ teaspoon salt
⅛ teaspoon freshly ground
  black pepper
8 savoy cabbage leaves,
  blanched

SAUCE
¼ cup Madeira
½ cup beef broth
1 teaspoon butter, softened
1 teaspoon all-purpose
  flour

1. To make the lamb chops: In a large sauté pan over high heat, warm the oil. When hot, add the chops in one layer. If necessary, cook in several batches. Cook for 2 to 3 minutes on each side, or until desired doneness. Remove from the pan and keep warm.

2. To make the stuffing: In the same sauté pan melt the butter. Add the shallot or onion and cook, stirring for 30 seconds. Add the mushrooms and thyme and continue to cook until the mushrooms begin to brown. Add the sausage meat and cook, breaking up with a fork, until the meat is cooked through. Transfer this sausage mixture to a bowl and let cool completely. When cool, add the heavy cream, parsley, salt, and pepper. Blend well.

3. For the sauce: Return the pan to the heat. Pour in the Madeira, scraping the bottom of the pan with a spoon. Add the beef broth, bring to a boil, and reduce heat to a simmer. Simmer for 5 minutes. In a small bowl, combine the softened butter with the flour until all the flour is incorporated. Whisk this into the sauce and cook until the sauce begins to thicken.

4. To serve, top each lamb chop with some of the sausage mixture, wrap with a cabbage leaf, and pour the Madeira sauce over the top. Serve immediately.

Pasta, Rice, and Potatoes

PASTA AND SQUID
REMI ◆ NEW YORK, NEW YORK

MAKES 4 SERVINGS

5 tablespoons olive oil
1 pound calamari (squid),
  cleaned and sliced into
  rings about ¼ inch wide
1 clove garlic, lightly
  crushed
½ cup dry white wine
Salt and freshly ground
  black pepper, to taste
½ medium onion, finely
  chopped
3 cups chopped canned
  plum tomatoes, with their
  juices
2 teaspoons chopped fresh
  thyme, or 1 teaspoon
  dried
6 quarts water
1 pound tagliolini or
  fettuccine pasta
¼ cup grated Pecorino
  Romano cheese

Remi is the Italian word for the oars that are used to row boats, like the ones that are painted on the walls of the restaurant Remi in New York. The mural depicts the Italian city of Venice, which is also the origin of the recipes created by owner-chef Francesco Antonucci. A lover of seafood and pasta, he combines the two in a dish of tagliolini pasta and squid.

1. In a sauté pan over medium to high heat, warm the olive oil, and sauté the calamari and garlic until the liquid evaporates.

2. Add the white wine and cook until the wine is almost evaporated. Add the salt and pepper.

3. Add the onion and sauté for 2 minutes. Add the tomatoes and thyme. Lower the heat to medium-low and cook uncovered until the calamari is tender, about 10 minutes, stirring occasionally.

4. In a large pot, bring the water to a boil and cook the pasta until just done. Drain the pasta and put it into a bowl.

5. Pour the sauce over the cooked pasta and top with the Pecorino Romano cheese.

◆

THE FOOD OF VENICE

The Italian city of Venice is actually made up of 118 little islands that sit in the center of a lagoon. The islands are connected with about 400 bridges, and the only way to get around town is by boat. It has been that way since the last years of the fifth century when a group of people headed over to the islands in the hope of escaping from an invading army that was ravaging the mainland. Venice was in an ideal location to handle seaborne trade, and by the ninth century it was a major commercial center. By the 1200s, Venice was the strongest sea power in Europe and in virtual control of the major trade routes between Europe and Asia. The influence of Asia and the Middle East on Venice can be seen in its architecture, art, cultural traditions, and its food.

Venice sat right smack in the middle of the trade routes that brought spices from Asia and the Middle East to the cities of Europe. The availability of rare spices and exotic foods from faraway places, plus the ingredients that were locally available, made the cooking of Venice quite magnificent.

◆

ABOUT SQUID

In most of the countries that border on the Mediterranean Sea, squid is a traditional seafood. You'll find it in the recipes of Spain, France, Greece, and especially Italy. In fact, squid was made popular in North America by the Italian cooks who arrived at the turn of the century. Even today most Americans who are familiar with squid know it by its Italian name, calamari.

Virtually all of the squid eaten in the United States comes from the waters off the coast of California. Squid is an excellent source of low-fat protein and can be found in most supermarkets. Sometimes you'll find them cleaned and ready to go into the recipe; sometimes they need a little work before cooking. Inside the squid is a thin, transparent bone. It is important to remove this. Just pull it and it usually comes out in one easy motion. Then check to see that you got all of it. Peel off any remaining skin; that also comes off very easily. Slice the squid or leave it whole according to your recipe. But don't forget the tentacles. Some of the best flavor is there, so chop them up and get them into the pot.

◆

PENNE AND BROCCOLI
IL NIDO ◆ NEW YORK, NEW YORK

MAKES 6 SERVINGS

¼ cup olive oil
4 cloves garlic, thinly sliced
4 cups coarsely chopped
   steamed broccoli
1 cup chicken stock
6 quarts water
1 pound penne pasta
Freshly ground black
   pepper, to taste
¾ cup shaved or grated
   Pecorino Romano cheese

Il Nido is one of New York's most respected Italian restaurants. It has the kind of warm and cozy atmosphere that is typical of the country inns of Tuscany. The chef, Luigi Campoverde, produces many of the complex dishes of Italy, but he is also a master of the simple Italian recipes that find their success in top-quality ingredients and attention to detail. The following is a good example of Luigi demonstrating the art of simplicity.

1. In a sauté pan over medium heat, warm the olive oil. Add the garlic and cook for 2 minutes.

2. Add the broccoli to the pan and sauté for 1 minute. Add the chicken stock, raise the heat to high, and cook until the liquid is almost evaporated, stirring occasionally.

3. In a large pot, bring the water to a boil and cook the pasta until just done. Drain the pasta and put into a bowl.

4. Toss the pasta with the broccoli sauce and season with the pepper. Add the Pecorino Romano cheese to the pasta, saving some for serving. Toss again and serve.

◆

ABOUT BROCCOLI

Broccoli is a member of the cabbage family and was probably first grown in Italy. The ancient Romans had recipes for it and used the florets as if they were cauliflower and the stems as if they were asparagus. The word "broccoli" is actually an Italian word and it's used without much change in most languages. This probably means that the Italians introduced broccoli to the other countries of Europe. The Italians also popularized broccoli in North America during the first part of the twentieth century. This happened to be the same time that scientists were getting serious about vitamins. What a break for broccoli.

Broccoli is packed with vitamins. It is a good source of vitamins A and B, and it has more vitamin C than an equal amount of orange. Broccoli also has significant amounts of calcium, iron, potassium, and fiber, and there are only forty calories in a full cup. To get the most nutrition from broccoli, make sure that the buds on the plant are closed and bright green when you buy it. If the buds are open or have started to turn yellow, then it's past its prime.

My favorite story about broccoli deals with the opening of the Suffolk Downs racetrack in Boston. Just before the track began operations, the Italian gardener in charge of the grounds was asked to plant something green that would grow fast and cover the infield. Broccoli was his choice.

PROHIBITION MADE ITALIAN RESTAURANTS POPULAR

On January 16, 1919, the government of the United States passed the Eighteenth Amendment to the Constitution. It prohibited the manufacture, sale, and distribution of alcoholic beverages. For years, until the repeal of Prohibition in 1933, distilled spirits, wine, and beer were no longer a legal line on our menus. However, in their "illegal" form they were still very much a part of the American way.

Prohibition has come and gone with very little effect on the way our nation drinks. But surprisingly, Prohibition had a powerful effect on the way we eat. Before Prohibition, when Americans went out to a restaurant they went to places where the food was basically English—steaks and roast beef—or dishes adapted from the French. Prohibition made it difficult to enjoy a glass of beer or wine with these meals, but that was not the case in the rooming-house restaurants in Italian immigrant neighborhoods. For decades these small establishments had produced modest amounts of wine and beer for their boarders. When the non-Italian population realized that they could pop into their town's "Little Italy" and have a drink with an excellent meal, the general interest in Italian restaurants exploded. These establishments gave the Americans their first look at ethnic food and made Italian restaurants the single most popular type of restaurant in North America.

RASTA PASTA
THE ENCHANTED GARDEN RESORT ◆ OCHO RIOS, JAMAICA

Rastafarians regard themselves as the descendent children of King Solomon and the Queen of Sheba from biblical Ethiopia. The Rastafarians were inspired by Haile Selassie. One of Selassie's titles was "Lion of Judah," and the rasta hairstyle known as "dreadlocks" is designed to resemble the mane of a lion. Rastas work toward a life with a minimal amount of materialism. Their ideas and ways of expression have had a major impact on international music. Today, Jamaica's most popular music is reggae, which has been described as not just a music but more a philosophy with the advice handed out to a danceable beat. Bob Marley became the first prominent international reggae star. And these days the Marley musical tradition is being carried on by members of his family. Four of his children, led by Ziggy Marley, have come together in a group called the Melody Makers, and they have gained an international reputation. The following recipe was suggested to me by Ziggy Marley, who is moving toward a vegetarian diet. It is called Rasta Pasta.

MAKES 6 SERVINGS

2 tablespoons vegetable oil
1 clove garlic, minced
1 medium onion, finely chopped
1 green bell pepper, thinly sliced
1 red bell pepper, thinly sliced
1 yellow bell pepper, thinly sliced
½ teaspoon dried oregano
½ teaspoon dried basil
5 drops Tabasco sauce
1 cup prepared tomato sauce
1 pound curly pasta, cooked and drained

1. In a sauté pan large enough to hold all of the ingredients including the cooked pasta, over medium heat, warm the oil. Add the garlic and cook, stirring for 1 minute. Add the onion and cook, stirring, for 3 minutes.

2. Add the bell peppers and cook, stirring, for 6 minutes. Add the oregano, basil, and Tabasco; cook, stirring, for 1 minute.

3. Add the tomato sauce and heat through. Add the pasta and heat through.

ORECCHIETTE WITH BROCCOLI
FOUR SEASONS HOTEL ◆ TORONTO, CANADA

MAKES 6 SERVINGS

4 quarts water
¼ cup plus 1 teaspoon
    vegetable oil
1 pound dried orecchiette
    (ear-shape pasta) or other
    thumb-size, shaped pasta
4 cups chopped broccoli
    rabe or broccoli florets
4 cloves garlic, minced
2 large tomatoes, peeled,
    seeded, and cut into strips
½ cup chopped fresh basil
Salt and freshly ground
    black pepper, to taste
10 sun-dried tomatoes, cut
    into strips
Freshly grated Parmesan
    cheese

In 1497 the first Italian, Giovanni Caboto, set foot in Canada. He was a skilled navigator who had anglicized his name to John Cabot and gone to work as an explorer for the British. Today, his historic influence is being celebrated in the kitchen of Toronto's Four Seasons Hotel by Chef Susan Weaver, who cooks up a bowl of orecchiette pasta.

1. In a large pot, bring the water to a boil. Add the teaspoon of oil and the pasta. Cook for 7 minutes.

2. Stir in the broccoli rabe or florets and cook for 3 minutes more, until the pasta is just cooked. Drain.

3. Meanwhile, in a large sauté pan, warm the remaining ¼ cup of oil over moderate heat. Add the garlic and sauté until soft, about 3 minutes. Add the tomatoes, basil, pasta-and-broccoli mixture, and toss to mix well. Season with salt and pepper. Cook just until all of the ingredients are heated through, 2 to 3 minutes.

4. Serve at once, sprinkled generously with freshly grated Parmesan cheese.

◆

JENIFER LANG'S CURRIED PASTA WITH SEAFOOD
CAFE DES ARTISTES ◆ NEW YORK, NEW YORK

One of the jewels in New York City's crown of fabulous restaurants is the legendary Cafe des Artistes. Originally built in 1901 as a haven for artists, Cafe des Artistes' reputation for culinary creativity has been displayed to such illustrious patrons as Rudolph Valentino, Isadora Duncan, and Noël Coward. Almost a century later, the artists are still at work designing culinary masterpieces in the kitchen of the café. Owners George and Jenifer Lang are committed to continuing this history of superior dining. The following dish is low in fat with lots of complex carbohydrates from the pasta and vegetables, garlic to keep away the vampires, and protein-packed seafood.

1.   In a large sauté pan over high heat, warm 2 tablespoons of the oil. Add the vegetables and garlic and sauté for 10 minutes. Add the apple, tomato, thyme, and bay leaf and cook for 5 minutes more. Remove the bay leaf and set the pan aside.

2.   In a medium sauté pan over high heat, add the remaining tablespoon of vegetable oil and the margarine. Add the mushrooms and sauté for 1 minute. Add the scallops and shrimp and sauté for 4 to 5 minutes, until the shrimp are pink and curled. Season with salt and pepper.

3.   Add the chicken stock, tomato paste, and curry powder to the vegetables and simmer for 5 minutes. Add the seafood and stir to combine. Add to the pasta and toss together. Serve immediately.

MAKES 4 SERVINGS

3 tablespoons vegetable oil
1 medium onion, chopped
2 carrots, peeled and chopped
2 stalks celery, chopped
3 cloves garlic, chopped
1 tart apple, MacIntosh or Granny Smith, cored and chopped
1 tomato, chopped
½ teaspoon dried thyme
1 bay leaf
1 tablespoon margarine
1 cup sliced mushrooms
½ pound uncooked scallops, cleaned
½ pound uncooked medium shrimp, shells removed, cleaned
Salt and freshly ground black pepper, to taste
½ cup chicken stock
1 tablespoon tomato paste
1 tablespoon curry powder, or more to taste
1 pound dried fettuccine pasta, cooked according to directions

◆

UPPER DECK LOBSTER AND PASTA
THE UPPER DECK ◆ HALIFAX, NOVA SCOTIA

MAKES 4 SERVINGS

2 tablespoons coarsely
   cracked black pepper, use
   more or less to taste
2 tablespoons dried
   tarragon
1½ cups dry white wine
Four 1-pound lobsters, or 4
   lobster tails, shelled, the
   meat cut into bite-size
   pieces
1 pound linguine
⅔ cup heavy cream

The town of Halifax in the Canadian province of Nova Scotia has a number of restaurants along the waterfront that have become well known for their seafood cookery. Perhaps the most famous is called the Upper Deck. The Upper Deck's chef is Chris Profit and one of his signature dishes is called Upper Deck Lobster.

1.   In a large skillet over medium heat, combine the pepper, tarragon, and wine. Add the lobster meat, cover, and simmer for 5 to 8 minutes, or until the lobster is thoroughly cooked.

2.   Meanwhile, in a pot of boiling water, cook the linguine until just done. Drain.

3.   Add the cream to the lobster mixture, and increase the heat to high. Cook, stirring constantly, for 3 minutes, or until the sauce thickens enough to coat the back of a spoon. Reduce the heat to low.

4.   Add the drained linguine and toss to coat with the sauce. Divide among 4 plates and serve at once.

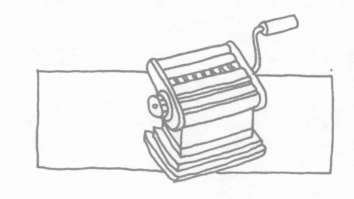

ABOUT LOBSTER

The waters off the Atlantic coast of North America have supplied lobsters to the native tribes for thousands of years. The first Europeans to have them as a regular part of their New World diet were the French and English colonists who settled down in Nova Scotia. Until recently, lobsters were so plentiful that all you had to do was walk along the beach and pick them up. An English visitor touring Nova Scotia in the mid-1800s wrote a letter home to London that said, "Lobster is found everywhere on the coast and in such extraordinary numbers that they are used by the thousands as fertilizer for the land." How times have changed. It was high-speed transportation that made fresh lobster available to a wide audience and increased both the demand and the price.

Nutritionally, lobsters are a good source of low-fat protein. They also contain amounts of calcium and are not as high in cholesterol as we used to think. It is important that lobster be alive when it is cooked. As soon as a lobster dies, its uncooked flesh attracts a bacteria that's dangerous. Lobsters should be moving when you start the cooking process. The restaurant lobster tank is a great idea.

♦

ABOUT WHEAT

Wheat is a form of grass and an essential element in the civilization of man. Historians tell us that our ancient ancestors were nomadic, wandering from place to place in search of food. But somewhere about seven thousand years ago, we began to settle down near stands of wild wheat and figure out how to plant the grain so we would have a dependable supply. Next thing you know we had jobs and mortgages, and wheat became the staff of life.

Wheat has also played a key roll in the stability of the nations that used it as a basic cereal. Every time a powerful nation has failed to supply its people with the wheat they needed, that nation went down the tubes. It happened in ancient Greece; it happened in ancient Rome; and most recently, it happened in Russia. For centuries Russia was not only able to produce the wheat that it needed for its own population, but was able to harvest so much wheat that it was an exporter. During its Communist period, however, production was so bad that Russia became an importer of wheat, bringing in thousands of tons each year from Canada and the United States. Shortly thereafter we witnessed the collapse of their economic system. When a country can no longer maintain a domestic source of its own basic foods, it is in deep trouble.

♦

SPAGHETTI ASPARAGUS LASAGNE
FOUR SEASONS OLYMPIC HOTEL ◆ SEATTLE, WASHINGTON

MAKES 6 TO 8 SERVINGS

1 tablespoon butter
2 tablespoons vegetable oil
1 tablespoon minced garlic
1 cup finely chopped onions
¼ cup finely chopped fresh
   basil leaves
4 medium tomatoes, peeled
   and roughly chopped,
   plus 2 thinly sliced
½ cup water
Salt and freshly ground
   black pepper, to taste
2 pounds asparagus,
   trimmed and blanched
12 ounces spaghetti,
   precooked and drained
2 cups grated mozzarella
   cheese
½ cup ricotta cheese

Kerry Sear.

Cool nights. Warm days. Clean, clear water flowing down from the mountains. Mineral-rich volcanic soil. These are the conditions that make Washington State the ideal place to grow asparagus. Most Washington asparagus have tips that are purple, which indicates a high sugar content. Washington State has about four hundred farmers that are dedicated to growing asparagus by hand and they produce about 100 million pounds each year. This practice gives great pleasure to chefs like Kerry Sear at Seattle's Four Seasons Olympic Hotel, who put Washington asparagus to good use.

1. Preheat the oven to 375° F. Butter a lasagne dish.

2. In a medium sauté pan over medium-high heat, warm the oil until hot. Add the garlic and onions and sauté until the onions are translucent, about 5 minutes.

3. Stir in the basil, chopped tomatoes, and water and bring to a boil. Add salt and pepper, remove from the heat, and set aside.

4. Arrange half of the asparagus in an even layer over the bottom of the prepared lasagne dish. Top with a layer of half of the sliced tomatoes, then a layer of half of the spaghetti and a layer of half the garlic/onion/tomato sauce. Evenly sprinkle half of the mozzarella over the tomato sauce and dot with half of the ricotta. Repeat layering, using all of the remaining ingredients.

5. Bake, uncovered, for 45 minutes, or until the top of the lasagne is golden brown.

A LITTLE SEATTLE FOOD HISTORY

Native Americans have been living in the Seattle area for about thirteen thousand years. For most of those years it was a perfect spot. The area has an unusually mild climate, considering how far north it is, and was literally Mother Nature's supermarket. The local rivers were home to hundreds of thousands of salmon, who each year returned from the ocean and swam upstream to spawn. While it was just sex for the salmon, it was a dependable supper for the tribes. The sea also offered dozens of other types of fish and shellfish, such as the famous Olympia oyster, the Dungeness crab, and a variety of clams. The forests were packed with elk, deer, and bear. Wild ducks and geese regularly passed through the area, and the wild berries and nuts were fabulous. Captain George Vancouver was a British explorer and the head of the first European expedition to explore Puget Sound. His logbooks indicate that he and his crew dined on oysters, clams, salmon, and local berries and loved it.

The first Europeans to settle in the region were agents of the Hudson Bay Company, who came for the fur trade. They planted gardens that surprisingly contained potatoes. These potatoes had come from the Spanish missionaries, who had learned about them in South America and taught the native Americans how to cultivate them. The native Americans, in turn, taught the fur traders. Today, Washington potatoes are a major crop for the state and a big deal to potato lovers all over the country. Washington has also become famous for its asparagus, which is still harvested by hand.

ABOUT ASPARAGUS

The ancient Greeks and Romans considered asparagus to be a gastronomic delight, but they also valued it for its medical properties. And were they on target! Asparagus contains large amounts of a substance called glutathione, which turns out to be one of the most powerful cancer blockers. Asparagus is also high in folic acid, which is important to cell growth, especially during pregnancy.

When you're buying asparagus in the market, look for spears with closed, compact tips and a firm stalk; those are signs of freshness. Pick out spears of the same size so they will cook evenly. Plump spears are the most tender. The best way to store asparagus is in a moist paper towel inside an open plastic bag. But not for long. It's best to eat asparagus the same day you buy it. Also, keep the cooking time short; five to seven minutes of steaming should do the trick.

PASTA, SHRIMP, AND LEEKS
FELIDIA RISTORANTE ◆ NEW YORK, NEW YORK

MAKES 6 SERVINGS

4 tablespoons olive oil
1 pound uncooked medium
  shrimp, shelled and
  deveined
2 large leeks
6 quarts water
2 tablespoons coarse salt
1 teaspoon minced shallot
  or onion
2 tablespoons unsalted
  butter (optional)
1 cup chicken stock
Salt and freshly ground
  black pepper, to taste
1 pound fresh tagliatelle or
  other fresh pasta
⅓ cup grated Pecorino
  Romano cheese, plus
  more for the table

1. In a sauté pan over medium-high heat, warm 2 table-spoons of the olive oil and quickly sear the shrimp for 2 min-utes. Set aside.

2. Trim the leeks and discard the top third of the tough green portion. Slice the remainder into ½-inch-thick rounds, and rinse in several changes of cold water to remove all soil and grit. Drain well.

3. Bring the water to a boil with the coarse salt.

4. In a sauté pan, heat the remaining 2 tablespoons of olive oil, add the leeks, and sauté over moderate-high heat, stirring until softened, about 5 minutes. Add the shallot or onion, and cook, stirring for 1 minute. Add the butter and the chicken stock, and simmer gently for 3 minutes. Add the shrimp and simmer for an additional 1 minute. Season with salt and pepper.

5. Add the pasta to the boiling water, stirring with a wooden spoon. The pasta will be done as soon as the water returns to the boil, 30 seconds to 1 minute.

6. Drain the pasta well, add the leek sauce, and toss thoroughly to coat the pasta with the sauce.

7. Sprinkle with Pecorino Romano cheese. Toss well and serve with additional Pecorino Romano on the side.

◆

DISCOVERING VITAMINS POPULARIZED ITALIAN FOOD IN THE UNITED STATES

Mark Twain used to say, "If you don't like the weather . . . just wait a minute." Sometimes I feel that the same approach could be used to describe the history of nutritional advice. If you don't like what the scientists are saying about something you eat or don't eat, just wait a minute and they'll tell you something different. One of my favorite examples is the flip-flop on nutritional advice that took place during the first two decades of this century.

For hundreds of years the idea of good eating meant fat. Then in the beginning of the twentieth century researchers discovered vitamins and dietary minerals, and all of the rules changed. Suddenly fruits and vegetables became "good foods." This was very important for the Italian community in North America. The basic diet for Italian immigrants to the New World was low in meat and fat, and very high in fruits and vegetables. Suddenly Italian food began to get great press. Magazines that dealt with the various aspects of homemaking were now looking for cooks who could do a good job with recipes for fruits and especially vegetables. The easiest place to find them was among the Italians. Italian cooking started to become the darling diet of food reporters. By the middle of the 1920s, Italian food had a highly regarded status among the middle class of North America. Today, it is our most popular ethnic cuisine and one of the original forces behind our interest in vegetables.

Lidia Bastianich.

PASTA WITH BEAN SAUCE
SAN DOMENICO ♦ NEW YORK, NEW YORK

MAKES 4 SERVINGS

2 pounds whole fava beans
(2 pounds in shell), or one
10-ounce package frozen
baby lima beans, thawed
¼ cup olive oil
2 medium shallots or
onions, finely chopped
Pinch of peperoncini (hot
pepper flakes)
1½ cups chicken stock
Salt and freshly ground
black pepper, to taste
6 quarts water
1 pound stricchetti,
pappardelle, or tagliatelle
pasta
¼ cup grated Pecorino
Romano cheese

Tony May.

The restaurant San Domenico sits on the edge of New York's Columbus Circle. Created by veteran restaurateur Tony May, it is an elegant establishment that features the specialties of Northern Italy. Chef Theo Schoenegger demonstrated his love of Tuscan regional cooking with this recipe for pasta with an unusual bean sauce.

1. Remove the fava beans from their shells. Blanch the beans in salted boiling water for 1 minute. Drain the beans and immediately plunge them into ice water. Drain the beans and peel off the outer skin. If using lima beans, just thaw and hold them at room temperature. Reserve ½ cup whole beans.

2. In a saucepan over medium-low heat, heat the olive oil with the shallots or onions and peperoncini and sauté until the onions are wilted. Add the chicken stock and turn up the heat to high, bring to a boil, and cook for 5 minutes. Add the beans and salt and pepper. Cook for 2 minutes.

3. Pour the mixture into a food processor or blender and puree.

4. In a large pot, bring the water to a boil and cook the pasta until just done. Drain the pasta and put into a bowl (reserve ½ cup of the pasta cooking water).

5. In a large sauté pan, warm the bean sauce. Add the pasta and whole beans to the sauce and toss gently, adding the reserved pasta water to moisten, if needed. Finish with the grated Pecorino Romano cheese and freshly ground black pepper, to taste.

♦

THE FOOD OF FLORENCE

When Americans talk about the food of northern Italy we are usually talking about the cooking of the Italian region called Tuscany. Since the third century B.C., Tuscany has been one of the great places for Italian cooking, and for hundreds of years the city of Florence has dominated this area. The cooks of Florence prefer natural dishes without complex preparation. They want the true flavors of the ingredients to come through without any disguises.

When Rome fell in A.D. 476, good food in Europe almost disappeared. Such cuisine didn't make a comeback until the Renaissance of the thirteenth century. It was at that time, and in Florence, that the first gourmet society was formed since the days of ancient Rome. The society was called the Company of the Cauldron and limited to twelve members. Each member was a painter or sculptor and had to create a new dish for every meeting of the group. The most famous member of the organization was an artist named Andrea del Sarto. He was often called the perfect painter because of his ability to produce a perfectly balanced composition, a skill that he also applied to his cooking.

One of the ingredients that was, and still is, very common in the cooking of Tuscany is the bean. In fact, the people of Tuscany are often referred to by other Italians as "bean eaters," and that is not meant to be a compliment. But to anyone interested in good nutrition, to be skilled in the art of bean cookery is a badge of honor.

◆

ABOUT LIMA BEANS

The most common of the shell beans in the United States is the baby lima bean. It is named after the capital city of Peru, where they have been growing lima beans for over six thousand years. But the capital of Peru, though it is spelled Lima, the same as the bean, is pronounced lee-ma, not lie-ma. So, if you are ever in Peru and you need some baby limas, you must remember to ask for lee-mas. Lima lovers should know that.

These days, however, baby limas no longer come from Lima. Most of them come from California. The dried variety is high in complex carbohydrates, protein, and dietary fiber. They are low in saturated fat and sodium, and they are easy to prepare. First, look through the beans and make sure that no small stones have come with them from the field. Wash the beans off and put them into a large pot. Remember that dried lima beans will increase by at least twice their volume when they finish absorbing water. Then pour in ten cups of hot water for every pound of beans. Bring the water to a boil and let it boil for three minutes. Turn off the heat and let the beans soak for four hours. At that point, drain off the water and they're ready for a soup, casserole, or a salad.

◆

PUERTO RICAN PASTA (GIUSEPPE'S PASTA)
SANDS HOTEL ◆ SAN JUAN, PUERTO RICO

MAKES 4 SERVINGS

2 tablespoons vegetable oil
8 cloves garlic, thinly sliced
1 teaspoon dried oregano
1 cup finely chopped onions
One 2-ounce can anchovy
  fillets, drained and
  chopped
1 teaspoon crushed red
  pepper flakes
1 cup sliced, stuffed green
  olives
1 cup sliced black olives
2 cups dry white wine
Two 8-ounce cans tomato
  sauce
1 pound linguine, just
  cooked until al dente and
  drained
½ cup freshly grated
  Parmesan cheese

Giuseppe Acosta is the chef at the restaurant Il Giardino, in the Sands Hotel of San Juan, Puerto Rico. He fully realizes that the strongest historic influences on the island's cooking come from the early native tribes, the Spanish explorers, and the Africans. But he is also quick to point out that the first European to arrive on these shores was Columbus, an Italian, who stopped by during his second voyage in 1493. Giuseppe has therefore taken it upon himself to protect the memory of this momentous event by producing the traditional dishes of Columbus's homeland.

1. In a large sauté pan over medium-high heat, warm the oil. Add the garlic, oregano, onions, anchovies, red pepper flakes, and both types of olives. Sauté until the onions are translucent, about 5 minutes.

2. Stir in the wine and tomato sauce and cook until the sauce is heated through, 3 to 5 minutes.

3. Add the linguine and toss to coat. Cook for 2 to 3 minutes, or until thoroughly heated through. Add the Parmesan cheese, stir well, and serve.

ABOUT TRADITIONAL PUERTO RICAN DISHES

Some of the best places to get a real look at what traditional Puerto Rican cooking is really like are the local fondas. Fondas are modest, small restaurants that cater to the tastes of their neighborhood. They serve up Ma's home cooking and it's usually Ma that actually does the cooking. The foods they serve are the most customary and familiar in Puerto Rico. Tostones are plantains deep-fried, then flattened out and fried again. As easily addictive as the ultimate potato chip. Bacalaitos are dried salt codfish fritters. Pasteles are grated plantains or green bananas with a spiced ground-beef filling wrapped in plantain leaves. Postalos is like a lasagne but the pasta is replaced with ripe plantains. Arroz con pollo is chicken and rice, virtually the national dish of Puerto Rico. And to drink, mabi made from the fermented root of the mabi tree, water, sugar, cinnamon, and cloves. This is very similar to a beverage that was made by the ancient Taino tribes that lived on the island starting in A.D. 300.

One of the most interesting programs for the appreciation and presentation of things Puerto Rican is a government project in the area of gastronomy. In the 1980s the government of Puerto Rico decided it was time to protect and promote the traditional gastronomy of the island's various regions. In order to do that it instituted a program called Mesones Gastronomico, which translates as "houses of gastronomy." Through the program fifty restaurants were set up, spread out all over the island, to serve authentic local specialties in an attractive location and with reasonable prices.

All of the restaurants in this program are outside of San Juan. Many are located in the most picturesque parts of the island—in small villages, along the seashore, and up in the mountains. The foods that they serve represent some of the best of Puerto Rican cooking and often at the best prices.

It's as if the U.S. federal government decided to help preserve the best recipes from each neighborhood in our country and helped set up restaurants to keep up the good cooking. Puerto Rico's Mesones Gastronomico project is doing just that, holding on to the island's culinary heritage for the Puerto Ricans and for other people who go and visit.

◆

ABOUT CHINESE MUSHROOMS

The Chinese are great lovers of mushrooms. They have been cultivating them on a commercial scale for about 1,500 years, which gives them a 1,000-year lead on everyone in the West. These days there are about three hundred edible types of mushrooms available to the Chinese cook. The three most commonly used to reproduce Chinese recipes in North America are the dried black, *the* straw mushroom, *and the* cloud ear. *Straw mushrooms are sold in cans and should be washed under running water before they are used. Any leftover straw mushrooms should be stored in water in an airtight jar in the refrigerator. They will keep there for about a week. It is still a good idea to use these small, delicate mushrooms as quickly as possible after you open the can.*

Cloud ears are thin and brittle. They are usually sold in the form of dry chips and need to be soaked in water for about 30 minutes before they go into a recipe. The eye of a cloud ear is normally quite hard, and you should cut it out before using the mushroom. Cloud ears do not absorb moisture when they go into a recipe, which is why they are traditionally used in dishes that have a good deal of sauce to coat the mushrooms and give them flavor. Cloud-ear mushrooms are really used only for their texture.

STIR-FRIED NOODLES, MING JIANG STYLE
THE GRAND FORMOSA REGENT HOTEL ◆ TAIPEI, TAIWAN

Chinese noodle making seems to have gotten its official start during the Han Dynasty, which ran from roughly 200 B.C. to A.D. 200. It was during this time that people mastered the technique for grinding wheat into flour, which made noodle production obvious and easy, since a noodle dough in its simplest form is just wheat mixed with water. This dish is called Noodles Ming Jiang Style. Ming Jiang is the name of a river in the province of Fukien. The recipe uses the common Chinese cooking technique of cooking the noodles with two different methods, first boiling, then stir-frying.

1. Cook the noodles in at least 1 quart of boiling water until they are just done. They should be firm to the bite, not soft.

2. While the noodles are cooking, heat the vegetable oil in a wok or high-sided sauté pan. As soon as the oil is hot, add the cabbage, mushrooms, carrots, green beans, and ham or bacon, and stir-fry for 2 minutes.

3. When the noodles are cooked, drain from the water and add to the wok. Stir-fry for 1 minute. Add the chicken stock, soy sauce, and pepper and stir-fry for 2 minutes more.

MAKES 8 SERVINGS

½ pound flat thin noodles
2 tablespoons vegetable oil
4 cups sliced cabbage
½ cup sliced mushrooms
2 cups sliced carrots
2 cups green beans, cut into
    bite-size pieces
1 cup precooked ham or
    precooked bacon, cut into
    bite-size pieces
1 cup chicken stock
¼ cup soy sauce
½ teaspoon freshly ground
    pepper

Daw-Ming Lee, Production Coordinator.

NYDIA'S RICE AND BEANS
EL SAN JUAN HOTEL ◆ SAN JUAN, PUERTO RICO

MAKES 6 SERVINGS

2 tablespoons vegetable oil
2 medium onions, roughly
  chopped
1 medium green bell
  pepper, seeded and
  roughly chopped
1 medium red bell pepper,
  seeded and roughly
  chopped
4 cloves garlic, crushed
2 medium tomatoes,
  roughly chopped
4 cups chicken broth or
  stock
1 pound red beans, soaked,
  cooked until tender, and
  drained
One 8-ounce can tomato
  sauce
Salt and freshly ground
  black pepper, to taste
4 cups freshly cooked white
  rice

1. In a large saucepan over medium-high heat, warm the oil until hot. Add the onions, bell peppers, and garlic and sauté until the onions are translucent, 5 to 7 minutes.

2. Stir in the tomatoes, chicken broth or stock, drained beans, and tomato sauce. Bring the mixture to a low simmer, and cook, stirring frequently, until most of the liquid has evaporated, 15 to 20 minutes.

3. Adjust the seasonings, adding salt and pepper as needed.

4. Divide the rice and the beans evenly among 6 plates and serve at once.

JAMAICAN RICE AND BEANS
THE ENCHANTED GARDEN RESORT ◆ OCHO RIOS, JAMAICA

In Jamaica this dish is called rice and peas, but what Jamaicans call peas are known in North America as beans. The recipe is a standard part of everyone's home cooking and comes as a side dish with many meals. It has an excellent nutritional balance. The peas and rice together provide all the amino acids that are needed to make up a complete protein.

1.   In a 4-quart saucepan or stockpot, bring the water to a boil. Add the prepared beans, vegetable oil, onion, scallions, thyme, garlic, and jalapeño pepper. Bring to a boil, then lower the heat and simmer, partially covered, for 45 minutes.

2.   Add the coconut milk or cream, rice, and salt and pepper. Bring to a boil, lower heat, cover, and simmer for 20 minutes. Allow to stand, covered, on stove for 5 minutes before serving.

NOTE: The best way to make coconut milk is to take the skin off the fresh coconut, put the coconut meat into a blender with a bit of water. Blend until the meat has a creamy texture, and strain the milk through cheesecloth.

MAKES 4 SERVINGS

4 cups water
1 cup pinto beans, covered
    with water, boiled for 2
    minutes, allowed to rest in
    the water for 1 hour and
    then drained
1 tablespoon vegetable oil
½ cup minced onion
½ cup scallions, cut into
    ¼-inch rounds
1 tablespoon fresh thyme,
    minced or ½ tablespoon
    dried
1 clove garlic, minced
1 teaspoon chopped
    jalapeño pepper
¼ cup unsweetened coconut
    milk (see Note) or canned
    coconut cream (optional)
1 cup uncooked rice
Salt and freshly ground
    black pepper, to taste

◆

ABOUT ALLSPICE AND SCOTCH BONNET

More than anything else, what makes Jamaican food Jamaican is the use of certain spices and chili peppers. The most notable spice on Jamaica is allspice. Most people think it's a mixture of many different spices. However, that is not true. Allspice is the hard, small, round berry of the pimiento tree. Pimiento trees seemed to have gotten their start in South America and the Caribbean. They grow particularly well in Jamaica. When European explorers arrived on Jamaica they took one whiff of the pimiento tree and concluded that it smelled like cinnamon, nutmeg, cloves, and pepper all in one. So, they called it allspice. Jamaicans use the ground berries in pies, cakes, and cookies. However, it is also a basic flavoring agent for pork and chicken dishes.

When it comes to chili peppers, the superstar in Jamaica is the Scotch Bonnet. It's actually the most popular chili in the Caribbean. Many cooks just pop it into a soup or stew to add flavor and take it out just before serving. The fact that the pepper has been kept whole reduces the heat, and as soon as you slice it open you "release the force." Remember, when you are handling hot chilies, if you have sensitive skin, use a kitchen glove, and wash your hands before you go from the chili peppers to your face, especially the area near your eyes. It's hot stuff.

◆

JAMAICAN
SCOTCH
BONNET

CANTONESE SHRIMP WITH FRIED RICE
THE GRAND FORMOSA REGENT HOTEL ◆ TAIPEI, TAIWAN

The ancient Chinese custom of balancing each meal between the **fan** *food of grains and the* **ts'ai** *food of meat, fish, and poultry, has made much of Chinese home cooking extremely healthful. A lot of complex carbohydrates with a very limited amount of saturated fat appears to be a perfect eating pattern. An excellent example of a recipe using the* **fan** *and* **ts'ai** *balance is this dish of Cantonese Shrimp with Fried Rice.*

1. In a wok over high heat, heat 2 tablespoons of the oil until it begins to shimmer. Add the ham and the shrimp and stir-fry for 1½ to 2 minutes, until the shrimp are opaque on the outside and cooked through. Remove the ham and the shrimp; wipe out the wok.

2. In the wok over high heat, heat the remaining 1 tablespoon of oil until hot. Add the eggs and cook until they are solid, about 2 minutes.

3. Add the cold rice and stir-fry vigorously, breaking the eggs into pieces and mixing them thoroughly with the rice until the mixture is hot, about 2 minutes.

4. Add the shrimp, ham, salt and pepper, scallions, and lettuce and stir-fry thoroughly to mix the ingredients, about 2 minutes. Serve at once.

MAKES 4 SERVINGS

3 tablespoons vegetable oil
1 cup diced smoked ham (about 6 ounces)
1 cup uncooked baby shrimp (about 8 ounces), deveined and shelled
4 eggs, beaten
3 cups cooked white rice, *cold*
Salt and freshly ground black pepper, to taste
1 cup chopped scallions
1 cup shredded iceberg lettuce

FAN AND TS'AI: THE BALANCE OF CHINESE FOOD

A group of scientists have been studying the history of Chinese food and have been able to document their work as far back as 5000 B.C. The result is a food tradition that has been going on longer than any other eating system that we know.

From the earliest of times, the Chinese believed that there was a clear relationship between food and health. They believed, and still believe, that your approach to eating will affect your general health. Additionally, your health at any particular time dictates the food you should be eating during that period. The Chinese developed a series of broad instructions which are particularly fascinating because they are being supported by some of our most recent medical research.

An example is the ancient concept of fan and ts'ai. The word fan *is used to describe grains and starches. Ts'ai is primarily fish, meat, and poultry mixed with fruits and vegetables. A properly balanced Chinese meal combines specific proportions of fan and ts'ai. The result is a seven-thousand-year-old recipe that gives the eaters about 70 percent of their calories from complex carbohydrates in the form of grains, fruits, and vegetables. The remaining 30 percent comes from meat, fish, or poultry. Most of the time that last 30 percent is low in fat.*

Night market, Taiwan.

CARIBBEAN MADRAS RICE
CLUB MED I

The Club Med I is the largest sailing vessel in the world. It is a 617-foot, five-masted ship with the soul of a private yacht. Dining rooms with magnificent views of the sea offer buffets at breakfast and lunch, and classic French service at dinner. If you like, you can take your meal right on the deck. And to work off those calories, there's a fitness center with floor-to-ceiling windows to keep your mind off your muscles. There are also two swimming pools, aerobic exercise classes, and a water sports program that could entice Captain Nemo. As we sailed through the Caribbean, the boat's kitchen reflected the cuisine of the islands. The following recipe comes from the large Indian population that took up residence in the Caribbean during the past two centuries.

MAKES EIGHTEEN ½-CUP SERVINGS

3 tablespoons vegetable oil
1 cup finely chopped onions
3 cups extra long-grain white rice
5 cups hot chicken stock
⅓ cup raisins
½ cup drained crushed pineapple
⅓ cup grated coconut
1 teaspoon salt
Freshly ground black pepper, to taste

1. Heat the vegetable oil in a pot large enough to accommodate the cooked rice (3 quarts). Over medium heat, sauté the onions until softened, about 10 minutes.

2. Add the rice and stir to coat with oil for 2 minutes.

3. Pour in the hot chicken stock, then the remaining ingredients. Bring to a boil, cover tightly, and lower heat to a simmer.

4. Simmer for 20 minutes, or until the liquid is absorbed. Allow the rice to rest, covered, for 5 to 10 minutes. Uncover, fluff with a fork, and serve.

BERMUDAN SPANISH RICE
CECILLE SNAITH-SIMMONS ◆ BERMUDA

MAKES 4 SERVINGS

6 strips bacon
1 onion, minced
1 green bell pepper, minced
2 cups chopped tomatoes
   and their juices
¼ cup tomato paste
1½ cups rice, medium grain
Salt and pepper, to taste
½ teaspoon dried thyme
2 cups water or chicken
   stock

Cecille Snaith-Simmons was born in Bermuda and by profession is a registered nurse. Her husband, Lionel Simmons, was for many years a member of Parliament. She is the author of The Bermuda Cookbook, *which contains recipes passed down from both her family and that of her husband. She was kind enough to stop by the kitchen of Bermuda's hotel school and demonstrate her recipe for Spanish Rice.*

A Spanish recipe makes excellent historic sense in Bermuda. The Spanish knew about Bermuda before the English. As a matter of fact, the name "Bermuda" comes from the Spanish explorer, Juan de Bermudez, who stopped there in 1511, about a hundred years before the English.

A rice dish like this is easy and convenient and tastes so good because rice has a natural ability to carry the flavors of the other ingredients. Long grain rice is best for a dish like this because it ends up extra-fluffy and each grain tends to stay separate and hold its shape.

1. Preheat the oven to 350° F.

2. In an oven-proof casserole or a sauce pan, large enough to hold 4 cups of finished rice and fitted with a cover to be used in step 3 below, over high heat, cook the bacon until crisp, remove from pan, let cool, and crumble into small pieces.

3.   In the pan drippings from the bacon, over medium heat, cook the onion for 3 minutes. Add the bell pepper and sauté for 1 minute. Add the tomatoes and their juices, the tomato paste, the rice, salt and pepper to taste, and the thyme, and sauté for 1 minute. Add the water and bring to a boil. Cover the pan and place it into the oven for 30 minutes. Remove the rice from the oven. Using a fork, fluff the cooked rice and mix in the crisp crumbled bacon before serving.

Cecille Snaith-Simmons.

A B O U T   T H E   P I N E A P P L E

When a new food arrives on the shores of a foreign country, it usually takes a long time before people start to eat it on a regular basis. Often hundreds of years will pass before the new food is a part of the local diet. An amazing exception to that rule is the pineapple. Pineapples have grown wild in South America and the Caribbean for thousands of years.

The first Europeans to see a pineapple were the men who sailed to Jamaica with Christopher Columbus on his second voyage. They saw it, tasted it, loved it, and took the fruit with them for their voyage home. New world explorers would take pineapples aboard their boats to feed the sailors. Pineapples are high in vitamin C, and that protected the crews from scurvy. When the boats came to a new land, the men would plant the pineapple crowns to see if they would grow. If they did, the sailors hoped they could come back to that place for fresh pineapples on a later voyage. Within fifty years, the pineapple was planted in almost every major tropical area from Jamaica to Java. The pineapple is a symbol of welcome for the people of Jamaica. It is present in the country's coat of arms and there is a pineapple watermark on Jamaican money.

POTATOES VAN GOGH
AMSTEL INTER-CONTINENTAL ◆ AMSTERDAM, HOLLAND

MAKES 4 SERVINGS

1¼ cups chicken broth or
  stock
6 juniper berries (optional)
1 bay leaf
3 thin slices peeled fresh
  ginger
1 tablespoon prepared
  mustard
2 large potatoes, peeled
2 medium onions, peeled

For Van Gogh, the peasant and the potato represented a simpler and purer world. He believed that peasants were in many ways much better than the more sophisticated people in the city and that their lives could provide a lesson for other people. When it comes to cooking, that is often true; much of the simpler farm food of Europe can teach us a lesson about good cooking. Robert Kranenborg, the executive chef at Amsterdam's Amstel Inter-Continental hotel, has used Van Gogh's painting of the **Potato Eaters** *as a starting point for a Dutch potato dish.*

1. Preheat the oven to 375° F.

2. In a small saucepan over medium-high heat, bring the chicken broth, juniper berries, bay leaf, ginger, and mustard to a boil. Reduce the heat to low and simmer for 5 minutes.

3. Meanwhile, using a mandoline, food processor, or sharp knife, cut the potatoes and the onions into ⅛-inch-thick slices.

4. Alternate the potato and onion slices over the bottom of a shallow, 6-×-9-inch casserole or baking dish.

5. Strain the chicken broth mixture through a medium sieve over the potatoes and onions. Bake for 30 minutes, or until the potatoes are tender.

◆

ABOUT VAN GOGH AND POTATOES

Vincent van Gogh was born in Holland in 1853 and died in 1890. Almost all of his paintings were made during the 1880s, and though he was able to sell only a few of his works during his lifetime, his paintings have since become the most valuable in the international art market. In 1990 a Van Gogh sold for more than $80 million. In the center of Amsterdam is the Van Gogh Museum, built to honor the great Dutch painter and to make his works available to the public. Over one hundred works of Van Gogh are on continual exhibition.

Food has always been an important subject for Dutch painters, and Van Gogh was no exception. He painted dozens of pictures of fruits—lemons, pears, apples, grapes, and oranges. The still life of apples and pears that he painted in 1887 was a color study. He wanted to produce a completely yellow picture. He also presented people eating and drinking in cafés and restaurants.

One of Van Gogh's favorite works was the **Potato Eaters,** *painted in April 1885. It depicts a family of Dutch farmers sitting down to a meal of potatoes. The fact that they were making a meal of potatoes is a reminder of how important the introduction of the potato was to European farming. Throughout the 1700s and 1800s the potato, because of its high nutritional content, was enough to keep farmers alive.*

There are ancient stone carvings that go back over six thousand years and clearly show people making beer. The ancient Egyptians even put beer into the tombs of their kings so the departed royalty could have a drink in the afterlife. Talk about a six-pack to go. In Amsterdam, the old Heineken Brewery is one of the most popular tourist attractions. The original facility was called the Haystack Brewery, and it opened in 1572. In 1863 it was taken over by Gerard Heineken who, at the age of twenty-two, decided that he could make a better beer. Today, the original plant is a museum devoted to the history of beer. They have a collection of art and artifacts that tell the story of the history of beer making. They also have an extensive collection of beer-drinking vessels.

At the Heineken Brewery, you can see the process pretty much the way it has been for the past two thousand years. It starts with barley, a grain that people have been eating since prehistoric times. Because barley has a shallow root system and grows well even in soil that has a high salt content, it was one of the first crops grown in Holland after the land was reclaimed from the Zuider Zee. When the barley grain is mixed with water, an enzyme starts a process called "germination." This process, which wakes up the grain, goes on for a week and then is stopped by toasting the barley. The germinated and toasted grain is called "malt." The malt is transferred into a big copper kettle, mixed with water, and heated. The starch in the malt changes to sugar. Hops, which are the leaves of a vine, are added to give flavor and help preserve the beer. The solids are filtered out and the remaining liquid is called "wort." The wort is mixed with a special yeast that converts the sugar in the wort to alcohol, the result is beer. The young beer rests in a storage tank for four to six weeks, at which time it's old enough to have its own bottle.

The main reason that beer has been so popular for so long in so many parts of the world is that for many people beer was the only safe thing to drink. The open water found in lakes and rivers was highly polluted, and though no one knew about bacteria as such, they knew from experience that the water was dangerous. Experience also taught them that beer was safe, and the cause is quite simple. During the beer-making process the water used to make the beer is boiled, which kills the dangerous bacteria. In addition, the alcohol formed during fermentation destroys even more bacteria. Beer was safe, while water could have killed you.

◆

VEGETABLES AND SALADS

SAUTÉED EGGPLANT WITH BASIL
THE GRAND FORMOSA REGENT HOTEL ◆ TAIPEI, TAIWAN

MAKES 4 SERVINGS

1 cup vegetable oil
1 large eggplant, cut into
  bite-size pieces (6 cups)
½ cup scallions, cut into
  1-inch strips
2 cloves garlic, minced
1 red bell pepper, coarsely
  chopped
½ teaspoon hot chili flakes,
  or 2 small hot red chilies,
  cut into thin strips
¼ cup soy sauce
2 cups basil leaves, or
  spinach leaves, lightly
  packed

The vegetarian diet of Buddhist monks may have gotten started out of necessity, or it may have originated in the Buddhist philosophy of responsibility to all living things. Most likely it was a little bit of both. The result, however, is that the kitchens of Buddhist temples have some of the world's best vegetarian cooking. An example of the style is this dish of sautéed eggplant with basil.

1.   In a wok or large high-sided sauté pan, heat the oil until just shimmering. Add the eggplant and fry for 30 seconds. Remove the eggplant from the oil, and remove all but 2 teaspoons of the oil from the wok.

2.   Reheat the wok. Add the scallions, garlic, red bell pepper, and hot chili flakes and stir-fry for 1 minute. Return the eggplant to the wok and continue stir-frying for 1 minute. Add the soy sauce and stir-fry for 30 seconds. Add the basil or spinach and stir-fry for 1 minute. Pour the wok's contents into a serving bowl.

ABOUT EGGPLANT

The eggplant is a native of southeastern Asia, where it has been cultivated for over 4,000 years. It probably got its start somewhere near, or actually in India, and moved east from there to China. It shows up in Chinese paintings and recipes somewhere around 600 B.C. and was a common ingredient in cooked dishes. It was also eaten raw as a fruit. In the thirteenth century it became one of the foods that were specifically recommended as an offering at the shrines of royal Chinese ancestors. It was also used as a cosmetic. At the time it was fashionable for Chinese women of social standing to stain their teeth black. The skin of the eggplant was often used to do the job. At some point about 1,500 years ago, Arab traders brought it from Asia to the Mediterranean area, and the Spanish appear to have been the first Europeans to take any real interest in cooking eggplant.

Most of the eggplant dishes that we see in North America today come from countries that border on the Mediterranean Sea. The French like to slice eggplant and grill it, or make it into ratatouille. Whatever the eggplant recipe, it usually tastes better if you start with young thin plants. As they get bigger and older they lose their best texture and taste.

ABOUT BUDDHISM

The people of Taiwan have managed to blend together three philosophies and an assortment of folk religions in order to produce a body of beliefs and customs to satisfy the spiritual needs of the community. Two of these systems, Taoism and Confucianism, were developed in China during the sixth century B.C. The third, Buddhism, also began in the sixth century B.C. but was imported to China from India.

Buddhism is based on the life and teachings of Siddhārtha Gautama. Siddhārtha is thought to have been born about 550 B.C. in a small town in Nepal. He was a local prince and lived in great luxury. In his late twenties he left his family and their palace in search of spiritual enlightenment. For years he wandered the countryside, avoiding all material comforts. At one point he began a long meditation under a fig tree and eventually found the enlightenment for which he had been searching. From then on he was known as the Buddha, the Enlightened One, and he traveled about teaching his philosophy.

His teachings center around the Four Noble Truths. The first truth is that all existence contains elements of suffering. The second states that the cause of the suffering is desire. The third suggests that the way to put an end to the suffering is to put an end to desire; this also leads to enlightenment. And finally, the fourth truth is that the path to enlightenment is available to everyone. Buddha rejected the difficult life of an ascetic, but he also opposed the pursuit of pleasure for its own sake. He recommended what he called "the Middle Way."

The same trade routes that brought Chinese spices, silks, and pottery to the West brought Buddhist monks to China. For centuries, Buddhist monks had been vegetarians; they introduced vegetarianism as a formal style of gastronomy to China, although the idea of a mostly vegetable diet had been around in China for a long time. The vegetarian diet came about out of simple necessity. China has always been short on land for cattle, and poultry and fish were not easy to come by. So vegetables were always on top of the shopping list.

These days there is a continual stream of scientific research clearly indicating that a diet high in vegetables is better for our overall health. The general rule is that 50 percent of our daily calories should come from complex carbohydrates in the form of fruits and vegetables. And Buddha knew it all along.

◆

ABOUT CHINESE FOOD AND THE SUNG DYNASTY

The Sung emperors ruled China from the middle 900s to the end of the 1200s. It was an era of peace and prosperity, which gave the royal families an opportunity to devote a considerable amount of their time and money to food and drink. Thousands of people worked in the imperial kitchens and produced meals that offered hundreds of different dishes; and this was going on everyday. Not only did these workers do the cooking for the royal family, their guests, and the supporting staff, but they also prepared the dishes that were offered at the temples to appease the gods and honored ancestors.

If, as it is often said, the choice is between guns and butter, a period of peace can easily increase your cholesterol level. That seemed to be the case with the Sungs. Their capital was in the middle of one of the best agricultural areas in China and right next to the port of Shanghai. If you could catch it, raise it, grow it, or import it, the chefs at the Sung court were interested. The Sung period was also the time when the first Chinese cookbook was published that described specific quantities for the ingredients. It was written by a Madame Wu, and because the Chinese had already invented printing, it had a quite reasonable distribution.

It was during the last years of the Sung Dynasty that Marco Polo showed up in China and took note of what was going on in the Asian kitchen. His accounts give us a second and confirming opinion as to the opulence of Chinese food at the time. After the Sung rulers came the Ming Dynasty and they made everything bigger and better. They even established a ministerial position to oversee court banquets. This was also the time that trade with European nations began to pick up. Spanish and Portuguese ships sailed into the neighborhood and introduced a whole new collection of ingredients, including potatoes, corn, and chili. The fact that the hot dishes of China, especially those from Hunan and Szechwan, were seasoned with chilies that were brought by European explorers, was quite a surprise to me. All those flaming hot peppers came from South and Central America and were dragged around the world by European traders.

DUTCH PEPPERS
AMSTEL INTER-CONTINENTAL ◆ AMSTERDAM, HOLLAND

MAKES 4 SERVINGS

6 red bell peppers, roasted
  and peeled
2 tablespoons vegetable oil
1 cup chopped onions
2 cups chopped, seeded
  tomatoes
2 teaspoons chopped garlic
¼ cup water
1 cup carrots julienne
1 cup leeks julienne
1 cup celery julienne
1 cup fennel julienne
4 medium mushrooms,
  sliced
1 cup chopped scallions
1 teaspoon dried tarragon
1 tablespoon chopped fresh
  cilantro leaves
Salt and freshly ground
  black pepper, to taste

The farmers of Holland have developed a large business based on the growing of top-quality vegetables. Much of the farming actually takes place in huge greenhouses where the quality of the environment can be carefully controlled. These farms are particularly well known for their sweet bell peppers, which are produced in dozens of different colors. The chefs at the Amstel Inter-Continental regularly take advantage of this excellent produce.

1. Cut off the 2 widest sides of each bell pepper. Reserve the 12 squares; roughly chop the remaining parts of the peppers.

2. In a small saucepan over medium heat, warm 1 tablespoon of the vegetable oil. Add the chopped bell peppers, onions, tomatoes, garlic, and water. Cover and simmer for 7 minutes, or until the onions are translucent. Allow to cool for 10 minutes. Puree the mixture in a blender until smooth. Set aside.

3. Preheat the oven to 350° F.

4. In a large sauté pan over medium-high heat, warm 2 teaspoons of the remaining vegetable oil and sauté the vegetables, stirring constantly, until they begin to soften, about 2 minutes. Remove from the heat, and stir in the seasonings.

5. Coat a large oven-proof baking dish with the remaining teaspoon of oil. Place 4 squares of bell pepper onto the baking dish. Spoon about 1 tablespoon of the vegetable mixture onto each square and top each one with another square of pepper. Repeat the procedure and top each one with the remaining squares of pepper.

6. Bake for 5 minutes, or until the peppers are heated through. Serve at once, drizzled with some of the pureed sauce.

ABOUT AMSTERDAM'S STREET FOODS

Each city around the world has its own customary street foods. Eating them as you move about the town has become almost a ritual for the citizens. In Amsterdam there are a group of very traditional street foods. Maybe it's because Amsterdam was originally founded some seven hundred years ago by herring fisherman, or maybe it's because the Dutch love herring. Whatever the reason, Amsterdam has dozens of small street stands where people eat herring. The fish is very fresh, lightly salted, cleaned, and served on a paper plate with some chopped onion. The herring is held in the air above your head and eaten bite by bite.

There are also street vendors for french fried potatoes freshly cut and deep-fried right in front of you. The french fries are served with mayonnaise, a peanut sauce, or ketchup. The third classic street food of Amsterdam is the waffle. Waffles are freshly made by the vendors and served with maple syrup. Although not exactly a street food, Amsterdam is also famous for its licorice. This anise-flavored candy is available in sweet and salty forms and in dozens of different shapes.

WARM FISH SALAD
AMSTEL INTER-CONTINENTAL ◆ AMSTERDAM, HOLLAND

MAKES 4 SERVINGS

2 to 3 cups water
Vegetable oil
1½ pounds firm-fleshed fish
   fillets or shellfish, such as
   swordfish, haddock, tuna,
   snapper, scallops, or
   shrimp
1 bunch spinach, well
   washed, stems removed
   and dried
1 small cucumber, thickly
   sliced
8 asparagus spears,
   steamed
½ red onion, sliced into
   rings, rings separated
1 clove garlic, minced
1 teaspoon Dijon mustard
Salt and freshly ground
   black pepper, to taste
3 tablespoons red wine
   vinegar or balsamic
   vinegar
½ cup olive oil

1. Choose a saucepan with a top rim just large enough to hold a large dinner plate so that most of the bottom surface of the plate is suspended over the pan. Make sure the plate can withstand exposure to hot steam. Bring the water to a boil in the saucepan. Set the dinner plate on top and brush it lightly with oil. Arrange the fish on the plate and invert another dinner plate over the fish to cover the fish completely. Steam the fish for 5 minutes.

2. Meanwhile, assemble the salad: In a large bowl, toss together the vegetables. In a jar, combine the garlic, mustard, salt and pepper, and vinegar. Cover and shake well. Add the olive oil, cover, and shake until thoroughly mixed.

3. Dress the salad greens with some of the dressing and toss to coat. Divide the greens among 4 plates. Place a portion of the fish on each plate and spoon a bit of the remaining vinaigrette on top.

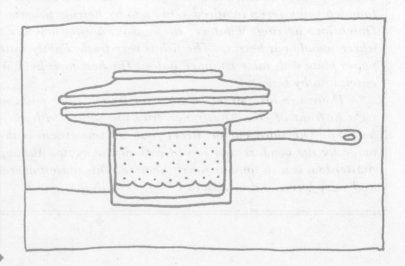

ABOUT THE DUTCH FRUIT AND VEGETABLE AUCTION

One day, back in 1887, a Dutch farmer took a boatload of cauliflower to the town market. He tied up his canal barge next to the market dock and got ready to do some business. However, for some reason or another, cauliflower was not on anyone's menu. To get rid of the stuff as fast as he could, he invented a new form of selling. He announced that the entire load was available for sale. He would start the sale by yelling out a price. Every few seconds he would yell out a lower price until someone took the offer and the cauliflower was sold. The first bid gets it. That is how the Dutch Fruit and Vegetable Auction System was born.

Today the farmer yelling out his ever-decreasing price has been replaced with a computer, and the purchasers have buttons next to their seats to signal their purchase. Farmers bring in their products, which are then checked for quality, a primary responsibility of the system. A particular batch is selected and the auction begins. The buyer wants the price to go down as far as possible, but there is always the danger that a competitive buyer will press his button first, purchase the lot, and force you to go home without the product that you need.

ABOUT SEATTLE'S PIKE PLACE MARKET

Seattle's Pike Place Market opened up in 1907. The basic idea behind the operation was very simple. Local farmers wanted to have a place where they could sell their produce directly to the public without price increases by middlemen. The farmers would get more money for their crops, and consumers would get lower food prices. The idea worked so well that within a few months there were over two hundred farmers renting space. The market continued to expand as a public source for good food, but it also began to develop as a social center. It did particularly well during the Great Depression of the 1930s, when people were looking for both low food prices and a place to hang out. Everything was fine until the end of the Second World War. People started moving to the suburbs and doing their shopping in supermarkets. For a while, it looked like the market area was going to be sold to real estate developers, who had a vision of a modern commercial development. But the people of Seattle wouldn't stand for that. They formed a grass-roots citizens group and started a "Save the Market" campaign. In 1971, the citizens of Seattle voted overwhelmingly to place the market under public ownership with the clear objective of preserving and restoring it to its former glory. I like that; I hope that as I get on in years someone will be interested in preserving and restoring me, too.

VEGETARIAN BURGERS
FOUR SEASONS OLYMPIC HOTEL ◆ SEATTLE, WASHINGTON

Kerry Sear is the executive chef at Seattle's Four Seasons Olympic Hotel. He runs a large staff that produces the meals for the hotel's restaurants, room service, and banquet facilities. And though his menus contain a complete range of foods for guests, at home Kerry's cooking is vegetarian. The following is his recipe for vegetarian burgers.

1. In a large sauté pan over medium-high heat, warm 2 tablespoons of the vegetable oil until hot. Add the onion and garlic and sauté for about 5 minutes, or until the onion is translucent.

2. Stir in the vegetables and herbs. Cook for 5 minutes.

3. Add the rolled oats, stirring thoroughly. Check for seasoning and add salt and pepper.

4. Transfer the mixture to a large bowl, add the mashed potatoes, and mix together thoroughly. Form the mixture into 8 patties.

5. In a large skillet over medium-high heat, heat the remaining 2 tablespoons of oil until it is hot. Fry the patties for about 3 minutes on each side, or until the burgers develop a crust.

Serve on the hamburger buns, with ketchup and mustard, if desired.

MAKES 8 BURGERS

4 tablespoons vegetable oil
1 medium onion, thinly sliced
1 teaspoon minced garlic
1 cup drained canned shredded beets
½ cup grated yellow squash
½ cup grated zucchini
1 cup grated carrots
½ cup grated turnip
1 tablespoon chopped fresh dill
1 tablespoon chopped fresh parsley
1⅓ cups rolled oats
Salt and freshly ground black pepper, to taste
1½ cups cooked mashed potatoes (not too moist)
8 hamburger buns
Ketchup and mustard (optional)

ABOUT WASHINGTON POTATOES

The Native American tribes called it Fire Mountain, and on May 18, 1980, it lived up to its name. After two hundred years of snoozing, Mount St. Helens woke up in a terrible mood and blew its stack. One hundred and fifty square miles of mountain took off and shot up over 60,000 feet into the sky. The eruption caused over $1 billion worth of damage and sent out clouds of ash circulating around the globe. But those clouds of ash had a silver lining for the potato farmers of Washington State: The ash was filled with valuable nutrients for the potatoes grown in the state. The Washington Russet is ideal for baking. It has a dry flesh that comes out fluffy when it's baked or mashed. Russets are also perfect as a thickener in soups and stews as they break up in the liquid and richen the texture.

Potatoes are an extraordinary food. Over 95 percent of their calories come from complex carbohydrates. Scientists are telling us that a diet made up mostly of complex carbos is the healthiest. Potatoes are also packed with vitamins, minerals, and protein. For years I have used baked potatoes as a snack food. I wash off the surface, rub them with a little vegetable oil, and bake them in a 400° F. oven for an hour. At that point, they go into the refrigerator, which will hold them properly for a couple of days. When I want a potato, it goes into the microwave for two minutes, and my low-calorie snack is ready. I have an exercise and diet program that was specifically designed to control my blood pressure. A low-fat, high-potassium food like potatoes is perfect. I don't want to blow my stack like Mount St. Helens.

NIKE STIR-FRIED VEGETABLES AND PASTA
NIKE KITCHENS ◆ BEAVERTON, OREGON

Nike is the number one sports and fitness company in the world, and their primary objective is to maintain that position. Their attitude is reflected in their company slogan: "There is no finish line." Nike corporate headquarters is in Beaverton, Oregon, just outside of Portland. It is an extraordinary facility called the "Nike World Campus." The buildings are named after leading sports figures who have been associated with the company: Michael Jordan, Alberto Salizar, Steven Prefontaine.

Nike's commitment to fitness is not limited to its customers. They are just as deeply interested in the fitness of the employees. To make their point, they have opened the Bo Jackson Sports & Fitness Center. It is one of the most comprehensive corporate health and fitness facilities ever developed and has had a powerful and positive impact on Nike employees. They are happier, more productive, and healthier. Nike's love of fitness also extends to their kitchen. A good example is this dish of stir-fried vegetables and pasta.

1. In a large sauté pan or wok over medium heat, warm the vegetable oil and 1 tablespoon of the sesame oil. Add the ginger and garlic and cook, stirring, for 1 minute.

2. Raise the heat to high, add the vegetables, and cook, stirring, for 5 minutes. Add the sprouts and stir.

3. Add the hoisin sauce, soy sauce, remaining tablespoon of sesame oil, and the water. Stir to blend.

4. Add the cooked spaghetti, toss to combine, and serve.

MAKES 4 SERVINGS

1 tablespoon vegetable oil
2 tablespoons sesame oil
2 teaspoons finely chopped fresh ginger
2 teaspoons finely chopped garlic
6 cups cut-up mixed vegetables, such as carrots, broccoli, scallions, red and yellow bell peppers, zucchini, or yellow squash
1 cup bean sprouts
3 tablespoons hoisin sauce
1 tablespoon soy sauce
1 tablespoon water
¾ pound spaghetti, cooked, drained, and tossed with a little vegetable oil to prevent the strands from sticking together

FUNGI WITH OKRA
GRAND PALAZZO HOTEL ◆ ST. THOMAS, U.S. VIRGIN ISLANDS

MAKES 6 SERVINGS

4 to 5 cups water
1 cup frozen sliced okra,
  thawed
½ cup butter or margarine,
  melted
1½ cups cornmeal
½ teaspoon salt

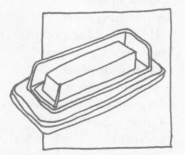

The Danish government took control of the island of St. Thomas in the middle of the 1700s. The old paintings of the town clearly show the Danish flag flying above the roof tops. Today the Danish flag still waves above St. Thomas; the street signs still bear Danish names; and, the port is still a major trading center housed in the original Danish buildings. But when it comes to the island's cooking, it's almost impossible to find a Danish influence, with one possible exception. Unlike most of the islands in the Caribbean, St. Thomas has a series of recipes that use butter, an ingredient that the Danes have always loved. A perfect example of a classic island dish using butter is called "fungi." It's a cornmeal mush that makes an excellent side dish.

1. In a large pot bring the water to a boil. When boiling, add the okra and cook for 2 minutes. Add ¼ cup of the butter or margarine. Slowly, in a thin stream, stir in the cornmeal and continue to cook and stir until a mush is formed and begins to leave the bottom of the pan. Season with salt. This is fungi.

2. Line a small soup bowl with 1½ to 2 teaspoons of the melted butter or margarine. Place 1 cup of the fungi into the bowl and swirl it around until all sides are smooth and rounded. Repeat this process 5 more times. Turn out onto plates and serve immediately.

◆

WILTED SPINACH SALAD
HOTEL 1829 ◆ ST. THOMAS, U.S. VIRGIN ISLANDS

The Hotel 1829 sits atop a small hill in the middle of Charlotte Amalie, which is the main town on the U.S. Virgin Island of St. Thomas. It has a small number of guest rooms, but it is best known for its restaurant and bar, both of which offer magnificent views of the harbor. The following recipe is prepared table side, and is so good that it can actually distract you momentarily from the vista.

1. In a serving bowl, toss together the spinach, onion, and mushrooms. Sprinkle with Parmesan cheese over the top.

2. In a sauté pan, melt the butter over medium-low heat. Mix in the mustard, bacon, brandy, and Cointreau. Heat this mixture for a minute, then carefully light the surface with a long match. The alcohol will flame off within the next minute; the Cointreau and brandy flavor will remain.

3. When the flame has gone out, stir in the lemon juice, oil, vinegar, and pepper.

4. Pour the hot dressing over the salad. Turn the sauté pan over the salad bowl as a lid, and hold it there for 1 minute. This will help wilt the spinach and warm the cheese.

5. Mix the salad and serve immediately.

MAKES 4 TO 6 SERVINGS

One 10-ounce bunch fresh spinach, washed carefully and trimmed of stems
1 red onion, thinly sliced
1 cup thinly sliced mushrooms
½ cup freshly grated Parmesan cheese
1 tablespoon unsalted butter
2 tablespoons Dijon-style mustard
4 strips cooked bacon, crumbled
3 ounces brandy
1½ ounces Cointreau liqueur
Juice of ½ lemon
⅓ cup vegetable oil
3 tablespoons red wine vinegar
Freshly ground black pepper, to taste

◆

Honey-Glazed Pork Salad
THE OBSERVATORY HOTEL ◆ SYDNEY, AUSTRALIA

MAKES 6 SERVINGS

One 1-inch piece fresh
    ginger, peeled and sliced
1 clove garlic, minced
2 teaspoons juniper berries
    (optional)
2 tablespoons honey
1 tablespoon soy sauce
¼ cup orange juice
2 scallions, minced
1 pound boneless pork loin
2 tablespoons vegetable oil
4 cups mixed greens
¼ cup vinaigrette
One 16-ounce can whole
    beets, rinsed and sliced,
    for garnish
One large Granny Smith
    apple, cored and thinly
    sliced, for garnish

1. In a large glass or ceramic dish, combine the ginger; garlic; junipers, if used; honey; soy sauce; orange juice; and scallions. Add the pork and toss to coat. Marinate at room temperature for 6 hours or overnight.

2. Preheat the oven to 400° F.

3. Scrape the excess marinade from the surface of the pork. Strain the marinade through a fine sieve and reserve both solid and liquid portions.

4. In a large sauté pan over high heat, warm the oil. When pan is hot, add the pork and cook for 3 to 5 minutes on all sides, until golden. Add the solids from the marinade. Cook, stirring, until nicely browned. Add ¼ cup of the reserved marinade. Place the pork in the oven and cook for 20 minutes, or until the pork reaches 170° F. internal temperature. Remove from the oven to a cutting board and let the pork rest for 10 minutes.

5. Toss the mixed greens with the vinaigrette, and garnish each plate with beets and apples.

6. Thinly slice the pork and lay on top of the salad greens.

A BRIEF INTRODUCTION TO THE HISTORY OF SYDNEY

In general, it's good to be king, but certain times are clearly better than others. If you were a European monarch, the last twenty-five years of the 1700s would not have been your favorite period. The ideas that resulted in the French Revolution were being spread all over and eventually led to thousands of royal folks having their heads cut off. A truly revolting idea to a king. There were also the British colonies in America, filled with more revolting people. The upper crust in England concluded that there was a dangerous and criminal class on their island nation and decided that the best thing to do was to ship them to some other part of the world before they caused even more trouble. For decades they shipped their convicts to the colonies in North America. But the American Revolution in 1776 put an end to that location. English jails began to fill up. The government was getting desperate. Then someone had what appeared to be a great idea. Let's transport the criminals to Australia, wherever that is.

In 1770, the English explorer, Captain Cook, had bumped into Australia, hung up a flag, and claimed the east coast for England under the name of New South Wales. No one in London actually had any idea of what New South Wales was really like, but that was just a detail. It was definitely far enough away to keep the troublemakers off the court. So, a fleet of eleven ships carrying 1,350 men, women, and children set sail. Eight months and one week later they arrived at Botany Bay. On Saturday evening, January 26, 1788, they flew the British flag over a spot they called Sydney Cove, and the history of the new colony was underway.

During the next fifty years, 80,000 convicts were shipped there. Another 70,000 people came over on their own to see if they could make a better life for themselves. During the 1850s, Sydney publicized the discovery of gold and thousands of people rushed in. Actually, the government had known about the gold fields for a long time; it just never told anyone. The government thought the news would attract a bad element to the neighborhood. But England had stopped shipping over convicts and the colony needed more people, so the powers that be let the word out about the gold. In ten years, the population of Sydney doubled, and the growth of the city has never stopped.

In 1932, the Sydney Harbor Bridge was opened and the northern part of the area began to develop. The bridge is called the "old coat hanger." After the Second World War, tens of thousands of immigrants came over from Europe and totally changed the city. It went from an isolated outpost of England to a vibrant cosmopolitan metropolis.

◆

BURT WOLF

MANY SMALLER MEALS ARE BETTER THAN THREE LARGE MEALS

Researchers are telling us that it is better for our health to eat five or six smaller meals a day instead of eating two or three large meals. When you think about it, it's quite natural. When we hunted and gathered our food, we ate small amounts throughout the day. It's the way we were set up for millions of years. Find it, eat it. Only when we developed a more industrial lifestyle did we set up a breakfast, lunch, and dinner mentality. Three big meals are fine for industry but not so fine for good health. Try and follow the advice of the nutritional experts. Smaller amounts of food spread out throughout the day. It's better for you.

◆

ABOUT COOKING BEANS

Beans are actually the seeds of plants in the legume family. There are about a dozen major varieties that have been grown all over the world for thousands of years. Beans are a rich source of iron, the B vitamins, and are packed with dietary fiber. Nutritionists at the American Dietetic Association suggest that we increase our intake of beans because they contain valuable nutrients and are very low in fat. When you are shopping for beans in the market, remember that dried beans are more nutritious than those that are canned or frozen.

Preparing dried beans is relatively simple. Sort through the beans and make sure that no pebbles or twigs have come along from the harvest. Place the beans in a large pot and cover them with water. The water should come up at least two inches over the beans. Bring the water to a boil, cover, and cook for two minutes. Then, uncover and let the beans soak for one hour. This is a better system than letting the beans soak overnight, because more of the nutrients are saved this way. Afterward, drain off the old water. Cover the beans with fresh water and let the beans simmer for thirty-five minutes, or until they are tender. That's it. Put those beans together with some whole-grain brown rice and you have a nutritional package with the same quality protein that you would find in meat, fish, or poultry.

◆

DESSERTS

BLUEBERRY PURSES
DON SHULA'S ♦ MIAMI LAKES, FLORIDA

MAKES 4 SERVINGS

2 tablespoons butter or
  margarine
1 cup fresh blueberries
Pinch ground allspice
Pinch ground cloves
Grated zest of 1 orange
¼ cup fresh orange juice
½ teaspoon cornstarch
  dissolved in 1 tablespoon
  cold water
5 sheets phyllo dough
2 tablespoons melted butter
  or margarine
2 teaspoons granulated
  sugar mixed with ½
  teaspoon ground
  cinnamon
¼ cup Mascarpone cheese
  or cream cheese
Confectioners' sugar, for
  dusting (optional)

For over twenty years Don Shula has been the coach of the Miami Dolphins. He has led the team to over 300 victories and is the "winningest" coach in the NFL . . . and still on active duty. But he's not just a coach, he's a culinarian with two restaurants in Miami Lakes, Florida. The first to open was Shula's Steak House, and now there is Shu's All-Star Cafe. The theme of the café is "the winning edge," and the Historical Association of South Florida has put together a collection of winning moments in South Florida sports to decorate the walls. One of the restaurant's most popular desserts is called a Blueberry Purse.

1. In a sauté pan over medium heat, melt the butter or margarine. Stir in the blueberries, allspice, cloves, orange zest, orange juice, and the cornstarch mixture. Simmer, stirring occasionally, for 6 minutes. Spread the blueberry mixture onto a plate and refrigerate for at least 1 hour.

2. Preheat the oven to 375° F. Very lightly grease a baking sheet with butter or margarine.

3. Lay out one sheet of phyllo dough on a flat surface. Brush it lightly with some of the melted butter or margarine. Continue layering and brushing 3 more sheets of dough. Set the top sheet in place, but do not coat with butter. Cut the layered stack of dough lengthwise and width-wise to make 4 equal rectangular quarters.

♦

4. Sprinkle the center of each rectangle of dough with a quarter of the cinnamon and sugar mixture. Mound 1 table-spoon of the cheese on top of the cinnamon and sugar. Spoon a quarter of the blueberry mixture over the cheese. Shape the dough around the filling to make a small purse, twisting the top to seal well. (The purses may be assembled beforehand and refrigerated for baking at a later time. Place them close to-gether in an airtight container and cover well to prevent the pastry from drying out.)

5. Place the purses on the prepared baking sheet and bake for 10 minutes, or until the dough is lightly browned. Sprinkle with the confectioners' sugar, if desired.

ABOUT BLUEBERRIES

Blueberries have been growing in North America for thousands of years. Native American tribes believed that the berries were a gift from heaven, sent down to earth to ease the hunger of children during an ancient period of famine. The Native Americans point to the star on the top of the blueberry as a reminder of that legend.

Over 95 percent of the world's blueberry crop comes from the United States, and blueberries are becoming more and more popular. They are probably the easiest fruit to prepare and serve. You need not peel, pit, core, or cut them. Just give them a quick rinse and chew. They're my kind of food.

From a nutritional point of view, they are a joy, having only forty calories in a half-cup serving with plenty of vitamin C and potassium. There is no salt and less than half a gram of fat, which makes them virtually fat-free. We are continuing to see more and more research that indicates that increasing the amounts of fresh fruits and fresh vegetables in our diets is one of the best ways to improve our health.

APPLE-ROSEMARY SHORTCAKES
THE HERBFARM ◆ FALL CITY, WASHINGTON

MAKES 6 SERVINGS

SHORTCAKES

1 cup all-purpose flour
¾ tablespoon baking
  powder
1½ tablespoons chopped
  fresh rosemary
¼ teaspoon salt
½ teaspoon granulated
  sugar
3 tablespoons butter
½ cup heavy cream
1 egg, separated
1 tablespoon packed dark
  brown sugar

APPLES

¾ cup granulated sugar
3 tablespoons butter
3 large tart apples, peeled,
  halved, and cored
3 rosemary sprigs, plus 6
  more, for garnish
  (optional)
6 tablespoons heavy cream
3 cups vanilla ice cream,
  softened

1. To make the shortcakes: In the bowl of an electric mixer fitted with a pastry blender, combine the dry ingredients and butter. Blend until just combined, then add the cream and egg yolk and continue to mix until the dough comes together in a ball.

2. Turn the dough out onto a lightly floured surface and roll to ½-inch thickness. Cut into twelve 3-inch rounds. Place 6 rounds on a lightly buttered and floured sheet pan. Freeze remaining rounds for a later use.

3. Brush the rounds with the reserved egg white and sprinkle with the brown sugar. Chill for 30 minutes. Meanwhile, preheat the oven to 375° F.

4. Bake the rounds for 20 minutes, until lightly golden. Remove from the oven and cool completely. Keep the oven on.

5. For the apples: In a medium-size oven-proof sauté pan over medium heat, add the granulated sugar. Cook the sugar until it turns to a caramel color and consistency, 3 to 5 minutes. Add the butter, apple halves, and rosemary sprigs. Place the pan in the oven and bake for 15 minutes. Turn the apples to the second side and bake for an additional 15 minutes, or until the apples are tender. Transfer the cooked apples to a platter, cover with foil, and keep warm. Return the pan to the top of the stove and stir in the heavy cream. Strain the sauce through a fine meshed sieve into a small bowl and keep warm.

◆

6. To assemble, slice the cooled shortcakes in half horizontally. Place half of the shortcake on a plate, place an apple half on top of the half shortcake. Top with ½ cup softened vanilla ice cream and spoon on some of the reserved sauce. Top with the other half of shortcake. Garnish with a rosemary sprig, if desired.

ABOUT STARBUCKS IN SEATTLE

If you wanted to try and find a reason for Seattle's passion for coffee, you might look at a number of factors. Seattle has a rather gray climate which tends to keep people indoors, stimulating themselves with hot coffee. You might give some credit to the large number of Seattle's creative artists who like to hang out in coffeehouses. But the most important element in the passionate relationship of Seattle to coffee is a company called Starbucks. It was started in Seattle in 1971 as a small coffee-roasting company with a few retail outlets serving freshly roasted coffee. Today, it is America's leading importer and roaster of specialty coffee with over 230 company-owned stores, making it the largest coffee retailer in North America. The company is run by a man named Howard Schultz, who seems to have perfectly brewed coffee running through his veins.

HOW WE CAME TO BE A NATION OF COFFEE DRINKERS

The United States has an interesting story when it comes to coffee. During the 1700s, London's drink of choice was clearly coffee. The town had over two thousand coffeehouses and drank more coffee than any other city. Consequently, the first English colonists to arrive in the New World came with a love of coffee. Boston opened its first coffeehouse in 1670 and waited twenty years before it opened a tearoom. The consumption of tea, however, kept increasing, and for one very simple reason. At the time, tea was much cheaper than coffee. Ultimately, economics turned England and its American colonies into tea drinkers, until the American Revolution of 1776. Of all of the taxes that England had placed on their American colonies, none was more offensive to the general public than the tax on tea. Eventually that frustration boiled over into the Boston Tea Party, and shortly thereafter, a general boycott of tea by the patriotic colonial housewife. Ships that were heading to colonial ports and carrying tea were scared off with stories about the violence in Boston. Eventually, the Congress passed a resolution against the drinking of tea. At that point, we began our national switch to coffee.

The history of how people eat and drink, however, clearly shows that politics rarely changes our diet. On the other hand, price is a powerhouse and constantly alters our eating patterns. When the Revolutionary War was over, we went right back to drinking tea because, once again, it was cheaper. Then, during the War of 1812, the price of tea went through the roof. Consequently, we went back to drinking coffee. Only this time, the coffee was coming up from South America and was not at all expensive. When the War of 1812 was over, tea began returning to American ports. But instead of coming from experienced English tea companies, the tea was coming from American shippers who were interested in tonnage, not taste. Most of the tea coming into the United States was inferior. The coffee coming in from Latin America, however, was excellent. Why drink a cup of terrible tea, when you could have a cup of exceptional coffee and for less money? That was when, and to a great extent why, America became a nation of coffee drinkers. We drink over a half-billion cups each day.

During the second half of the 1800s, a conflict arose between the eating habits of the Italian immigrants to North America and the scientific community of the time. Researchers began to develop a series of theories about the relationship between what people eat and drink, and their overall well-being. The scientists began to teach these theories to the general public as if they were new scientific truths. They had a few interesting ideas. They thought that tomatoes were poisonous and could cause cancer. Fruits and vegetables were made up almost completely of water and practically useless in terms of nutrition, especially green vegetables; they were the worst. If you ate different foods together at the same meal, for instance, a meat, a vegetable, and a grain all at the same time, you were stressing your body's digestive system to the point of danger. Having meat loaf, mashed potatoes, and carrots on one plate was virtually flirting with death. Finally, garlic was the last straw. To eat garlic was clearly a self-inflicted wound punishable by court-martial.

What a fabulous place to move to, especially if you happened to be a southern Italian immigrant. Your new government was telling you not to eat what you loved, what your heart told you was good for you, and even more important, what your mother told you was good for you. Well, it has taken over a hundred years, but the Italian immigrant cooks have finally been vindicated. Almost everything they believed was good for you turned out to be just that.

PLUM PUDDING
LILIANFELS ♦ BLUE MOUNTAINS, AUSTRALIA

MAKES 16 SERVINGS

2 cups dried currants
3 cups raisins
1 cup chopped dried
    apricots
1 cup blanched, sliced
    almonds
½ cup dark rum or orange
    juice
1 pound (4 sticks) plus 2
    tablespoons unsalted
    butter, at room
    temperature
1 cup light or dark brown
    sugar
½ cup dark Karo syrup
8 eggs
1 tablespoon ground
    cinnamon
1 tablespoon ground
    allspice
Grated zest of 2 medium
    lemons
1 teaspoon salt
3 cups self-rising flour

The Blue Mountains just outside Sydney, Australia, were an obstacle that prevented access to the west, until the construction of the railroad in the 1860s. The railroad transported the wealthy people of Sydney to the area and they began to build country homes. Perhaps the most beautiful of these homes was Lilianfels. It was constructed as the summer residence of Sydney's chief justice, Sir Frederick Darley, and named after his daughter Lilian. Today it is a graceful and elegant guest house. The original residence area has been restored as the setting for Darley's Restaurant. Chef Ralph Potter presides over the kitchen. The following is his recipe for traditional Plum Pudding.

1. Preheat the oven to 375° F.

2. In a large mixing bowl, combine the currants, raisins, apricots, and almonds. Stir in the rum or orange juice and set aside.

3. In another large mixing bowl, beat together 1 pound of the butter, the brown sugar, and the Karo syrup. Add the eggs, cinnamon, allspice, and lemon zest and beat until well mixed. Add the salt and flour and beat well. Add the plumped fruit and mix together thoroughly.

4. Using the remaining 2 tablespoons of butter, lightly butter sixteen 6-ounce pudding molds and one side of sixteen 3-inch squares of parchment paper. Divide the mixture equally among the molds. Bang each mold on the work surface to settle the mixture. Top each pudding with a square of the parchment paper, buttered side down.

5. Place the puddings in a large roasting pan, set the pan on the middle rack of the oven, and add hot water to the pan to reach halfway up the sides of the puddings. Bake for 1 hour, until a toothpick inserted in the center of a pudding comes out clean. Remove from the molds and serve hot.

Ralph Potter.

ABOUT AUSTRALIAN WINE

When the first fleet arrived in Sydney Cove in 1788, the settlers brought with them the first vines to be planted in Australia. The vines had weathered the voyage without difficulty and were planted soon after the fleet came into port. The vines grew rather well in the fertile areas near the coast. The long hours of warm Australian sun produced ripe grapes, which in turn produced excellent wines. In fact, the wines were so good that when they were entered in a wine-judging competition in Europe, the judges refused to rate them. The judges thought the wines were too good and accused the Australians of putting French wine in bottles with Australian labels. They would probably make the same mistake today. The Australian wine industry is topnotch, and one of the reasons for the high quality is the dedication of the country's early wine makers.

One of the first wine makers was Dr. Henry John Lindeman. Dr. Lindeman had been a medical officer with the British navy and immigrated to Australia in the mid-1800s. He had come to the conclusion that wine was a source of great happiness to all mankind and decided to start making his own. My kind of doctor. These days Lindeman wines are some of the finest, and they are produced in the Hunter Valley just north of Sydney.

RUMMED BANANAS
EL SAN JUAN HOTEL ◆ SAN JUAN, PUERTO RICO

MAKES 4 SERVINGS

2 cups granulated sugar
2 tablespoons butter
¼ cup light rum
¼ cup heavy cream
2 bananas, peeled, halved
   lengthwise and then
   crosswise
1 quart vanilla ice cream

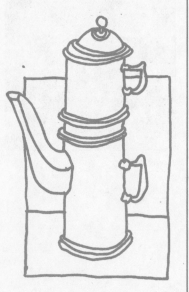

For almost 500 years rum has been the most important distilled alcoholic drink in Puerto Rico. It has been a major item of export from the very beginning of its manufacture. Puerto Rican rums are lighter in both color and intensity than many of the other rums of the Caribbean. That has helped Puerto Rican rums gain a worldwide popularity over the past 20 years. As a drink its fame is legendary, but it is also a basic part of many recipes, especially in the area of desserts. Chef John Carey of the El San Juan Hotel uses rum to make the sauce for a dish that is clearly Puerto Rico's answer to Bananas Foster of New Orleans.

1.   In a small, heavy saucepan over high heat, stir the sugar constantly with a wooden spoon until it melts and caramelizes to a rich brown color, about 8 minutes.

2.   Add the butter and stir vigorously to combine it with the sugar. Add the rum and then the cream, stirring vigorously to incorporate.

3.   Add the bananas and stir to coat with the sauce. Spoon portions over vanilla ice cream and serve at once.

ABOUT PUERTO RICO AND MOLASSES

It was during Columbus's second voyage to the New World in 1493 that he first set foot on the island of Puerto Rico. That was also the voyage during which he brought sugarcane to the Caribbean. He brought it from the Canary Islands, which are in the Atlantic just off the coast of Africa. By 1515 the Spanish colonists on Puerto Rico had planted fields of sugarcane and were very busy building up a sugar export business. Sugar was a rather new commodity in Europe and the demand for it was very high, as were the profits of the owners of sugar plantations.

The process of turning sugarcane into sugar is fairly straight forward. The juice of the cane is pressed out and boiled down to a concentrate. The concentrate is spun around and centrifugal force causes the sugar crystals to form. The crystals are removed and what is left is a thick, brown syrup called "molasses." During the American colonial period molasses was a major export from the Caribbean to the colonies. It was an important sweetener at the time and much cheaper than white sugar. Today we have three grades of molasses: First boil is the finest and used as a table sweetener; second boil is darker and less sweet; and the third form is called blackstrap and is very dark. Molasses is an excellent sweetener in baking recipes that use baking soda. It acts as a natural preservative that helps keep cakes and cookies moist for long periods of time.

FROM MOLASSES TO RUM

Columbus's introduction of sugarcane to Puerto Rico has had the longest standing impact on the economy of the island. The production of sugar as a commodity for export has come and gone, but a by-product of sugar refining has become a permanent and important part of Puerto Rican business. It was during the early 1500s that the owners of the Puerto Rican sugar plantations noticed that when the sugar was extracted from the cane, the molasses that was left over had a natural tendency to ferment into a kind of wine. Yeast in the air turns the sugar in the molasses into alcohol. The Spanish understood the process of distillation and so they boiled the molasses and produced rum.

For decades, rum was the most important distilled drink in the American colonies. Not only did we import it from the Caribbean, but we had major rum-producing facilities of our own throughout New England. Only when the British introduced the taxation of sugar and molasses did Americans reduce their rum drinking as part of the American Revolution. But these days the popularity of rum is returning. U.S. federal legislation encouraged the development of the Puerto Rican rum industry, and today Puerto Rico is the home of the world's largest producers of rum.

◆

Sesame Walnuts
THE GRAND FORMOSA REGENT HOTEL ◆ TAIPEI, TAIWAN

1. In a wok or large sauté pan, over high heat, bring 3 cups of water to the boil. Add the walnuts and cook for 1 minute. Drain the nuts from the water and pour the water out of the wok.

2. Return the wok to the heat and over high heat, bring ½ cup of water to the boil. Add the nuts. Add one cup of the sugar. Cook and stir until almost all of the water has evaporated. Remove the nuts from the wok and drain them away from any remaining water.

3. Over high heat, warm the empty wok. Return the nuts to the wok. Add the remaining cup of sugar and 1 tablespoon of water. Stir-fry for 2 minutes. Remove the nuts from the wok.

4. In the wok, over medium heat, heat the vegetable oil. Add the nuts and deep-fry for 2 minutes. Drain the nuts from the oil and place them into a mixing bowl. Blend in the sesame seeds.

MAKES 2 CUPS

2 cups shelled walnuts
2 cups sugar
2 cups vegetable oil
2 tablespoons sesame seeds

Thousand-Mile Eyes.

The Ming Dynasty of China began in the middle of the 1300s and ran for almost three hundred years. It was one of the great periods in Chinese history. Artists, writers, poets, and scientists were supported by the Ming rulers. Their works produced one of the golden ages of Chinese culture. By the early 1600s, however, the administration had became totally self-serving and corrupt. At the same time, their Manchu neighbors to the northeast developed a well-trained and efficient army. When the Manchu forces attacked, the Ming defenses disintegrated. The troops were totally destroyed or forced to retreat to the south.

The last great Ming defender was a war-lord named Cheng Ch'eng-kung. With an army of over 100,000 men he tried to hold back the Manchu advance. But by 1661 he was forced to abandon the mainland and move his troops to the island of Taiwan. Taiwan, however, was a major trading post for the Dutch, who controlled the area from Fort Zeelandia. Under the theory that "This town ain't big enough for both of us," Cheng Ch'eng-Kung laid siege to the fort. The battle lasted for two years, at which point the Dutch were compelled to surrender, and Cheng Ch'eng-Kung took control of Taiwan.

When Cheng Ch'eng-Kung arrived in Taiwan, he brought his army, as well as hundreds of writers, artists, teachers, monks, and cooks. He did everything possible to preserve the best of the Chinese culture and the lifestyle that had flourished during the Ming period. It is quite amazing, but virtually the same story was repeated some three hundred years later when Chiang Kai-shek moved over 2 million people from the mainland in 1948 in order to avoid the Communists. Once again, Taiwan is the repository of ancient Chinese culture and cuisine.

◆

CHOCOLATE ROLL
FOUR SEASONS HOTEL ◆ TORONTO, CANADA

1. In a microwave oven or the top of a double boiler, melt the chocolate with the butter until just melted. Remove from the heat, add the sugar, and stir until smooth.

2. Stir in the cookies, dried fruit, nuts, and raisins and mix until well coated and combined.

3. Spread out an 18-inch-long sheet of plastic wrap on a work surface. Spoon out the chocolate mixture in a long mound, situating it about 2 inches from the bottom edge of the plastic wrap. Pat the mixture with your fingers to compact it into a long, 2-inch tube of chocolate, and tightly roll it up in the plastic wrap. Fold in the ends to cover completely.

4. Set the roll on a small baking sheet and refrigerate until solid, at least 3 hours.

5. Unwrap the chocolate roll and cut into slices. Serve with ice cream.

MAKES 6 SERVINGS

12 ounces semisweet chocolate, coarsely chopped
¼ cup unsalted butter, cut into bits
¼ cup granulated sugar
½ cup crumbled cookies—your choice
1 cup diced dried fruit, such as cherries or apricots
1 cup shelled pistachio nuts
½ cup coarsely chopped macadamia nuts
½ cup sliced almonds
¾ cup raisins
Ice cream, for serving

CHOCOLATE SOUFFLÉS
HOTEL PLAZA ATHÉNÉE ◆ PARIS, FRANCE

MAKES 6 SERVINGS

8 ounces semisweet
  chocolate
7 tablespoons water
¼ cup butter
4 egg yolks
¼ cup granulated sugar
10 egg whites
Confectioners' sugar, for
  serving (optional)

1. Preheat the oven to 400° F. Lightly butter and sugar 6 individual soufflé molds.

2. Melt the chocolate in a double boiler with the water. Remove from the heat and stir in the butter. Cool to room temperature.

3. Whisk the egg yolks and sugar together until they're a light lemon-yellow color, then add to the chocolate.

4. Beat the egg whites until stiff peaks form. Stir ⅓ of the egg whites into the chocolate mixture to lighten, then gently fold the chocolate into the egg whites.

5. Divide the butter evenly among the molds and bake for 10 minutes. Sprinkle with powdered sugar, if desired, and serve immediately.

ABOUT VEUVE CLICQUOT, THE GREAT LADY OF FRENCH CHAMPAGNE

In 1772, Philippe Clicquot announced that he was going into the wine business. Philippe's family had lived in the district of Champagne since the 1400s and had become prosperous middle-class merchants. It was not unusual for this type of family to be making and selling a little wine from the vineyards on their land. But now Philippe was getting serious about champagne.

In 1778, Philippe's son François became a partner in his father's business. He developed a plan for the expansion of the company through the use of traveling salesmen who would visit any town in Europe where they could get a respectable order. The operations were expanding at a considerable rate when François suddenly died. His widow, who was only twenty-eight at the time, took over the business. What a time it was, too. The Napoleonic wars were under way and Europe was a wreck.

Nobody was interested in ordering champagne and it was almost impossible to deliver it. The English navy was blockading the ports, and the overland roads were unsafe. If by some miracle you got an order and actually delivered it, there was a good chance you would not get paid. It was in this wonderful business climate that Madame Clicquot spent her first years in the company. You've got to love her; she must have been made of steel.

As soon as the war ended and the royal house of France was restored, Madame Clicquot made a shipment of wine to Russia. The Russians loved the quality and very soon Clicquot became a household name. Of course, it was the household of the Czar, but it's always been important to have your name mentioned in places of power.

During the following years Madame Clicquot saw a meteoric rise in profits. In 1819 she wrote a note to her associate that read, "I am forced to reduce all orders received from old friends by half and to refuse any orders from new clients." She increased the distribution of her champagne throughout Europe and purchased key vineyards in order to ensure her supply of grapes. Madame Clicquot died in 1866 at the age of eighty-nine. Today, the champagne is called Veuve Clicquot, and it is literally named after this woman. The word veuve means "widow."

CAKES

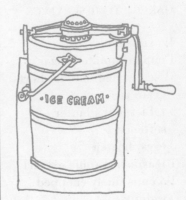

RICE AND WALNUT CAKE
RIHGA ROYAL HOTEL ◆ NEW YORK, NEW YORK

MAKES 8 TO 10 SERVINGS

4¼ cups milk
1 cup granulated sugar
1½ cups medium- or short-
   grain rice
3 tablespoons butter,
   softened
3 eggs, beaten
1 teaspoon vanilla extract
1¼ cups finely chopped
   walnuts
Grated zest of 1 lemon
½ cup chopped mixed
   candied fruit or fruit peel
Sifted confectioners' sugar,
   for dusting

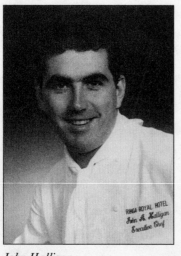

John Halligan.

The great migration of Italians to the United States that occurred in the late 1800s took place only a few years after the unification of Italy into a single nation. The immigrants arriving in this country still thought of themselves as coming from a specific region as opposed to a nation. Accordingly, they cooked the dishes of their old neighborhood using their old neighborhood ingredients. One of the classics is Bologna's rice and walnut cake. The following recipe is from Chef John Halligan at New York's Rihga Royal Hotel.

1. In a large saucepan over medium-high heat, combine the milk and sugar. Bring to a boil, stirring to dissolve the sugar. Stir in the rice and cook, stirring from time to time, until the rice is tender and has absorbed almost all of the milk, 20 to 25 minutes. Set aside to cool to room temperature.

2. Preheat the oven to 400° F. Generously butter a 10-inch-wide baking dish or cake pan.

3. Stir the butter into the rice mixture and mix well. Add the eggs, vanilla, walnuts, lemon zest, and candied fruit or fruit peel and mix well until thoroughly combined.

4. Spoon the mixture into the prepared pan and smooth the top. Bake for 30 to 35 minutes, until lightly browned on top and a toothpick inserted in the center comes out clean.

5. Cool the cake in the pan on a rack. Unmold and serve, sprinkled with the confectioners' sugar.

1810 LEMON SPONGE CAKE
FORT YORK ◆ *TORONTO, CANADA*

Fort York was the defensive garrison for the British-Canadians during the early years of the 1800s. In the spring of 1813 it was also the site of the only meaningful victory that the U.S. forces had in Canada. Today, the reconstructed fort is a teaching museum dealing with early nineteenth-century Canadian life. Tourists and students come from all over to see what was going on in the old days. Part of the Fort York program is devoted to reproducing recipes from the early 1800s. Fiona Lucas is the historical researcher who teaches the techniques. The following recipe is adapted from one that was written in 1810.

1. Preheat the oven to 350° F. Move the top rack to the middle position. Butter a 10-inch (or larger) bundt or tube pan.

2. In a bowl, beat the egg whites until stiff peaks form.

3. In another large bowl, beat the egg yolks. Add the lemon zest, lemon juice, rose water, and sugar and whisk to combine well. Gently whisk the yolk mixture into the beaten egg whites. Add the flour and blend in until just combined.

4. Spoon the batter into the prepared pan and tap gently to level the mixture. Bake for 55 to 60 minutes, until a cake tester comes out clean. Expect the cake to rise above the top of the pan.

5. Cool the cake in the pan on a rack. Loosen the sides, if necessary, and unmold.

MAKES 10 SERVINGS

10 large eggs, separated
Grated zest and juice of 1
  lemon
3 tablespoons rose water, or
  1 tablespoon lemon juice
  diluted in 2 tablespoons
  water
2 cups granulated sugar,
  sifted
3 cups all-purpose flour

NEW YORK CHEESECAKE
TAVERN ON THE GREEN ◆ NEW YORK, NEW YORK

MAKES 12 TO 16 SERVINGS

One 9-ounce box chocolate
  wafer cookies, finely
  crushed
2 pounds cream cheese, at
  room temperature
1½ cups granulated sugar
4 eggs
1 cup sour cream
2 cups heavy cream
Seeds from 2 vanilla beans,
  or ½ teaspoon vanilla
  extract

GARNISHES
¾ cup sour cream
  (optional)
Sliced fresh strawberries
  and/or pureed strawberry
  sauce

Cooks in Europe have been preparing cheesecakes for thousands of years. The ancient Greeks and Romans made them, and they left us the recipes to prove it. There are English cheesecakes and Italian cheesecakes. But it took a group of dairymen of German ancestry working in New York State to come up with cream cheese, the essential ingredient in New York Cheesecake. Here is how New York Cheesecake is prepared by Chef Marc Poidevin at New York's Tavern on the Green Restaurant.

1. Preheat the oven to 300° F. Generously butter the bottom and sides of a 10-inch round baking pan with sides at least 2 inches deep. Press the cookie crumbs onto the bottom and sides of the pan, coating evenly. Set aside.

2. In a large mixing bowl, beat the cream cheese with the sugar until smooth and fluffy. Add the eggs and beat well. Add the sour cream, heavy cream, and vanilla seeds or vanilla extract; beat until well combined and smooth.

3. Set the cookie crumb–lined pan into a larger pan. Carefully pour the mixture into the cookie crumb–lined pan. Place the 2 pans on the top rack of the oven. Add enough hot water to the larger pan to reach halfway up the sides of the baking pan. Bake for 1 hour, or until the top of the cheesecake is lightly browned in spots. The texture will be soft.

4. Remove the cheesecake from the water bath. Set the pan on a wire rack and let the cake cool to room temperature. Cover with plastic wrap and refrigerate until chilled through and set, at least 3 hours or overnight.

5. To serve, spread the sour cream over the top of the cheesecake, if desired. Cut the cake into thin wedges and serve with sliced fresh berries or in a pool of strawberry puree.

FUDGEY RUM-CHOCOLATE CAKE
THE OBSERVATORY HOTEL ◆ SYDNEY, AUSTRALIA

MAKES 10 SERVINGS

8 ounces unsweetened
  chocolate
2 teaspoons instant coffee
2 teaspoons rum
2 tablespoons boiling water
4 eggs
½ teaspoon vanilla extract
2 cups confectioners' sugar
2 tablespoons arrowroot
1 cup heavy cream
One 10-ounce package
  frozen strawberries in
  light syrup, thawed
One pint vanilla ice cream
One pint fresh strawberries

The Observatory Hotel in Sydney, Australia, was based on the design of one of Sydney's historic buildings called the Elizabeth Bay House. The hotel feels like a grand Australian home, luxuriously furnished with Australian antiques, original oil paintings, and fine tapestries. With only 100 guest rooms, there is a feeling of great privacy and personal attention. One of the most popular desserts at the hotel is this Fudgey Rum-Chocolate Cake, made by Sous Chef Anthony Musarra.

1. Preheat the oven to 350° F. Lightly butter and flour an 8-inch round loose-bottomed cake pan.

2. Melt the chocolate and allow it to cool to room temperature, about 15 minutes. Place the melted chocolate into a mixing bowl and blend in the instant coffee, rum, and boiling water.

3. Break the eggs into a second mixing bowl. Whisk in the vanilla extract. In a third bowl, mix the confectioners' sugar with the arrowroot and whisk that mixture into the egg mixture. Using an electric beater, beat the egg mixture until it is about double its original volume, that should take about 4 minutes.

4. In a mixing bowl, beat the heavy cream until it is stiff and stands in peaks. Combine the chocolate mixture with the egg mixture. Then fold in the whipped cream. Pour the mixture into the prepared cake pan, and bake for 1 hour, or until the center of the cake is fully cooked.

◆

5. Remove the pan from the oven and let cool on a rack. Meanwhile, puree the defrosted strawberries in a food processor or blender until you have a sauce.

6. Cut the cake into slices. Place some of the berry sauce on serving plates and shake the plates until you have a thin coating of the sauce covering most of the plate. Put a piece of the cake onto the sauce. Put a scoop of the ice cream on the cake and garnish each slice with the fresh berries.

Anthony Musarra.

ABOUT AUSTRALIAN RUM

In 1793 an American trading ship named The Hope *arrived in Sydney Harbor. On board were supplies that were badly needed by the new settlers. The military officers of the colony saw this as a unique commercial opportunity and formed a group to purchase the ship's entire cargo for resale to the colonists. The cargo included 7,500 gallons of rum. The deal made a fantastic profit for the men, and they decided that their regiment would, from then on, hold a monopoly on rum. In fact, the regiment became so involved in the business of rum that it became known as the "Rum Corps." The Rum Corps soon found itself so wealthy that it issued its own currency, which was actually preferred to the official currency of the government. Of course, rum itself was the best currency of all.*

Rum is made by raising cane, pressing out its juice, boiling down the juice to molasses, and distilling the molasses to rum. There is, however, an exception. In Australia there is a company called Stubbs that makes a rum from the fresh juice of sugarcane, rather than molasses. Stubbs was established as a distillery in 1884, which makes it the oldest distillery in Australia. It produces a very clean, dry, and smooth rum with a distinct flavor.

If you read the book Mutiny on the Bounty, *or saw any one of the three films based on it, you will remember the character of Captain Bligh. Well,* Mutiny on the Bounty *was a true story, but that was only the first mutiny against Captain Bligh. After he survived the revolt led by Mel Gibson or Marlon Brando, depending on which film you saw, he was sent into service again by the King of England. He ended up as the governor of Britain's colony in Australia. When he tried to interfere with the activities of the Rum Corps, he was faced with a second mutiny. The only difference was that this time the men put him in prison instead of casting him adrift. Poor old Bligh . . . he was just not in touch with what was going on, kind of like our federal government.*

◆

ITALIANS INTRODUCED ICE CREAM TO NORTH AMERICA

The Chinese have been making something like ice cream for thousands of years, but it was the cooks of Italy who introduced ice cream to Europe and eventually to the general public in North America. The Italians have been making various forms of ice cream for at least two thousand years. The old Roman emperors loved it. They would send a military runner into the mountains to bring back snow. The cooks mixed the snow with fruits and cream to produce a reasonable facsimile of what we have today. But the story of ice cream in ancient Rome followed a rocky road. If the runners didn't get the ice to the cooks before it melted, they were executed. And you think the guys at Domino's are in a hurry.

George Washington had an ice-cream-making machine, and Thomas Jefferson had his own recipe. But it was up to the Italian immigrants to North America to make it the big deal it is today. The first advertisement for commercially produced ice cream appeared in a New York newspaper on May 12, 1777. The manufacturer was an Italian named Philip Lenzi. More than two hundred years have passed since that first call for ice cream made by an Italian in America, but throughout those two centuries, the Italians have maintained an important roll in the production of this frozen delight. From Sedutto in New York to Ghirardelli in San Francisco, the Italians have garnished their just desserts.

MINT–CHOCOLATE CHIP ICE CREAM CAKE
THE COMPASS ROSE INN ◆ LUNENBURG, NOVA SCOTIA

MAKES 10 TO 12 SERVINGS

2 quarts mint–chocolate
  chip ice cream
1 cup finely crushed
  chocolate wafer cookie
  crumbs
3 tablespoons melted butter
2 tablespoons green crème
  de menthe (optional)

The Irish influence in the Canadian province of Nova Scotia has been there since the mid-1700s, and it's still going strong. Irish traditions are part of the religion, literature, folklore, as well as the food. I always thought that the idea of coloring food green for St. Patrick's Day was a twentieth-century fashion. But the old recipe books in Nova Scotia clearly show that it has been going on since at least the early 1800s.

At the Compass Rose Inn in the town of Lunenburg, Rodger Pike and his wife Suzanne have taken an old recipe from Suzanne's Irish heritage and used it to give new meaning to the St. Patrick's Day idea of "the wearing of the green." It's an ice cream cake and it's, quite frankly, irresistible.

1. Remove the ice cream from the freezer and allow it to soften slightly.

2. In a medium bowl, combine the cookie crumbs and melted butter, tossing until evenly moistened. Press the mixture over the bottom of a 9-inch springform pan.

3. Using a large, sturdy spoon, mix the ice cream until spreadable, but not melted. Spread 1 quart of the ice cream evenly over the cookie crumbs. Drizzle the crème de menthe over the ice cream.

4. Spread the second quart of ice cream over the crème de menthe. Cover with plastic wrap and place the pan in the freezer for at least 3 hours, or overnight.

◆

5. To remove the cake from the pan, warm the blade of a knife with hot water and run it around the perimeter of the cake. Unlatch the springform side and remove.

ABOUT THE IRISH IN NOVA SCOTIA

Halifax, Nova Scotia, on the northeast coast of Canada, was founded by the English in 1749. Shortly thereafter, a law was passed which forbade the immigration of the Irish to the colony. Nevertheless, within ten years, one out of every three people living in Halifax was of Irish ancestry. By the last years of the 1700s the local St. Patrick's Day celebration was attended by His Royal Highness Prince Edward and the anti-Irish laws had disappeared. On August 31, 1843, the Church of Our Lady of Sorrows was erected in a single day. Two thousand parishioners showed up and built the entire structure by dinnertime. A record of the event described the meal that was served at the end of the day's celebration— corned beef, cabbage, soda bread, potatoes, fruit pies, and green pastry cakes.

Today there are tens of thousands of Nova Scotia citizens who are of Irish ancestry and their traditional foods are eaten throughout the community. Besides the potatoes, corned beef, soda bread, and green colored St. Patrick specialties, they were responsible for many of the local beef and pork recipes and the habit of porridge for breakfast.

ABOUT MINT

Mint is one of the most widely used of all aromatic herbs. There are about forty different species of true mint, but the two most important are spearmint and peppermint. Spearmint is thought to be the oldest and may be the type of mint described in the Bible. The name "mint" comes from an ancient Greek myth about a nymph called Minthe. She was kissing the god Pluto when Pluto's wife came in and discovered them. Pluto's wife, a goddess of considerable power, trampled Minthe into the ground. Pluto saw to it, however, that Minthe lived on in the sweet smell of the herb.

Elizabethan gardeners in England picked up the idea and planted their garden paths with mint. As people strolled along they crushed the herb, which proceeded to perfume the area. The pungent smell of mint comes from a volatile oil in the stems and leaves called "menthol." The menthol gives your mouth that characteristic cool sensation, which was probably very popular, if not essential, in the days before toothbrushes. Mint is not native to the New World; it had its first planting in Nova Scotia when English colonists arrived in the 1600s.

PIES AND TARTS, A BREAD, A MUFFIN, AND A SCONE

TriBeCa Apple Tart
TRIBECA GRILL ◆ *NEW YORK, NEW YORK*

MAKES 6 SERVINGS

½ cup confectioners' sugar
One 9-inch round unbaked
  piecrust
⅓ cup ground hazelnuts
¼ cup butter
⅔ cup granulated sugar
4 large red apples, peeled,
  halved, cored, and thinly
  sliced
Ice cream or frozen yogurt,
  for serving

There were no native American apples growing when the first Pilgrims arrived in Massachusetts in the 1620s. But within a few years English colonists were planting apple trees wheresoever they could. Apples had been a very important crop in Great Britain. It was only natural for the colonists to continue this crop where the climate was favorable. We often hear the phrase "as American as apple pie." It would be much more accurate to say "as English as apple pie," or, in this case, apple tart. Pastry Chef George McKirdy prepares this recipe for apple tart at New York City's TriBeCa Grill.

1. Sprinkle a work surface with about ¼ cup of the confectioners' sugar. Set the round of pie dough on the sugar and sprinkle the remaining ¼ cup of confectioners' sugar on top. Rub the sugar all over the pie dough, making it adhere as well as possible. Sprinkle the nuts over the top of the dough and lightly press into the dough with a rolling pin. Cut the dough into 6 equal wedges.

2. Line a large baking sheet with a length of parchment paper. Arrange the wedges of dough close together but not touching on the baking sheet. Refrigerate for 1 hour.

3. Preheat the oven to 375° F.

4. Bake the pastry wedges for about 15 minutes, until lightly browned and cooked through. Remove the baking sheet to a rack to cool to room temperature.

◆

5. Melt the butter in a nonstick skillet over moderately high heat. Add the granulated sugar and stir until almost melted. Add the apple slices and cook, stirring from time to time, until the apples are browned, well glazed, and caramelized, 15 to 20 minutes. Remove from the heat.

6. Puree half of the apple mixture in a food processor or blender. Spread some of the puree over each pastry wedge. Arrange the remaining apple slices over the puree. (If possible, avoid assembling these tarts too far ahead of time as the puree tends to soak into the pastry.) Top with ice cream or frozen yogurt and serve.

◆ *Don Pintabona.*

ABOUT THE ENGLISH AND THEIR FOOD

When we read about the English coming to the New World, the story is usually about the pilgrims on the Mayflower and their search for religious freedom. The first English to set sail for America, however, were sent by Sir Walter Raleigh in the 1500s and they had a very clear set of instructions: Find gold! By the year 1700, 90 percent of the colonists were English. They never would have been able to survive their first years in the New World if the Native American tribes had not taught them to hunt for local fish and game and use pumpkins, beans, and corn. But as soon as they could grow or import traditional English foods, they returned to their old food ways—food ways that have become a basic part of the way we eat in North America. When you see roast beef, a pie that has a top crust, a cup of steamed pudding, marmalade, oatmeal, and most of the food around our traditional celebration of Christmas, you are looking at foods that were brought to America by the English. One of their most important undertakings was the planting of English fruit trees—pears, apricots, cherries, peaches, and dozens of different apple varieties were introduced to the New World by English farms. Our language is English, our system of law is English, and even today, our most common food ways are still English.

◆

HAWAIIAN PINEAPPLE TART
HALEKULANI HOTEL ◆ HONOLULU, HAWAII

MAKES 4 SERVINGS

1 pineapple, fully ripe
One 8-inch-wide disc of
  your favorite piecrust,
  baked
½ cup melted orange
  marmalade, warm

Chef George Mavrothalassitis is the executive chef at the Halekulani Hotel on Waikiki Beach in Hawaii. His specialty is taking local ingredients and using them with the traditional recipe techniques of his native France. The following tart is a clear example of that approach.

1. Preheat a nonstick pan.

2. Remove the crown, stem, end, and outside rind of the pineapple and slice it lengthwise into 8 pieces. Cut the core strip off each piece and slice the remaining pineapple into bite-size wedges.

3. Place the pineapple wedges onto the surface of the pan. The pan should not contain any oil or butter. The heat of the surface of the pan will caramelize the natural sugar in the pineapple and give the wedges a crust. Turn the pineapple pieces in the pan until the crust forms, about 2 minutes on each side.

4. Spoon or brush the piecrust with half of the marmalade. Arrange the pineapple wedges in overlapping concentric circles on top of the crust. Brush the top of the pineapple with the remaining marmalade and serve.

◆

ABOUT HAWAIIAN LEIS

The Hawaiian lei is a delicate necklace usually made from flowers but sometimes constructed of shells, leaves, nuts, or feathers. It is made with care and offered with great affection. Each part of a lei has a specific significance. Traditionally, it was worn as a head wreath, necklace, and bracelet during religious dances and considered an important offering to the gods. A lei used in a sacred ceremony was regarded as the personal property of the deity to whom the ceremony was dedicated. Even today leis are a very important part of Hawaiian society. Many tourists receive them when they arrive on the islands. But leis are also used by Hawaiians for all major and many minor occasions—births, weddings, funerals, parties, and anytime you want to express trust and affection.

TARTE TATIN
AIR FRANCE CONCORDE KITCHENS

MAKES 8 SERVINGS

2 tablespoons unsalted
   butter
⅔ cup plus 2 tablespoons
   granulated sugar
10 Granny Smith apples,
   peeled, cored, and set
   aside in water
1 egg
⅓ cup milk
1 sheet frozen puff pastry,
   thawed

A while ago I had the opportunity to fly to Paris on the Air France Concorde. It took three hours and forty-five minutes and was truly an amazing experience. I could actually see the curvature of the earth as we crossed the ocean. I could also see that Michel Martin, the head chef at Air France, was someone I wanted to meet. When I returned to New York, I made arrangements to visit Michel's kitchen and get some of his recipes. The following is his version of the classic tarte tatin, basically an apple tart cooked in a frying pan with the pastry on top. When it is finished, it is reversed onto a serving dish.

1. Preheat the oven to 350° F.

2. Butter the bottom of an oven-proof 12-inch skillet with 1 tablespoon of the butter. Sprinkle the ⅔ cup sugar evenly onto the buttered skillet.

3. Dry 8 of the apples and cut into ½-inch-thick wedges. Arrange the wedges, overlapping them in a circular pattern, over the bottom of the skillet.

4. Chop the remaining apples into ¼-inch cubes and scatter them over the sliced apples. Sprinkle the remaining 2 tablespoons of sugar on top, and dot the remaining tablespoon of butter evenly over the apples.

5.   In a small mixing bowl, beat the egg and whisk in the milk. Place the sheet of pastry over the top of the skillet. Pat down, seal, and trim the edges so that the pastry fits the skillet. Brush the pastry with the egg wash. Evenly pierce the pastry with a fork about 10 times.

6.   Place the skillet in the oven and bake for 30 to 45 minutes, or until the pastry is golden brown.

7.   Remove the skillet from the oven and put it on the stovetop over medium-high heat. Cook for 8 to 12 minutes, or until the bottom is caramelized. You will be able to smell the sugar caramelizing on the apples; use your sense of smell to make sure that the sugar doesn't burn.

8.   Place a large plate over the top of the skillet. Quickly and carefully invert the two. Tap the bottom of the skillet to loosen the mixture. Remove the skillet. Serve hot, at room temperature, or chilled.

KEY LIME PIE

JOE'S STONE CRAB RESTAURANT ◆ MIAMI BEACH, FLORIDA

MAKES 6 TO 8 SERVINGS

CRUST
⅓ cup plus 1 teaspoon
   melted margarine
1¼ cups crushed graham
   crackers
¼ cup granulated sugar

FILLING
Two 14-ounce cans
   sweetened condensed milk
5 egg yolks
Grated zest of 1 lime
1 cup fresh lime juice (5 to
   6 limes)

Joe's Stone Crab is the oldest restaurant on Miami Beach. It was started in 1913 when Joe and Jennie Weiss moved to Miami Beach from New York City. They bought a bungalow on South Beach, cooked inside, and served on the front porch. Today their restaurant is in its own sprawling building and is one of the most successful in the world. Currently the fourth generation of Joe's family is being trained. Stephen Sawitz is Joe's great-grandson, and he worked with me to adapt their famous Key Lime Pie recipe for home use.

1. To make the crust: Preheat the oven to 350° F. Coat the inside of a 9-inch pie pan with 1 teaspoon of the melted margarine.

2. In a mixing bowl, combine the crushed graham crackers, sugar, and ⅓ cup of melted margarine. When the ingredients are fully combined, use the mixture to line the bottom and sides of the pie pan. Place the pie pan into the preheated oven and bake for 10 minutes.

3. While the crust is baking, in a mixing bowl, make the filling by whisking together all the ingredients.

4. When the crust is baked, remove it from the oven and pour in the filling. Return the filled piecrust to the oven and bake for 10 minutes more. Let cool to room temperature.

ABOUT STONE CRABS AND JOE'S

Miami Beach is surrounded by the warm waters of the Atlantic, home to bathing beauties, boating enthusiasts, and some of the world's best seafood. Perhaps the most famous of the local specialties is the stone crab. Although stone crabs are found along the coast from North Carolina to Mexico, they are commercially landed only in Florida.

Stone crabs have the amazing ability to drop off their claws and then grow new ones. It was a protection adaptation. If an enemy of the crab got hold of a claw, the crab just gave it up and took off. Each claw can exert over 13,000 pounds of pressure per square inch, which is used to open oysters, a favorite meal for the crab. When Florida fishermen harvest stone crabs, they take off a claw and return the crab to the sea where the claw grows back.

The restaurant that put stone crabs on the gastronomic map is called Joe's Stone Crab and it sits on the southern tip of Miami Beach. It's only open from October to May, which happens to be the stone crab season. The restaurant serves almost a ton of crab everyday. Because the meat is so rich, there are only three to five claws to a serving, and that's more than enough. They are served with a light mustard sauce, coleslaw, and fried sweet potatoes.

The original Joe's.

BURT WOLF

ABOUT CRAB

An American statesman named John Hay once pointed out that he believed politicians are very similar to crabs. They both seem to be coming when they are actually going and seem to be going when they are actually coming.

There are over four thousand different species of crab, and the one thing they all have in common is that they are edible. North America is fortunate in having the largest variety of crab in the world. Consequently, we have made crab our second favorite shellfish; only shrimp are more popular. Most of the crab that we cook at home comes as precooked meat, but it is not always as free of crab shell as we would like it to be. It's a good idea to go through the precooked crab meat and make sure you've gotten all of the shell out before you continue with the recipe.

If you are going to buy live crab, always pick out those that are heavier and more active; the heavier the better. Make sure the claws are bound and can't grab you. Also remember that crabs are cannibals and will eat each other, so don't leave them together. Like lobsters, crabs must be cooked while they are still alive to be safe to eat.

WHEN TO ADD BAKING SODA OR BAKING POWDER

Baking soda and baking powder are chemically active ingredients that make dough rise. The actual chemical activity starts when the soda or powder first comes in contact with moisture, but you really want it to do its stuff while the dough is in the oven. The trick, then, is to shorten the time between the contact with the wet ingredients and the dough going into the oven. The last-minute blending helps.

BERMUDA BANANA BREAD
WYNDHAM'S ELBOW BEACH RESORT ◆ BERMUDA

The island of Bermuda is warmed by an ocean current that comes out of the Gulf of Mexico. The result is a mild climate that encourages the growing of fruits and vegetables that are usually associated with the tropics. A perfect example is the banana, which is cultivated throughout Bermuda.

The banana, by the way, is neither a fruit nor a vegetable. The banana is, in fact, an herb. Actually, it is the world's largest herb.

1. Preheat oven to 300° F. Butter and flour a 3 × 5 × 8-inch loaf pan.

2. In a mixing bowl, cream together the sugar and the butter. One at a time, add the eggs. Add the bananas and the walnuts and mix until everything is well combined.

3. In a second bowl, sift together the baking soda, salt, and flour. Mix the moist ingredients into the dry ingredients. Pour the batter into the loaf pan and bake in the oven for 2 hours or until a wooden toothpick inserted into the center of the loaf comes out free of moist batter. If the top of the loaf starts to get too dark, cover the pan with aluminum foil.

MAKES 1 LOAF

1 cup sugar
4 ounces butter
2 eggs
3 very ripe bananas,
  mashed
½ cup chopped walnuts
1 teaspoon baking soda
¼ teaspoon salt
2 cups all-purpose flour

◆

BLUEBERRY-OATMEAL MUFFINS ✓
THE SILVER SPOON ◆ HALIFAX, NOVA SCOTIA

MAKES 2 DOZEN MUFFINS

2 cups rolled oats
2 cups fresh orange juice
Grated zest of 1 orange
2 cups whole-wheat flour
½ cup all-purpose flour
2 teaspoons baking soda
2 teaspoons baking powder
1 tablespoon salt
10 tablespoons (1¼ sticks)
  butter or margarine, at
  room temperature
1 cup light brown sugar,
  packed
2 eggs
2 teaspoons vanilla extract
¼ cup molasses
2 cups frozen blueberries
  or fresh blueberries,
  stemmed and washed

The Silver Spoon restaurant in Halifax, Nova Scotia, is famous for its warm and hospitable atmosphere. It is owned by a woman named Deanna Silver. She never thought that she would end up in the restaurant business. But she was forced into opening up the restaurant because her friends loved her baking. A good example is her Blueberry-Oatmeal Muffins.

1. Preheat the oven to 350° F. Place paper cupcake liners into two 12-cup muffin tins. (If you don't have paper liners, lightly butter the muffin cups.)

2. In a mixing bowl, combine the oats, orange juice, and orange zest.

3. On a sheet of wax paper, combine both of the flours, the baking soda, baking powder, and salt.

4. In the large bowl of an electric mixer, cream together the butter and sugar until thoroughly mixed. Add the eggs and mix well. Add the oat mixture and mix. Gradually add the dry ingredients. Beat in the vanilla and the molasses.

5. Add the blueberries and gently fold them in by hand. Divide the batter among the muffin cups, filling them about three-quarters full.

6. Bake for 25 minutes, or until a toothpick inserted in the center comes out clean. Cool the muffins on a wire rack.

◆

ABOUT THE SCOTS IN NOVA SCOTIA

Nova Scotia is Latin for New Scotland. It is the ancestral home of the Native American Micmac tribe, the original French colony in North America, an outpost for the English, a welcome residence for tens of thousands of immigrants from the United States, and a joyous haven for Germans who escaped from world poverty in the 1700s. The only group of people that had a consistently terrible time going to "New Scotland" were the Scots. They were forced to go there when the Clan system of Scotland collapsed. They were poor, uneducated, and unable to deal with the problems of survival in the New World. Yet through the traditional Scottish determination and frugality they managed to hang on, and eventually introduced Nova Scotia to the foods of their home country.

Their beloved oats took hold in the soil. Mills were built, and before long oatmeal, oat cakes, oat breads, and any other oat-based recipe that you could think of became part of the cooking of Nova Scotia. The Scots are famous for their open hospitality, which has an effect on their recipes, especially when it comes to baking. They love quick breads and cakes made with baking soda. A famous Scottish cook once told me that she only used cake recipes that could be produced in the time it took guests to come up the driveway, enter her home, and settle in.

♦

ABOUT OATS

Oats are the berries of a cultivated grass that is native to central Europe. They have been grown by European farmers since the Bronze Age, which started in about 3500 B.C. Oats grow best in cool, wet climates and have become a basic part of the diets in places like England, Wales, Scotland, and Ireland. In Scotland, oats are the staff of life. They are made into oat porridge, soups, sausages, cakes, cookies, and muffins. I've even seen Scottish cooks toast oatmeal and sprinkle it on ice cream.

A few years ago researchers at Northwestern University in Chicago conducted a study that indicated that two ounces of oatmeal or oat bran everyday can help reduce cholesterol levels. What actually does the job is the soluble fiber that appears to reduce cholesterol as it passes through the body. Oats are also one of the best sources of soluble fiber in the North American diet. Two cups of breakfast-style oatmeal or two medium-size oat muffins contain the two ounces of oat fiber that you need. But please remember that if you take in oat muffins that are packed with saturated fat you are not doing yourself any good. The oat fiber needs to be part of a low-fat diet to really do its job.

♦

RAISIN-NUT SCONES ✓
ROYAL YORK HOTEL ◆ TORONTO, CANADA

MAKES 16 SCONES

2 eggs
½ cup milk
2 cups all-purpose flour
2 teaspoons baking powder
½ teaspoon salt
¼ cup granulated sugar,
   plus ¼ cup, for tops
6 tablespoons (¾ stick)
   unsalted butter
½ cup raisins
½ cup roughly chopped
   dried apricots
½ cup roughly chopped
   walnuts

The west coast of Canada is one of the most beautiful parts of our planet. The Hydah people had been there for thousands of years when Captain Cook showed up in 1793. Ever since then, English culture has been in the neighborhood. It is particularly evident in the daily afternoon service of English tea with scones.

1. Preheat the oven to 450° F. Line 2 cookie sheets with parchment paper or use them unlined; either way, do not grease the pans.

2. In a small bowl mix together the eggs and milk and set aside.

3. Sift together the dry ingredients. Cut the butter into small squares and blend it into the dry ingredients.

4. Stir in the raisins, apricots, and walnuts.

5. Add the egg-milk mixture all at once and stir with a fork until the dry ingredients are combined. Do not mix more than is necessary.

6. Drop tablespoon-size batter onto the baking sheets at least 1 inch apart, and sprinkle the tops lightly with additional sugar. If you would like your scones flatter, you can lightly press them down.

7. Bake for 12 to 15 minutes, until the scones are golden. Serve immediately.

◆

COOKIES

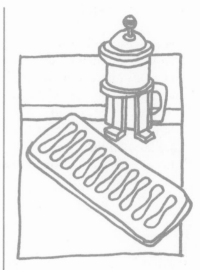

COCONUT DROP COOKIES ✓
GRAND PALAZZO HOTEL ◆ ST. THOMAS, U.S. VIRGIN ISLANDS

MAKES 4 DOZEN COOKIES

6 cups shredded coconut
5 cups granulated sugar
3 cups all-purpose flour
6 eggs
¼ cup melted unsalted
  butter
1 tablespoon light rum
2 teaspoons vanilla extract

The European explorers of the Caribbean spent a great deal of effort describing everything that grew in the New World. But they never said anything about the coconut. It appears that the coconut came to the Americas from the South Pacific, after the landing of Columbus. For one third of the world's population the coconut is a very important food, especially for people living in the tropics.

Fabrice Dubuc is a French pastry chef who performs his art at the Grand Palazzo Hotel on the U.S. Virgin Island of St. Thomas. His specialty is adapting classic recipes to local ingredients. These Coconut Drop Cookies are a delicious example.

1. In the large bowl of an electric mixer, combine all of the ingredients and beat until thoroughly mixed. Cover the bowl and refrigerate for 1 hour.

2. Preheat the oven to 375° F. Line a baking sheet with parchment or wax paper.

3. Roll the cookie dough into 1-inch balls and place them 2 inches apart on the baking sheet.

4. Bake for 10 minutes, or until browned on the bottom and around the edges. Cool the cookies on a wire rack. Store in an airtight container.

◆

REGGIE ROBY'S COOKIES FOR KICKS
DON SHULA'S ◆ MIAMI LAKES, FLORIDA

Reggie Roby is a superstar punter who ranks among the top kickers in the history of the NFL. He is also a cookie lover. A while ago he was interested in having some home-baked chocolate chip cookies, and he was willing to do the baking. His taste memory told him that the all-star cookie recipe was his mother's and he called her for the details. The following is Reggie's mother's recipe, with Reggie's twist.

1. Preheat the oven to 375° F. Lightly grease a cookie sheet.

2. In a mixing bowl, combine all of the ingredients and beat until well mixed. Spoon out 2 tablespoon–size mounds of dough onto the cookie sheet, keeping the mounds about 2 inches apart.

3. Bake the cookies for 10 to 13 minutes, until lightly browned on the top and bottom. Let cool.

MAKES APPROXIMATELY
2½ DOZEN COOKIES

2½ cups all-purpose flour
¾ cup granulated sugar
¾ cup brown sugar, packed
1 teaspoon baking powder
2 eggs
¾ cup butter (1½ sticks)
¼ cup sour cream
1 teaspoon vanilla extract
12 ounces semisweet
  chocolate chips

DUTCH BUTTER COOKIES
AMSTEL INTER-CONTINENTAL ◆ AMSTERDAM, HOLLAND

MAKES ABOUT 2 DOZEN

1 pound unsalted butter, at
   room temperature
1¾ cups granulated sugar
1 egg
3½ cups all-purpose flour
1 teaspoon vanilla extract
1 egg beaten with 2
   tablespoons milk, for egg
   wash

The Dutch city of Amsterdam is a visual treat with its tree-lined canals, magnificent old houses, and picturesque streets. Amsterdam can also be a gastronomic treat. The point is made at Amsterdam's Amstel Inter-Continental hotel by Pastry Chef Jos van Velzen's recipe for Dutch Butter Cookies.

1. Using an electric mixer or a hand whisk, beat the butter until fluffy. Add the sugar and beat until pale in color. Beat in the egg. Add the flour, ½ cup at a time, until incorporated. Beat in the vanilla.

2. Spread out 2 long sheets of plastic wrap, overlapping one long edge. Place the dough on the plastic wrap and press out with your fingers into a large rectangle, roughly ½ inch thick and 12 inches by 16 inches in diameter. Cover the dough with 2 more sheets of plastic wrap and fold the edges over. Keeping the dough flat, refrigerate for at least 1 hour.

3. Preheat the oven to 350° F. Line 2 baking sheets with parchment paper.

4. Remove the dough from the refrigerator and set on a work surface. Without unwrapping it, roll out as needed until smooth and evenly ½ inch thick. Remove the top sheets of plastic. Score the top of the dough in a crisscross pattern. Using 3-inch round cookie cutters (or whatever largish shape suits you), cut out the dough. Transfer each cookie *with its cutter* to the prepared baking sheets. Brush the top of each cookie with some of the egg wash.

5.   Bake the cookies for 30 to 35 minutes, or until the edges are browned and the tops lightly golden. Cool on a rack and store airtight.

NOTE: Instead of buying cookie cutters or circular baking forms, I use empty tuna cans with the tops and bottoms cut out, well washed and labels removed.

Hazelnut and Raspberry Chocolate-Dipped Cookies

Four Seasons Olympic Hotel ◆ Seattle, Washington

MAKES APPROXIMATELY
1½ DOZEN COOKIES

6 (1½ sticks) ounces butter,
  at room temperature
½ cup confectioners' sugar
¾ cup toasted, ground
  hazelnuts
1 tablespoon ground
  cinnamon
5 egg whites
1¼ cups all-purpose flour
½ cup raspberry jam
4 ounces semisweet
  chocolate, melted

The Four Seasons Olympic Hotel in Seattle, Washington, has a great reputation for good food, which is usually based on local ingredients. The pastry chef, Regis Bernard, makes a cookie that uses local hazelnuts and raspberries.

1. Preheat the oven to 350° F. Lightly butter and flour a baking sheet.

2. In the bowl of an electric mixer, cream the butter and sugar. Add the hazelnuts, cinnamon, egg whites, and flour. Blend until the dough just comes together.

3. Transfer the dough to a pastry bag (see Note) fitted with a small round tip. Pipe the batter in thin 4-inch-long strips onto the baking sheet. Bake for 15 to 20 minutes, or until the cookie edges are golden. Cool completely.

4. Turn every other cookie over and spread with raspberry jam. Place another cookie on top, forming a sandwich.

5. Dip one end of each sandwich in the melted chocolate. Set on wax paper to harden.

NOTE: If you don't have a pastry bag you may substitute a resealable plastic bag. Simply make a small hole in one corner of the bag. Continue with the recipe directions.

◆

A LITTLE SEATTLE HISTORY

The first European settlement in the Seattle area was built by a group of fur traders. They had been sent during the 1840s by The Hudson Bay Company. The fur traders bartered goods with the Native Americans and did a little trading. However, the 1849 discovery of gold in California brought hundreds of thousands of immigrants to the West Coast and pushed out the fur traders. At that time, the idea of a group of people getting together with the specific objective of building a new city was quite common. A handful of entrepreneurial settlers would get together, stake out a claim to some land, draw up a plan for a new city, and do everything they could to get other people to buy in. They were the Donald Trumps of the time.

In the case of Seattle, the first developer was David Denny, who arrived with a group of some twenty people in September of 1851. Denny was soon joined by three other visionaries, Charles Boren, William Bell, and Dr. David Maynard. Together they worked out the grand plan for the city. One of Doc Maynard's friends was a Native American chief named "Sealth," and sometimes called "Seattle." It was the Doc's suggestion that the new city be named after his pal.

The next heavy to arrive in town was Henry Yesler, who built a saw mill and made lumber the area's major industry. To get the logs from the top of the hill to the water below, a road was built and covered with wood. The wood helped the logs skid down easily and was called a skid road. Eventually it became a hangout for drunken loggers and miners at the bottom of their luck. At that point, the area became known as "skid row," a phrase which is now synonymous with the down-and-out neighborhood of any city in North America.

During the 1850s, the local Native Americans began to understand just what the settlers were doing to the area. There was a small uprising, which was quickly put down by the U.S. military. The Native American leader named Leschi was caught and tried for murder. The lawyer that defended him was H. R. Crosby. Crosby lost the case, and Leschi lost his life. The leader eventually became a local hero, and today one of Seattle's most popular parks is named after him.

Meanwhile, up in Alaska gold was about to be discovered. When the story of the Yukon gold hit the newspapers in 1897, Seattle became the jumping-off point for thousands of miners. In one year, the gross sales of Seattle merchants went from less than a half-million dollars to over 25 million. The joint was jumping, and Seattle became the center of trade and commerce in the northwestern part of the United States.

◆

MACADAMIA BROWNIES ✓
KAHALA HILTON ◆ HONOLULU, HAWAII

MAKES 2 DOZEN BROWNIES

2 cups granulated sugar
½ teaspoon salt
9 ounces butter or
  margarine, at room
  temperature
¼ cup light corn syrup
4 eggs
1 cup unsweetened cocoa
  powder, Dutch processed
  preferred
1 teaspoon vanilla extract
1 cup all-purpose flour
2 cups coarsely chopped
  macadamia nuts

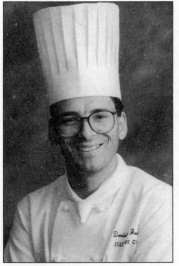

Dominique Jamain.

The Kahala Hilton sits on the edge of a secluded white sandy beach on the Hawaiian island of Oahu. For over twenty-five years it has lured travelers in search of a peaceful, and private, rest. Paddle boating, snorkeling, wind-surfing, scuba diving, and just lazing on a raft in the brilliant Hawaiian sun are some of the activities that visitors enjoy. There is an oceanside pool for those who prefer freshwater swimming and a man-made lagoon which has become home to three bottle-nosed dolphins. The Kahala's waterfalls, lush gardens, and an oceanside lounge were a regular setting for scenes in the television series "Magnum, P.I." The Kahala Hilton is also well known for its food.

Executive Chef Dominique Jamain was trained in a number of fine restaurants in his homeland of France and perfected his skills in Montreal, Canada, before coming to Hawaii. Chef Jamain uses the local macadamia nut in this recipe for Hawaiian brownies.

1. Preheat the oven to 325° F. Put a light coating of butter or margarine onto an 11-×-17 or 15-×-10-inch jelly-roll pan, then line the pan with parchment paper.

2. In a large mixing bowl, cream together the sugar, salt, butter or margarine, and corn syrup.

3. Add the eggs, cocoa, vanilla, flour, and 1½ cups of the nuts. Mix together thoroughly.

4. Pour the batter into the prepared pan and sprinkle with the remaining ½ cup of nuts. Bake for 30 to 35 minutes. You can test for doneness by inserting a wooden toothpick into the center of the pan. If the toothpick comes out free of moist batter, the brownies are fully cooked. Let cool to room temperature.

ABOUT MACADAMIA NUTS

Macadamia nuts are the seeds of a tropical tree that was originally a native of Australia. It was named after John Macadam, a chemist who lived during the mid-1800s and promoted the plant in Australia. Macadamias were brought to Hawaii in the 1880s as an ornamental plant and were not thought of as a source of nuts for many years . . . probably because they're a tough nut to crack. When automobiles were first brought to Hawaii, one of their uses was to open macadamia nuts. The nuts would be placed between boards, and cars were driven over them to open up the protective shell. These days the job is done with rollers that carry three hundred pounds of pressure. Inside is a delicate, crisp meat that seems to melt into a creamy flavor. Today, Hawaii produces 90 percent of the world's macadamia nuts, and local companies continually search for new ways of presenting them.

Macadamia nuts have about 100 calories in a half-ounce portion, and their <u>fat content is unsaturated</u>. They're good sources of <u>phosphorous, iron, and vitamin B_1,</u> and have <u>a fair amount of calcium</u>. The vacuum-packed variety of nuts will last up to two years, but they should be refrigerated in an airtight container after opening.

BERMUDA TRIANGLE COOKIES
WYNDHAM'S ELBOW BEACH RESORT ◆ BERMUDA

MAKES 48 TRIANGLES

THE PASTRY CRUST
3 cups all-purpose flour
½ cup sugar
Pinch of salt
10 ounces, cold sweet
  butter, cut into small
  pieces
2 eggs, lightly beaten

THE ALMOND TOPPING
1 cup sugar
¼ cup honey
½ cup heavy cream
1 ounce butter
8 ounces sliced almonds

Chef Norbert Stange at Wyndham's Elbow Beach Resort bakes something he calls a Bermuda Triangle Cookie, which is subject to unexplained disappearances, and in extremely large numbers. The following recipe will allow you to have a firsthand encounter with the problem.

TO MAKE THE PASTRY CRUST

1.   In a large mixing bowl, combine the flour, sugar, and salt. Add the butter, and using two knives or a pastry blender, blend the butter into the flour until the mixture resembles coarse oatmeal. Add the eggs and mix until the dough can be formed into a compact ball. Wrap the ball in plastic wrap and refrigerate for 1 hour.

2.   Preheat the oven to 350° F. Prepare a 12 × 17-inch jelly roll pan by lining it with parchment paper.

3.   Roll out the pastry into a ⅛-inch-thick sheet that will cover the entire inside of the pan and up along the sides. Fit the dough into the jelly roll pan, and using the tines of a fork, poke holes into the dough every few inches. The holes will let the steam out of the dough while it is cooking and thereby prevent the dough from developing bubbles and bulges. Chill the dough for 10 minutes.

4.   Bake until lightly golden brown, about 20 to 25 minutes. *Do not turn the oven off.*

TO MAKE THE ALMOND TOPPING

1.   In a heavy sauce pan, over medium-high heat, combine the sugar, honey, heavy cream, and butter. Bring the mixture to a boil and cook for 5 to 7 minutes or until a deep caramel color appears. Mix in the almonds.

2.   Pour the mixture over the pastry crust in the jelly roll pan. Spread the almond mixture into an even layer.

3.   Return the pan to the oven and bake for 20 minutes. Remove from the oven and allow to cool in the pan. When the pastry is completely cool, cut it into triangles.

A B O U T   B E R M U D A   S H O R T S

In Bermuda, Bermuda shorts are considered to be a preferred form of dress for men. They are actually thought of as conservative. I could wear them to the most serious business meeting and be properly dressed. Of course, they must be regulation length, which is four inches above the knee, and they should be of a solid color. The people of Bermuda got the idea for these shorts from the British Army, who started wearing shorts during the early years of this century. And let me tell you, they're very comfortable.

ABOUT THE BERMUDA TRIANGLE

In 1964 Argosy magazine ran an article that described the unexplained disappearance of an extraordinary number of ships and planes in a triangular area between Bermuda, the coast of Florida, and the island of Puerto Rico. The article told the story of a British ship named the Ellen Austin. In 1881 the Austin came upon an abandoned vessel in the triangle. The craft was in perfect working order but there was no crew on board. The captain of the Austin put some of his own men onto the empty ship and instructed them to head for Nova Scotia, on the coast of Canada. A few days later the two ships met up and once again the crew on the mystery ship had vanished.

The legend of the Bermuda Triangle also includes the story of a flight of five U.S. Air Force fighter planes that took off on a routine patrol from Fort Lauderdale, Florida, in 1945. At one point the flight leader of the group radioed ground control that he was lost. A rescue plane was sent out to help. All six planes disappeared without a trace.

Since the original article on the Bermuda Triangle was published, there have been dozens of additional newspaper and magazine stories, plus a few books, television specials, and a movie. Eventually a librarian at Arizona State University used his research skills to evaluate the information. He checked through documents from the 1800s; he got hold of the military transcript of the radio conversations between the ground controllers and the five fighter planes; he looked into all the legends of the Bermuda Triangle.

When each Bermuda Triangle story is subjected to serious evaluation, the conclusion is clear. There is no greater loss of aircraft or naval vessels in this geographic area than in any similar place on the globe.

◆

The islands of Bermuda were well known to the Spanish explorers who followed Columbus to the New World. Their ships, filled with valuable cargo, started home by sailing north along the coast of Florida. The islands of Bermuda were the navigational markers that told them it was time to make a right and head east across the Atlantic.

The first detailed account of the area was written by a Spanish captain whose ship ran aground at Spanish Point. The document is of particular interest to me because, more than anything else, it is the islands' first grocery list with recipes. I quote, "The birds came to us and perched on our heads. We brought more than 500 to the ship. We cooked them with hot water and they were so fat and good that every night the men went hunting and we dried and salted more than 1,000 for the voyage home. We also caught great numbers of fish: groupers, parrot fish, and especially red snappers which were so plentiful that we were able to catch them with our hands." So, from the very beginning, Bermuda was a great spot for a good meal.

The story of England's involvement with Bermuda begins with Sir George Somers. He was the admiral of a small fleet that had set sail from England with colonists who intended to settle in Virginia. On July 28, 1609, a huge storm drove the admiral's ship onto the rocks that surround Bermuda. On board the ship was Sir Thomas Gates, who was going to Virginia to become the governor of the colony.

Somers, the professional seaman, and Gates, the professional politician, had different views on building a ship to continue the voyage to Virginia. As a result, each built to their own design. A full-sized replica of Gates's ship, named Deliverance, now stands on a small island in front of the town of St. George.

Somers's craft was called Patience, and both ships arrived in the Virginia colony of Jamestown in 1610. Jamestown was in sad shape and Somers was not very interested in hanging around. So he told everyone that he was going back to Bermuda to get food, and cut out. He was on his way back to England when he stopped in Bermuda, but while he was there, he died. His heart was removed and kept in Bermuda while the rest of him was shipped back to Great Britain. And that made him the first tourist to leave his heart in Bermuda.

The description of Bermuda given by Sir George's nephew Matthew was so positive that it convinced the King to grant a new charter for the development of Bermuda. In 1612 the first "intentional" settlers arrived on the islands.

◆

MERINGUE COOKIES
CLUB MED I

MAKES ABOUT 5½ DOZEN
COOKIES

½ cup egg whites (about 4
   large)
Pinch of salt
½ cup granulated sugar
½ cup finely ground
   almonds
½ cup confectioners' sugar,
   sifted

1. Preheat the oven to 225° F. Line 2 cookie sheets with parchment paper.

2. Place the egg whites into a bowl and beat with an electric mixer until foamy. Add the salt and continue beating until soft peaks form. Gradually add the sugar while beating until stiff peaks form and the mixture is smooth and shiny, 4 to 5 minutes.

3. Using a spatula, gently fold the almonds into the beaten egg whites, alternating with the confectioners' sugar. Fold only until blended.

4. Fill a pastry bag with a plain no. 3 tip with the mixture and pipe 1½-inch dots onto the lined cookie sheets, or drop the batter from a tablespoon, keeping the meringue cookies about 1½ inches apart.

5. Bake for 1 hour. Turn off the oven, but leave the oven door open. Allow the cookies to remain in the oven for 2 to 3 minutes. Remove the cookie sheets to racks to cook (keep out of drafts). Store cookies in a tightly sealed container.

INDEX

Upper Deck Lobster and Pasta, 180
Lucas, Fiona, 241

Mabi, 189
Macadamia nuts, 272–73
Macao, 9
McKirdy, George, 252
McNeill, George, 154, 156
Mangoes, 101
   Chicken in Mango Sauce, 100
   Fish with Mango Sauce, 64
Manioc, 141
Marley, Bob, 177
Martin, Michel, 68–69, 256
Mavrothalassitis, George, 48, 254
May, Tony, 186
Mead, 143
Meats, 132–70
   Beef Casserole, 144–45
   Beef Tarragon, 138
   Beef with Scallions, 134
   Breaded Veal Chops, 169
   Chinese Beef with Broccoli, 132
   Cola-Basted Baked Ham, 162
   Grilled Medallions of Beef, 137
   Herbed Tenderloin of Lamb, 163
   Lamb Tortillas, 164–65
   Pan-Roasted Beef, 136
   Pork and Prunes, 158
   Pork in Spicy Garlic Sauce, 153
   Puerto Rican Stuffed Beef, 140–41
   Roast Pork with Papaya Stuffing, 160–61

Ruth-Anne's Meat Loaf, 146–47
   Sautéed Pork Loin with Honey Sauce, 148
   Stir-Fried Beef and Broccoli, 135
   Stuffed Cabbage, 154–55
   Stuffed Lamb Chops, 170
   Stuffed Pork Chops, 156–57
Menthol, 250
Mesones Gastronomico (Puerto Rico), 189
Ming, Fred, 160
Mint, 250
   Chicken Adobo, 104
   Mint-Chocolate Chip Ice Cream Cake, 248–49
Molasses, 45, 98, 142, 231, 232, 246
   blackstrap, 231
Monkfish, 68–69
Morrow, Rob, 146
Mosimann, Anton, 163
Muffins, 262
Murray, Bill, 13
Musarra, Anthony, 164–65, 244
Museum Van Loon (Amsterdam, Holland), 10
Mushrooms, Chinese, 190

Napkin folding, 133
Niacin, 51, 147
Nike Kitchens (Beaverton, Oregon), 215
Noodles
   Baked Salmon Fillets Over Buckwheat Noodles, 61
   Stir-Fried Noodles, Ming Jiang Style, 191

tan tan, 8, 81
"Northern Exposure" Cookbook, 146
Nova Scotia, 249
Nuts
   cashews, 110
   hazelnuts, 270
   macadamia, 272–73
   walnuts, 233, 240

Oatmeal, 263
   Blueberry-Oatmeal Muffins, 262
Oats, 263
Observatory Hotel (Sydney, Australia), 163, 164, 218, 244
Okra, 36
   Fungi with Okra, 216
Old Drovers Inn (Dover Plains, New York), 128
Once Upon a Table (Hamilton, Bermuda), 22, 72–73
Onions, 26
   Bermuda, 27
   Fish Baked with Onions and Bell Peppers, 58–59
Orange roughy, 25
Ortanigue, 108
Orzo, 70
Otaheite, 108
Oysters, 6, 183, 259
Oyster sauce, 123

Pancakes, 34
Papaya, 49
   Fish Steaks with Papaya Salsa, 48
   Fish with Papaya, 66–67
   stuffing, 160

Red Snapper with Black Bean
  Salsa, 47
Rummed Bananas, 230
Shrimp Asopao, 35
Sofrito, 37
Puerto Rico, history, 142, 231
Pumpkins, 253
  Jamaican Pumpkin Soup, 14

Qantas Jet Base (Sydney,
  Australia), 24, 61, 116–17

Railroads and food, 54, 84, 118,
  119
Raisin-Nut Scones, 264
Raleigh, Sir Walter, 253
Rastafarians, 177
Recaito, 35
Religion
  Buddhism, 206
  Chinese, 88, 95
  Confucianism, 88, 206
  folk, 88, 95
  Taoism, 126, 206
Remi (New York, New York),
  172
Riboflavin, 51
Rice, 82, 140–41, 189
  Bermudan Spanish Rice,
    198–99
  Cantonese Shrimp with Fried
    Rice, 195
  Caribbean Madras Rice, 197
  Crabs Over Steamed Fried
    Rice, 89
  Jamaican Rice and Beans,
    193
  Nydia's Rice and Beans, 192
  Rice and Walnut Cake, 240

Rihga Royal Hotel (New York,
  New York), 240
Roby, Reggie, 267
Rockpool Restaurant (Sydney,
  Australia), 62, 86
Rosario, Ramon, 38, 100
Royal York Hotel (Toronto,
  Canada), 135, 154–55, 156,
  264
Rum, 232
  Australian, 246
  Fudgey Rum-Chocolate Cake,
    244–45
  Rummed Bananas, 230
Russian foods, 112–13
The Russian Tea Room (New
  York, New York), 112

St. Croix, Virgin Islands, 15, 32,
  44, 46, 67, 98
St. John, Virgin Islands, 46, 67
St. Thomas, Virgin Islands, 46, 66,
  67, 102, 144, 216, 217, 266
Salads
  Honey-Glazed Pork Salad,
    218
  Warm Fish Salad, 210
  Wilted Spinach Salad, 217
Salle, Gerard, 56, 120
Salmon, 25, 183
  Baked Salmon Fillets Over
    Buckwheat Noodles, 61
Salsa, papaya, 48
Salt. *See* Sodium
San Domenico (New York, New
  York), 186
Sands Hotel (San Juan, Puerto
  Rico), 38, 43, 100, 188
El San Juan Hotel (San Juan,

  Puerto Rico), 35, 47, 104,
    140–41, 192, 230
Sanna, Paolo-Arpa, 10, 114
Sauces
  chili, 123
  citrus, 74–75
  garlic, 148
  hoisin, 123
  honey, 148
  lemon, 94
  lime, 43, 68–69
  mango, 64, 100
  orange, 80
  oyster, 123
  pesto, 50
  port wine, 118
  pungent, 121
  red pepper, 44–45
  soy, 123
Sawitz, Stephen, 258
Scallions, 134
Schoenneger, Theo, 186
Schultz, Howard, 225
Scones, 264
Scotch Bonnet, 194
Scottish foods, 263
Seafood, 42–92
  auctions, 63
  Cantonese Shrimp with Fried
    Rice, 195
  Crabmeat and Corn Soup, 20
  Crabs Over Steamed Fried
    Rice, 89
  farms, 25
  Florida, 92
  Grilled Jumbo Shrimp with
    Citrus Sauce, 74–75
  Hummus with Shrimp, 86
  Jamaican Shrimp, 77